W9-BVW-544

The American Civil War and Reconstruction

People, Politics, and Power

America at War

The American Civil War and Reconstruction

People, Politics, and Power

Edited by Jeff Wallenfeldt, Manager, Geography and History

IN ASSOCIATION WITH

ROSEN
EDUCATIONAL SERVICES

Published in 2010 by Britannica Educational Publishing
(a trademark of Encyclopædia Britannica, Inc.)
in association with Rosen Educational Services, LLC
29 East 21st Street, New York, NY 10010.

Distributed exclusively by Rosen Educational Services.
For a listing of additional Britannica Educational Publishing titles, call toll free (800) 237-9932.

First Edition

Britannica Educational Publishing
Michael I. Levy: Executive Editor
Marilyn L. Barton: Senior Coordinator, Production Control
Steven Bosco: Director, Editorial Technologies
Lisa S. Braucher: Senior Producer and Data Editor
Yvette Charboneau: Senior Copy Editor
Kathy Nakamura: Manager, Media Acquisition
Jeff Wallenfeldt: Manager, Geography and History

Rosen Educational Services
Hope Lourie Killcoyne: Senior Editor and Project Manager
Nelson Sá: Art Director
Matthew Cauli: Designer
Introduction by Therese Shea

Library of Congress Cataloging-in-Publication Data

The American Civil War and Reconstruction: people, politics, and power / edited by Jeff Wallenfeldt.
p. cm.—(America at war)
"In association with Britannica Educational Publishing, Rosen Educational Services."
ISBN 978-1-61530-007-5 (library binding)
1. United States—History—Civil War, 1861–1865. 2. Reconstruction (U.S. history, 1865–1877)
I. Wallenfeldt, Jeffrey H.
E464.A44 2010
973.7—dc22

2009033551

Manufactured in the United States of America

On the cover: The Battle of Port Hudson, a nearly seven-week siege ending in July of 1863, marked a decisive victory for the Union over the vastly outnumbered Confederates. *Library of Congress Prints and Photographs Division*

CONTENTS

44

94

103

117

152

195

234

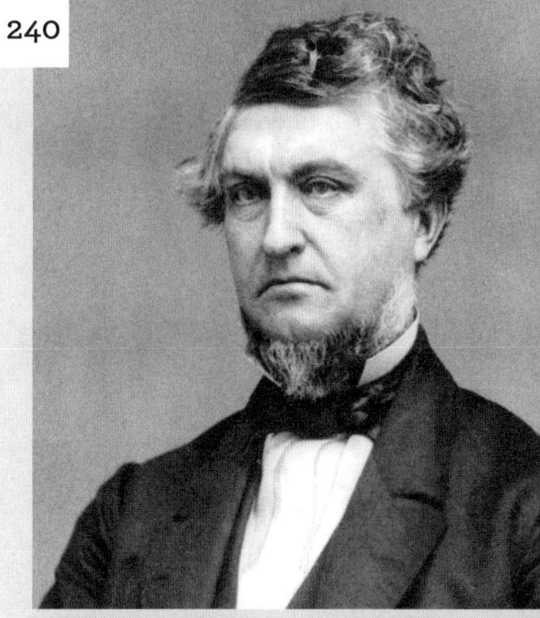

240

242

INTRODUCTION

Although the Civil War is the best known conflict on American soil, it is by no means an isolated episode of violence. Consider the history of North America. From the arrival of European explorers, historical records report skirmishes with Native Americans. As settlers built colonies, friction with native peoples defending their land eventually ended with assimilation or banishment to reservations. Europeans fought with other Europeans over territory. Eventually, thirteen colonies went to war with their parent country of Great Britain, resulting in the founding of the United States of America.

And yet it is the conflict between Northern and Southern states in the 1860s that most readily captures the public's attention and fires the imagination. Perhaps the fascination with the Civil War is due to the concept that a young country, recently united against a common enemy, was now at odds with itself. No other conflict has ever so divided the country, pitting state against state, family against family, friend against friend. Maybe the grand scale of carnage is as compelling as it is tragic. More American lives were lost during the four years of the American Civil War than in any other war in U.S. history. And arguably, more has been written about the various aspects of the Civil War than any other American conflict. This book, beginning with the precursors to war and continuing through the rocky period of Reconstruction, provides readers with a complete, concise, and detailed picture of the War between the States.

The truth is, there are any number of reasons why the Civil War remains such a seminal event in American history. This makes sense, given that the reasons for the war itself also are more complicated than any single issue. What's more, the last shots fired did not end the struggle as quickly or as easily as many history books might suggest.

The American Civil War is inextricably linked with slavery, an issue that has deep roots in the United States. Slaves had arrived with settlers as early as 1619, and their labour in the fertile soil of the South helped a nation become prosperous. The right to own slaves was a sticking point during the Constitutional Convention of 1787. While creating a document that would name the powers and duties of the government of the new nation, the question of what rights individual states should maintain came into play. Did the states' powers include authority over the slavery issue? This question would be revisited again and again. Considering

A reenactment of the Battle of Cedar Creek, Va., staged on the site of the original battle, which took place October 19, 1864. The Union victories in the Shenandoah Campaign of 1864 marked the beginning of the end for the Confederates. © www.istockphoto.com/Dennis Guyitt

that the conflict over slavery had been brewing as early as the writing of the U.S. Constitution, it is surprising that this issue, for which many were willing to give their lives, did not boil into an all-out war until 1861.

Indeed, the Founding Fathers had worried that focusing on slavery would divide the newly created country, so they did nothing to end the practice. Instead, they trusted that a stronger, more stable government in the future would resolve the matter. Thomas Jefferson stated: "Nothing is more certainly written in the book of fate than that these people are to be freed." Although the representatives believed they had avoided argument, they had actually watered the seeds of the conflict that would entangle their descendants. Likely, they did not realize that this judgment would push the country beyond legislative fixes and into the bloodiest conflict ever on American soil.

As the United States matured, slavery helped shape the basic economic differences and interests of the lands above and below the Mason-Dixon Line. The North, with its colder climate and natural harbours, became increasingly industrial with an economy based on manufacturing, trade, and transportation. A steady workforce was supplied by large numbers of European immigrants. By contrast, the South had few cities or centres of manufacturing. Instead, large plantations that relied on slavery dominated the agricultural economy. In 1790, the South produced about 3,000 bales of cotton per year, a bale weighing about 500 pounds. By 1860, an annual crop of over 3.8 million bales was a staple of the Southern economy. During this time, the number of slaves rose from about 650,000 to 3.8 million.

Slavery was an institution so well integrated into the Southern lifestyle that the thought that it would cease to exist was next to impossible for many to imagine. Some believed that the loss of slaves would ruin the Southern economy, its politics, and the very structure of its society. To some, it was only natural that two separate nations should exist if a single government could not make decisions to support both economies.

Congress made attempts to balance the needs of the North and South and the number of slave and free states. In 1820, Congress passed the Missouri Compromise (also known as the Compromise of 1820) to create a nation of twelve slave states and twelve free states. In addition, the compromise stated that any state formed from the Louisiana Territory above the 36° 30' latitude line, with the exception of Missouri, would be a free state. Later, the Compromise of 1850 introduced a concept called popular sovereignty, which allowed individual states to decide if slavery would be permitted within their borders.

Attached to the Compromise of 1850 was the Fugitive Slave Act, which called for citizens to turn in runaway slaves.

Illustration depicting federal troops entering the arsenal at Harpers Ferry, Va., which was defended by John Brown's men. Kean Collection/Hulton Archive/Getty Images

The law also took away an escaped slave's right to a trial. Because of this act, many fugitive slaves, as well as free blacks, were transported from the North to the South. The Fugitive Slave Act gave rise to a renewed urgency and fervour in the Underground Railroad. With the help of "conductors" such as Harriet Tubman, slaves were directed through a network of routes out of the slave-holding South and into freedom in the North.

Compromises and concessions never seemed to be enough, however. Pockets of crisis arose. The Kansas-Nebraska Act of 1854 introduced two new states into the union. Popular sovereignty dictated that these new states could determine their own fate when it came to the question of slavery. Both proslavery and antislavery voters in Kansas and Nebraska rushed to the polls. Rather than aiding in a peaceful democratic resolution, the voting erupted into violence. Skirmishes broke out along the Kansas-Missouri border. The episode, which New York newspaper reporter Horace Greeley dubbed "Bleeding Kansas," was yet another instance of violence escalating tensions between free and slave states.

The role of media in spreading ideas prior to the Civil War should not be understated. William Lloyd Garrison's abolitionist newspaper, *The Liberator*, and Harriet Beecher Stowe's novel *Uncle Tom's Cabin* led to more support for ending slavery. In addition, Frederick Douglass's *Narrative of the Life of Frederick Douglass* gave the public a true account of the life of a slave. As a reactionary measure, angry Southerners wrote as well. In their articles and books, slaves were depicted as being happier with their lives in the fields than poor, suffering Northern white factory workers.

Memorable civilian figures surfaced from the turbulence in the pre–Civil War period. Dred Scott, the slave who unsuccessfully sued his owner for his freedom, brought the states' rights issue over slavery to the forefront of national matters. With his raid on Harpers Ferry in 1859, John Brown's actions foreshadowed the violence that would erupt on a grand scale across the nation.

The political will of the North was embodied in lawyer, politician, and abolitionist Abraham Lincoln; that of the South in the reluctantly secessionist Jefferson Davis. The election of the former was directly responsible for the ascension to power of the latter. On March 4, 1861, Lincoln emphasized in his inaugural speech that he wished to preserve the Union, not to abolish slavery. However, the Confederacy was already established and war inevitable.

From the beginning, the resources of the Union far outweighed those of the Confederacy. However, military strategy and sheer force of will would fortify the Confederate forces in many victories. On April 12, 1861, the first show of power took place when the Confederates began shelling the federally held Fort Sumter in South Carolina. The conflict many feared had begun.

Most of the Civil War battles took place in the states along the border between the Union and the Confederacy. In July 1861, the First Battle of Bull Run in Virginia strengthened the confidence of the South and reflected that the war would not be easily won. In fact, the Union would not make much headway against Confederate forces until May 1862 at the Battle of Seven Pines. Union General George McClellan, leader of the eastern

Abolitionist pamphlet, published in 1762. MPI/Hulton Archive/Getty Images

A SHORT ACCOUNT Of that PART of *AFRICA*, Inhabited by the NEGROES.

With Reſpect to the *Fertility* of the Country; the *good Diſpoſition* of many of the *Natives*, and the *Manner* by which the SLAVE TRADE is carried on.

Extracted from divers Authors, in order to ſhew the *Iniquity* of that TRADE, and the *Falſity* of the ARGUMENTS uſually advanced in its *Vindication*.

With Quotations from the Writings of ſeveral Perſons of Note, *viz.* GEORGE WALLIS, FRANCIS HUTCHESON, and JAMES FOSTER, and a large Extract from a Pamphlet, lately publiſhed in *London*, on the Subject of the SLAVE TRADE.

The Second EDITION, with large Additions and Amendments.

Do you the neighb'ring, blameleſs *Indian* aid;
Culture what he neglects, not his invade,
Dare not, Oh! dare not, with ambitious View
Force or demand Subjection, never due.
* * * * * * * * * * * * * *
* * * * * * * * * * * * * *
Why muſt I *Africk*'s ſable Children ſee
Vended for Slaves, tho' formed by Nature free?
The nameleſs Tortures cruel Minds invent,
Thoſe to ſubject whom Nature equal meant?
If theſe you dare, altho' unjuſt Succeſs
Impow'rs you now, unpuniſh'd, to oppreſs
Revolving EMPIRE you and yours may doom;
Rome all ſubdued, yet *Vandals* vanquiſh'd *Rome*.

RICHARD SAVAGE, *on publick Spirit*.

PHILADELPHIA:

Printed by W. DUNLAP, in the YEAR MDCCLXII.

forces, was frequently hesitant to strike. Confederate General Robert E. Lee often counteracted with surprise and swiftness to dismantle Union forces, as at the Second Battle of Bull Run in August 1862. (Lee, a remarkable leader, had been against secession; he fought to defend his native state of Virginia. His motivations were not unique among Confederate leaders.)

Lee next took his Confederates into Maryland, the first attempt to capture territory in a Union state. McClellan stopped him at Sharpsburg, Md., on Antietam Creek. On September 17, the two forces clashed in one of the most deadly days in the war, ending in a very slim Northern victory. President Lincoln chose this time to issue the Emancipation Proclamation, stating that all slaves in the Confederate states would be "forever free" as of Jan. 1, 1863. He hoped this would weaken the Southern economy and encourage blacks to help the Northern effort.

In late May 1863, General Lee and his forces moved into Union territory. At the beginning of July, they suffered a loss at Gettysburg, Pa., that changed the South's fortunes. On July 3, the third day of the Battle of Gettysburg, 15,000 Confederates attacked the Union army's centre formation. Only about half of these Confederate soldiers survived "Pickett's Charge." Lee was never again to march into Union territory. Abraham Lincoln commemorated this victory with the Gettysburg Address—both honouring the dead and assuring the public that the Union would never "perish from the earth."

Areas west of the Appalachian Mountains also hosted many crucial battles. General Ulysses S. Grant's forces focused on capturing Confederate forts, waterways, and supplies. Some in the North called Grant "a butcher" after an estimated one out of four men died in Tennessee at the Battle of Shiloh in April 1862. Lincoln, though, admired his courage: "I can't spare this man. He fights."

Not until the Union surrounded Petersburg, Va., the rail centre that provided supplies to Richmond, did Grant, who had taken command of the Union army following his successful Vicksburg campaign, gain the final advantage over Lee. The Siege of Petersburg began in June 1864. Without supplies, Confederates suffered not only from a lack of food but also a lack of hope. Across the nation, the Union forces swelled while the Confederate army dwindled. Lee had no choice but to surrender at Appomattox Court House, Va., on April 9, 1865. The war, in efffect, was over.

Abraham Lincoln then turned to the Herculean task of reuniting and rebuilding the nation. Though this period is called Reconstruction, Lincoln preferred the term "Reconciliation" because he knew winning the hearts of the secessionists was imperative. However, five days after Lee's surrender, Lincoln was assassinated. It was left to Southern sympathizer Andrew Johnson, the vice president, to carry on the process.

After the Radical Republicans began directing Reconstruction following their sweeping election victory in 1866, the South (with the exception of Tennessee) came under military administration. The former Confederate states were permitted to rejoin the Union only after passing the Fourteenth, or if readmitted after its passage, the Fifteenth constitutional Amendment, intended to ensure the civil rights of freedmen after the Thirteenth Amendment abolished slavery. Millions of former slaves were now free, but the road to equality was a long one, and blacks continued to suffer great hardship in the postwar years.

Many countries that engage in civil war do not emerge whole. Lingering differences demand that separate nations be set up. Bearing in mind the expanse of the American conflict—fought both east and west of the Appalachian Mountains—the continuation of the Union after the war was an even greater and more impressive feat—one that required millions of Americans to pledge allegiance to their country, rather than their state. It was a feat that required accepting former slaves as citizens, ultimately paving the way for civil rights. It was a feat that ultimately became Abraham Lincoln's legacy, and salve for a wounded nation.

CHAPTER 1

PRELUDE TO WAR

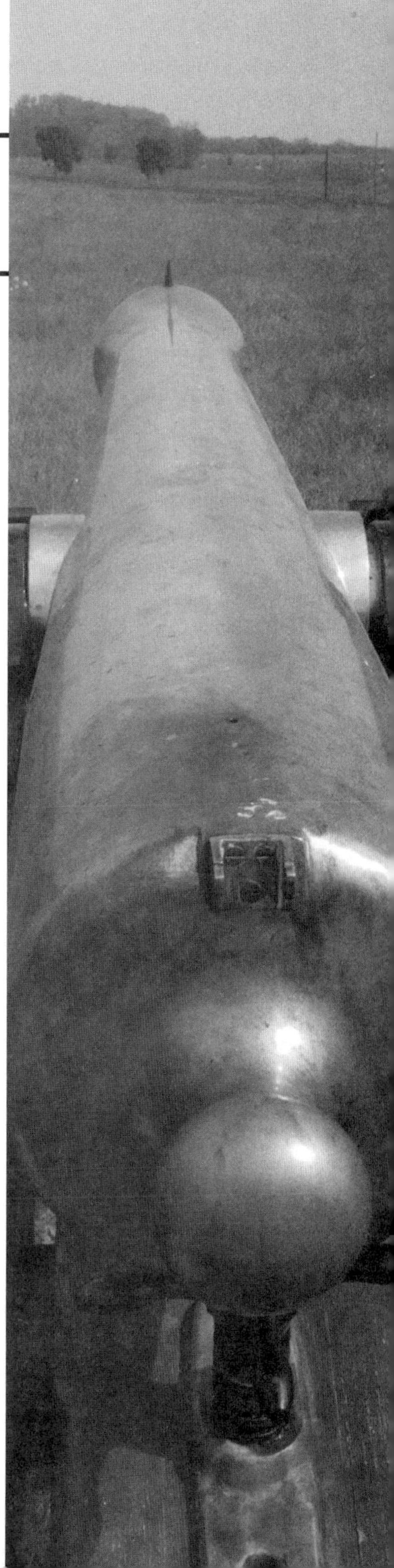

Before the Civil War, the United States experienced a whole generation of nearly unremitting political crisis. Underlying the problem was the fact that America in the early 19th century had been a country, not a nation. The major functions of government—those relating to education, transportation, health, and public order—were performed on the state or local level, and little more than a loose allegiance to the government in Washington, D.C., a few national institutions such as churches and political parties, and a shared memory of the Founding Fathers of the republic tied the country together. Within this loosely structured society every section, every state, every locality, every group could pretty much go its own way.

Gradually, however, changes in technology and in the economy were bringing all the elements of the country into steady and close contact. Improvements in transportation—first canals, then toll roads, and especially railroads—broke down isolation and encouraged the boy from the country to wander to the city, the farmer from New Hampshire to migrate to Iowa. Improvements in the printing press, which permitted the publication of penny newspapers, and the development of the telegraph system broke through the barriers of intellectual provincialism and made everybody almost instantaneously aware of what was going on throughout the country. As the railroad network proliferated, it had to have central direction and control; and national railroad corporations—the first true "big businesses" in the United States—emerged to provide order and stability.

For many Americans the wrench from a largely rural, slow-moving, fragmented society in the early 1800s to a bustling, integrated, national social order in the mid-century was an abrupt and painful one, and they often resisted it. Sometimes resentment against change manifested itself in harsh attacks on those who appeared to be the agents of change—especially immigrants, who seemed to personify the forces that were altering the older America. Vigorous nativist movements appeared in most cities during the 1840s; but not until the 1850s, when the huge numbers of Irish and German immigrants of the previous decade became eligible to vote, did the antiforeign fever reach its peak. Directed both against immigrants and against the Roman Catholic church, to which so many of them belonged, the so-called Know-Nothings emerged as a powerful

In Focus: Know-Nothing Party

Formally known as the American Party, the Know-Nothing party flourished in the 1850s as an outgrowth of the strong anti-immigrant and especially anti-Roman Catholic sentiment that started to manifest itself during the 1840s. A rising tide of immigrants, primarily Germans in the Midwest and Irish in the East, seemed to pose a threat to the economic and political security of native-born Protestant Americans. In 1849 the secret Order of the Star-Spangled Banner formed in New York City, and soon after lodges formed in nearly every other major American city.

Members, when asked about their nativist organizations, were supposed to reply that they knew nothing, hence the name. As its membership and importance grew in the 1850s, the group slowly shed its clandestine character and embraced its official name. As a national political entity, the American Party called for restrictions on immigration, the exclusion of the foreign-born from voting or holding public office in the United States, and a 21-year residency requirement for citizenship.

By 1852 the Know-Nothing party was achieving phenomenal growth. It did very well that year in state and local elections, and with passage of the Kansas-Nebraska Act in 1854 it won additional adherents from the ranks of conservatives who could support neither the pro-slavery Democrats nor antislavery Republicans. When Congress assembled on Dec. 3, 1855, 43 representatives were avowed members of the Know-Nothing party.

That, however, was the peak of Know-Nothing power. At the American Party convention in Philadelphia the following year, the party split along sectional lines over the pro-slavery platform pushed through by Southern delegates. Party presidential candidate Millard Fillmore carried just one state (Maryland) in the 1856 election, and congressional strength dropped to 12 representatives.

Caught in the sectional strife disrupting all national institutions, the American Party fell apart after 1856. Antislavery Know-Nothings joined the Republican Party, while Southern members flocked to the pro-slavery banner still held aloft by the Democratic Party. By 1859 the American Party's strength was largely confined to the border states. In 1860 remnants of the Know-Nothings joined old-line Whigs to form the Constitutional Union Party, nominating John Bell of Tennessee for president. Bell finished fourth in popular votes in the four-man contest of that year, won by the Republican Abraham Lincoln.

Two other groups that took the name American Party appeared in the 1870s and '80s. One of these, organized in California in 1886, proposed a briefly popular platform calling mainly for the exclusion of Chinese and other Asians from industrial employment.

political force in 1854, increasing the resistance to change.

SECTIONALISM AND SLAVERY

A more enduring manifestation of hostility toward the nationalizing tendencies in American life was the reassertion of strong feelings of sectional loyalty. New Englanders felt threatened by the West, which drained off the ablest and most vigorous members of the labour force. Further, once the railroad network was complete, western states produced wool and grain that undersold the products of the poor New England hill country. The West, too, developed a strong sectional feeling, blending a sense of its uniqueness, a feeling of being looked down on as raw and uncultured, and an awareness that it was being exploited by the businessmen of the East.

The most conspicuous and distinctive section, however, was the South—an area set apart by climate, by a plantation system designed for the production of such staple crops as cotton, tobacco, and sugar, and, especially, by the persistence of slavery, which had been abolished or prohibited in all other parts of the United States. It should not be thought that all or even most white Southerners were directly involved in the section's "peculiar institution." Indeed, in 1850 there were only 347,525 slaveholders in a total white population of about 6,000,000 in the slave states. Half of these Southerners owned four slaves or fewer and could not be considered planters. In the entire South there were fewer than 1,800 persons who owned more than 100 slaves.

Nevertheless, slavery did give a distinctive tone to the whole pattern of Southern life. If the large planters were few, they were also wealthy, prestigious, and powerful; often they were the political as well as the economic leaders of their section; and their values pervaded every stratum of Southern society. Far from opposing slavery, small farmers thought only of the possibility that they too might, with hard work and good fortune, some day join the ranks of the planter class—to which they were closely connected by ties of blood, marriage, and friendship. Behind this virtually unanimous support of slavery lay the universal belief—shared by many whites in the North and West as well—that blacks were an innately inferior people who had risen only to a state of barbarism in their native Africa and who could live in a civilized society only if disciplined through slavery. Though by 1860 there were in fact about 250,000 free blacks in the South, most Southern whites resolutely refused to believe that the slaves, if freed, could ever coexist peacefully with their former masters. With shuddering horror, they pointed to a number of incidents—an insurrection of blacks that had occurred in Santo Domingo; a brief slave rebellion led by the African American Gabriel in Virginia in 1800; a plot of Charleston, South Carolina, blacks headed by Denmark Vesey in 1822; and, especially, a bloody and determined Virginia insurrection led by Nat Turner in 1831—as evidence that African Americans had to be kept under iron control. Facing increasing opposition to slavery outside their section, Southerners developed an elaborate pro-slavery argument, defending the institution on biblical, economic, and sociological grounds.

A DECADE OF POLITICAL CRISES

In the early years of the republic, sectional differences existed, but it had been possible to reconcile or ignore them because distances were great, communication was difficult, and the powerless national government had almost nothing to do. The revolution in transportation and communication, however, eliminated much of the isolation, and the victory of the United States in its brief war with Mexico left the national government with problems that required action.

POPULAR SOVEREIGNTY

The Compromise of 1850 was an uneasy patchwork of concessions to all sides that began to fall apart as soon as it was enacted. In the long run, the principle of popular sovereignty proved to be most unsatisfactory of all, making each territory a battleground where the supporters of the South contended with the defenders of the North and West.

The seriousness of those conflicts became clear in 1854, when Stephen A. Douglas introduced his Kansas bill in Congress, establishing a territorial government for the vast region that lay between the Missouri River and the Rocky Mountains. In the Senate, the bill was amended to create not one but two territories—Kansas and Nebraska—from the part of the Louisiana Purchase from which the Missouri Compromise of 1820 had forever excluded slavery. Douglas, who was unconcerned over the moral issue of slavery and desirous of getting on with the settling of the

West and the construction of a transcontinental railroad, knew that the Southern senators would block the organization of Kansas as a free territory. Recognizing that the North and West had outstripped their section in population and hence in the House of Representatives, Southerners clung desperately to an equality of votes in the Senate and were not disposed to welcome any new free territories, which would inevitably become additional free states (as California had done through the Compromise of 1850). Accordingly, Douglas thought that the doctrine of popular sovereignty, which had been applied to the territories gained from Mexico, would avoid a political contest over the Kansas territory: it would permit Southern slaveholders to move into the area, but, as the region was unsuited for plantation slavery, it would inevitably result in the formation of additional free states. His bill therefore allowed the inhabitants of the territory self-government in

In Focus: Compromise of 1850

On Dec. 3, 1849, the territory of California requested admittance to the Union with a constitution prohibiting slavery. This request brought to a head several outstanding issues related to slavery, creating a crisis that threatened dissolution of the Union. Among the problems was the unresolved question of slavery's extension into other areas ceded by Mexico the preceding year.

To maintain an even balance between free and slave states, a series of measures was offered by the "great compromiser," Sen. Henry Clay of Kentucky. In an attempt to give satisfaction to both pro-slavery and antislavery forces, the important sections of the omnibus bill that resulted called for the admission of California as a free state, the organization of the territories of New Mexico and Utah with the slavery question left open, settlement of the Texas–New Mexico boundary dispute, a more rigorous provision for the return of runaway slaves, and the prohibition of the slave trade in the District of Columbia.

With the influential support of Sen. Daniel Webster and the concerted unifying efforts of Sen. Stephen A. Douglas, the five compromise measures were enacted in September. These measures were accepted by moderates in all sections of the country, and the secession of the South was postponed for a decade. The Compromise, however, contained the seeds of future discord. The precedent of popular sovereignty led to a demand for a similar provision for the Kansas Territory in 1854, causing bitterness and violence there. Furthermore, the application of the new Fugitive Slave Act triggered such a strong reaction throughout the North that many moderate antislavery elements became determined opponents of any further extension of slavery into the territories. While the Compromise of 1850 succeeded as a temporary expedient, it also proved the failure of compromise as a permanent political solution when vital sectional interests were at stake.

all matters of domestic importance, including the slavery issue. This provision in effect allowed the territorial legislatures to mandate slavery in their areas and was directly contrary to the Missouri Compromise. With the backing of Pres. Franklin Pierce (served 1853–57), Douglas bullied, wheedled, and bluffed congressmen into passing his bill.

POLARIZATION OVER SLAVERY

Sectional differences

Northern sensibilities were outraged. Although disliking slavery, Northerners had made few efforts to change the South's "peculiar institution" so long as the republic was loosely articulated. (Indeed, when William Lloyd Garrison began his *Liberator* in 1831, urging the immediate and unconditional emancipation of all slaves, he had only a tiny following, and a few years later he had actually been mobbed in Boston.) But with the sections, perforce, being drawn closely together, Northerners could no longer profess indifference to the South and its institutions. Sectional differences, centring on the issue of slavery, began to appear in every American institution. During the 1840s the major national religious denominations, such as the Methodists and the Presbyterians, split over the slavery question. The Whig Party, which had once allied the conservative businessmen of the North and West with the planters of the South, divided and virtually disappeared after the election of 1852. When Douglas's bill opened up slavery to Kansas and Nebraska—land that had long been reserved for the westward expansion of the free states—Northerners began to organize into an antislavery political party, called in some states the Anti-Nebraska Democratic Party, in others the People's Party, but in most places, the Republican Party.

Bleeding Kansas

Events of the mid-1850s further exacerbated relations between the sections, strengthening this new party. Sponsors of the Kansas-Nebraska Act (May 30, 1854) expected its provisions for territorial self-government to arrest the "torrent of fanaticism" that had been dividing the nation regarding the slavery issue. Instead, a small civil war erupted between pro-slavery and anti-slavery advocates for control of the new territory of Kansas under the doctrine of popular sovereignty. Free-soil forces from the North formed armed emigrant associations to populate Kansas, while pro-slavery advocates poured over the border from Missouri. Regulating associations and guerrilla bands were formed by each side, and only the intervention of the Governor prevented violence in the Wakarusa War, launched in December 1855 over the murder of an antislavery settler. On May 21, 1856, "Bleeding Kansas" became a fact with the Sack of Lawrence, in which a proslavery mob swarmed into the town of Lawrence and wrecked and burned the hotel and newspaper office in an effort to wipe out this "hotbed of abolitionism." The next day, the U.S. Capitol became the site of violence when Preston S. Brooks, a South Carolina congressman, brutally attacked Sen. Charles Sumner of Massachusetts at his desk in the Senate chamber because he had presumably insulted the Carolinian's "honour" in a speech he had given in support of Kansas abolitionists. On May 24, back in Kansas, an antislavery band led by John Brown retaliated in the Pottawatomie Massacre. Periodic bloodshed along the border followed as the two factions fought battles, captured towns, and set prisoners free. A political struggle to determine the future state's position on slavery ensued, centred on the Lecompton Constitution proposed in 1857. The question would not be settled until Kansas was admitted as a free state in January 1861, but, meanwhile, "Bleeding Kansas" had furnished the newly formed Republican Party with a much needed antislavery issue.

The 1856 presidential election made it clear that voting was becoming polarized along sectional lines. Though James Buchanan, the Democratic nominee, was elected, John C. Frémont, the Republican candidate, received a majority of the votes in the free states.

The Dred Scott Decision

The next year the U.S. Supreme Court hear a case that would have a profound impact on the debate over slavery, *Dred Scott* v. *John F. A. Sandford.*

Dred Scott was a slave who was owned by Dr. John Emerson of Missouri. In 1834 Emerson, because of his service in the U.S. military, undertook a series of moves, taking Scott from Missouri (a slave state) to Illinois (a free state) and

Dred Scott. Library of Congress, Washington, D.C. (digital file no. 3a08411u)

finally into the Wisconsin Territory (a free territory under the provisions of the Missouri Compromise). During this period, Scott met and married Harriet Robinson, who became attached to the Emerson household. In the early 1840s Dr. Emerson, along with his wife (whom he had married in 1838), and the Scotts returned to Missouri, and Dr. Emerson died in 1843.

Dred Scott reportedly attempted to purchase his freedom from Emerson's widow, who refused the sale. In 1846, with the help of antislavery lawyers, Harriet and Dred Scott filed individual lawsuits for their freedom in the Missouri state courts, arguing that their residence in a free state and a free territory had liberated them from the bonds of slavery. It was later agreed that only Dred's case would move forward, though the decision in that case would apply to Harriet's case as well.

Dred Scott v. *Irene Emerson* took years to reach a definitive decision. The case was initially filed in the Saint Louis Circuit Court. In 1850 a lower court declared Scott free, but the verdict was overturned in 1852 by the Missouri Supreme Court. Mrs. Emerson soon left Missouri and gave control of her late husband's estate to her brother, John F. A. Sanford, a resident of New York; his last name was incorrectly spelled Sandford on court documents. Because Sanford was not subject to suit in Missouri, Scott's lawyers filed a suit against him in the U.S. federal courts. The case eventually reached the U.S. Supreme Court, which announced its decision on March 6, 1857, just two days after the inauguration of Pres. James Buchanan.

Though each justice wrote a separate opinion, Chief Justice Roger B. Taney's opinion is most often cited on account of its far-reaching implications for the sectional crisis. As one of the seven justices denying Scott his freedom (two dissented), Taney declared that an African American could not be entitled to rights as a U.S. citizen, such as the right to sue in federal courts. In fact, Taney wrote, African Americans had "no rights which any white man was bound to respect." The decision might have ended there, with the dismissal of Scott's appeal. But Taney and the other justices in the majority went on to declare that the Missouri Compromise of 1820 (which had forbidden slavery in that part of the Louisiana Purchase north of the latitude 36°30', except for Missouri) was unconstitutional because Congress had no power to prohibit slavery in the territories. Slaves were property, and masters were guaranteed their property rights under the Fifth Amendment. Neither Congress nor a territorial legislature could deprive a citizen of his property without due process of law. As for Scott's temporary residence in a free state, Illinois, the majority said that Scott had still been subject then to Missouri law.

The decision—only the second time in the country's history that the Supreme

NOW READY:

THE

Dred Scott Decision.

OPINION OF CHIEF-JUSTICE ROGER B. TANEY,

WITH AN INTRODUCTION,

BY DR. J. H. VAN EVRIE.

ALSO,

AN APPENDIX,

BY SAM. A. CARTWRIGHT, M.D., of New Orleans,

ENTITLED,

"Natural History of the Prognathous Race of Mankind."

ORIGINALLY WRITTEN FOR THE NEW YORK DAY-BOOK.

THE GREAT WANT OF A BRIEF PAMPHLET, containing the famous decision of Chief-Justice Taney, in the celebrated Dred Scott Case, has induced the Publishers of the DAY-BOOK to present this edition to the public. It contains a Historical Introduction by Dr. Van Evrie, author of "Negroes and Negro Slavery," and an Appendix by Dr. Cartwright, of New Orleans, in which the physical differences between the negro and the white races are forcibly presented. As a whole, this pamphlet gives the *historical*, *legal*, and *physical* aspects of the "Slavery" Question in a concise compass, and should be circulated by thousands before the next presidential election. All who desire to answer the arguments of the abolitionists should read it. In order to place it before the masses, and induce Democratic Clubs, Democratic Town Committees, and all interested in the cause, to order it for distribution, it has been put down at the following low rates, for which it will be sent, free of postage, to any part of the United States. Dealers supplied at the same rate.

Single Copies	$0 25
Five Copies	1 00
Twelve Copies	2 00
Fifty Copies	7 00
One Hundred Copies	12 00
Every additional Hundred	10 00

Address

VAN EVRIE, HORTON, & CO.,
Publishers of DAY-BOOK,
No. 40 Ann Street, New York.

Newspaper notice for a pamphlet on the U.S. Supreme Court's Dred Scott decision. Library of Congress (ng. No. LC-USZ62-132561)

Court declared an act of Congress unconstitutional—was a clear victory for the slaveholding South. Southerners had argued that both Congress and the territorial legislature were powerless to exclude slavery from a territory. Only a state could exclude slavery, they maintained. This seemed a mortal blow to the Republican Party. It also forced Stephen A. Douglas, advocate of popular sovereignty, to come up with a method (the "Freeport Doctrine") whereby settlers could actually ban slavery from their midst. President Buchanan, the South, and the majority of the Supreme Court hoped that the Dred Scott decision would mark the end of antislavery agitation. Instead, the decision increased antislavery sentiment in the North, strengthened the Republican Party, and fed the sectional antagonism that burst into war in 1861. (The Scotts were later bought by the Blow family, who had sold Dred Scott to Dr. Emerson, and they were freed in 1857. Dred Scott died of tuberculosis the following year. Little is known of Harriet Scott's life after that time.)

An Irrepressible Conflict?

By this point many Americans, North and South, had come to the conclusion that slavery and freedom could not much longer coexist in the United States. For Southerners the answer was withdrawal from a Union that no longer protected their rights and interests; they had talked of it as early as the Nashville Convention of 1850, when the compromise measures were under consideration, and now more and more Southerners favoured secession.

For Northerners the remedy was to change the social institutions of the South; few advocated immediate or complete emancipation of the slaves, but many felt that the South's "peculiar institution" must be contained. In 1858 William H. Seward, the leading Republican of New York, spoke of an "irrepressible conflict" between freedom and slavery; and in Illinois a rising Republican politician, Abraham Lincoln, who unsuccessfully contested Douglas for a seat in the Senate, announced that "this government cannot endure, permanently half *slave* and half *free*."

That it was not possible to end the agitation over slavery became further apparent in 1859 when on the night of October 16, John Brown, who had escaped

In Focus: Lincoln-Douglas Debates

A series of seven debates were held between Democratic senator Stephen A. Douglas and Republican challenger Abraham Lincoln during the 1858 Illinois senatorial campaign, largely concerning the issue of slavery extension into the territories.

The slavery extension question had seemingly been settled by the Missouri Compromise nearly 40 years earlier. The Mexican War, however, had added new territories, and the issue flared up again in the 1840s. The Compromise of 1850 provided a temporary respite from sectional strife, but the Kansas-Nebraska Act of 1854—a measure Douglas sponsored—brought the slavery extension issue to the fore once again. Douglas's bill in effect repealed the Missouri Compromise by lifting the ban against slavery in territories north of the 36°30′ latitude. In place of the ban, Douglas offered popular sovereignty, the doctrine that the actual settlers in the territories and not Congress should decide the fate of slavery in their midst.

The Kansas-Nebraska Act spurred the creation of the Republican Party, formed largely to keep slavery out of the western territories. Both Douglas's doctrine of popular sovereignty and the Republican stand on free soil were seemingly invalidated by the Dred Scott decision of 1857, in which the Supreme Court said that neither Congress nor the territorial legislature could exclude slavery from a territory.

When Lincoln and Douglas debated the slavery extension issue in 1858, therefore, they were addressing the problem that had divided the nation into two hostile camps, threatening the continued existence of the Union. Their contest, as a consequence, had repercussions far beyond determining who would win the senatorial seat at stake.

When Lincoln received the Republican nomination to run against Douglas, he said in his acceptance speech that "a house divided against itself cannot stand" and that "this government

cannot endure permanently half slave and half free." Douglas thereupon attacked Lincoln as a radical, threatening the continued stability of the Union. Lincoln then challenged Douglas to a series of debates, and the two eventually agreed to hold joint encounters in seven Illinois congressional districts.

The debates, each three hours long, were convened in Ottawa (August 21), Freeport (August 27), Jonesboro (September 15), Charleston (September 18), Galesburg (October 7), Quincy (October 13), and Alton (October 15). Douglas repeatedly tried to brand Lincoln as a dangerous radical who advocated racial equality and disruption of the Union. Lincoln emphasized the moral iniquity of slavery and attacked popular sovereignty for the bloody results it had produced in Kansas.

At Freeport Lincoln challenged Douglas to reconcile popular sovereignty with the Dred Scott decision. Douglas replied that settlers could circumvent the decision by not establishing the local police regulations—i.e., a slave code—that protected a master's property. Without such protection, no one would bring slaves into a territory. This became known as the "Freeport Doctrine."

Douglas's position, while acceptable to many Northern Democrats, angered the South and led to the division of the last remaining national political institution, the Democratic Party. Although he retained his seat in the Senate, narrowly defeating Lincoln when the state legislature (which then elected U.S. senators) voted 54 to 46 in his favour, Douglas's stature as a national leader of the Democratic Party was gravely diminished. Lincoln, on the other hand, lost the election but won acclaim as an eloquent spokesman for the Republican cause.

punishment for the Pottawatomie massacre, staged a raid on Harpers Ferry, Virginia (now in West Virginia), designed to free the slaves and to help them begin a guerrilla war against the Southern whites. Even though Brown was promptly captured and Virginia slaves gave little heed to his appeals, Southerners feared that this was the beginning of organized Northern efforts to undermine their social system. The fact that Brown was viewed by many as a fanatic and an inept strategist whose actions were considered questionable even by most abolitionists did not lessen Northern admiration for him.

The presidential election of 1860 occurred, therefore, in an atmosphere of great tension. Southerners, determined that their rights should be guaranteed by law, insisted upon a Democratic candidate willing to protect slavery in the territories. They rejected Stephen A. Douglas, whose popular-sovereignty doctrine left the question in doubt, in favour of John C. Breckinridge. Douglas, backed by most of the Northern and border-state Democrats, ran on a separate Democratic ticket. Elderly conservatives, who deplored all agitation of the sectional questions but advanced no solutions, offered John Bell as candidate of the

View of the town of Harpers Ferry, now in West Virginia, and railroad bridge. Library of Congress, Washington, D.C. (LC-B8171-7187 DLC)

Constitutional Union Party. Republicans, confident of success, passed over the claims of Seward, who had accumulated too many liabilities in his long public career, nominating Lincoln instead. Voting in the subsequent election was along markedly sectional patterns, with Republican strength confined almost completely to the North and West. Though Lincoln received only a plurality of the popular vote, he was an easy winner in the electoral college.

CHAPTER 2

The Peculiar Institution

ORIGINS OF SLAVERY IN THE UNITED STATES

Between the 16th and 19th centuries an estimated total of 12 million Africans were forcibly brought to the Circum-Caribbean world—that is, to the islands of the Caribbean and to South and North America. Slaves first were brought to Virginia in 1619. Subsequently, Africans were transshipped to North America from the Caribbean in increasing numbers. Initially, however, the English relied primarily on indentured servants from the mother country for their dependent labour. But in the two decades of the 1660s and 1670s the laws of slave ownership were clarified (for example, Africans who converted to Christianity no longer had to be manumitted), and the price of servants may have increased because of rising wage rates in prospering England; soon thereafter African slaves replaced English indentured labourers. Tobacco initially was the profitable crop that occupied most slaves in the Chesapeake. The invention of the cotton gin by Eli Whitney in 1793 changed the situation, and thereafter cotton culture created a huge demand for slaves, especially after the opening of the New South (Alabama, Mississippi, Louisiana, and Texas). By 1850, nearly two-thirds of the plantation slaves were engaged in the production of cotton. Cotton could be grown profitably on smaller plots than could sugar, with the result that in 1860 the average cotton plantation had only about 35 slaves, not all of whom produced cotton. During the reign of "King Cotton," about 40 percent of the Southern population consisted of black slaves; the percentage of slaves rose as high as 64 percent in South Carolina in 1720 and 55 percent in Mississippi in 1810 and 1860. More than 36 percent of all the New World slaves in 1825 were in the southern United States. Like Rome and the Sokoto caliphate, the South was totally transformed by the presence of slavery. Slavery generated profits comparable to those from other investments and was only ended as a consequence of the American Civil War.

THE LAW AND NATURE OF AMERICAN SLAVERY

By definition slavery must be sanctioned by the society in which it exists, and such approval is most easily expressed in written norms or laws. Both slave-owning and slave societies that were part of the major cultural traditions borrowed some of their laws about slavery from the religious texts of their respective civilizations. While the Hebrew Bible prescribed that Hebrew slaves were to be manumitted after six years (Exodus 21:2; Deuteronomy 15:12) and many Islamic slave-owning societies adhered to a similar general recommendation that slaves be freed after six years, in Christian slave societies such as the American South, the principle that the tenure of slavery should be limited was almost completely ignored.

Because England had no law regarding slavery from which to borrow, the English colonies in the Caribbean and North America were free to create their own. The first code established was that of Barbados of 1688, whose origins are unknown. It was imitated by the South Carolina code of 1740. Beginning with Virginia in 1662, each colony in North America worked out its own ex post facto law of slavery before independence, a process that continued after the creation of the United States and until the Civil War. Slavery was mentioned only three times and referred to at most 10 times (and then only indirectly) in the antebellum U.S. Constitution, and, except for a handful of measures on fugitives, there was no federal slave law. The basic protection for the institution of slavery was the Tenth Amendment of 1791, the reserved powers clause, which left the issue of slavery and other matters to the states.

The master–slave relationship was the cornerstone of the law of slavery in all societies, and yet it was an area about which the law often said very little. A major touchstone of the nature of a slave society was whether or not the owner had the right to kill his slave, and in many parts of the American South before 1830 an owner could do so with impunity. The Code of Justinian and the Spanish Siete Partidas deprived cruel owners of their slaves, and that tradition went into the Louisiana Black Code of 1806, which made cruel punishment of slaves a crime. But while brutality and sadistic murder of slaves by their owners were rarely condoned on the grounds that such episodes demoralized other slaves and made them rebellious, few slave owners were actually punished for maltreating their slaves. Moreover, in the pre-1830 American South, where the owner's control over his slave was total, the law said little or nothing about how long he could work him, and whether his slave had a right to food and clothing. There were exceptions, however; for example, the Alabama Slave Code of 1852 mandated that the owner had to provide slaves of working age a sufficiency of healthy food, clothing, attention during illness, and necessities in old age.

The slave could not own property because the master owned not only his slave's body but everything that body might accumulate. This did not mean, however, that slaves could not possess and accumulate property, but only that their owners had legal title to whatever the slaves had. In the South the master also automatically had sexual access to his slaves. Moreover, slave marriages were not recognized in law. In general, a slave had far fewer rights to his offspring than to his spouse. Southern slave owners thought nothing of breaking up both the conjugal unit and the nuclear family. Nevertheless, slaves formed what they considered marriages and had children. Some Southern slave owners recognized such marriages (even across estate boundaries) as well as their offspring, because to have done otherwise would have interfered with production.

Because many more men than women were imported as slaves in most societies, it is not surprising that slaves rarely reproduced themselves in bondage. The American South was a major exception to the rule. There, slaves began to procreate in significant numbers in the mid-18th century. This fact helped the slave owners survive the cutting off of imports that was first enforced in 1808. Between the censuses of 1790 and 1860, the slave population of the South expanded enormously—from 657,327 to 3,838,765—one of the fastest rates of population growth ever recorded prior to the advent of modern medicine. Paradoxically, although the Southern slave regime was one of the most dehumanizing ever recorded, it was one of the most favourable on record demographically, because the nutritional and general living environments were highly conducive to explosive population growth. Without significant imports, the Southern slave population increased fourfold between the early 1800s and 1860.

SLAVE PROTEST

Throughout history human beings have objected to being enslaved and have responded in myriad ways ranging from individual shirking, alcoholism, flight, and suicide to arson, murdering owners, and mass rebellion. Perhaps the most common individual response to enslavement was sluggishness, passivity, and indifference. A nearly universal stereotype of the slave was of a lying, lazy, dull brute who had to be kicked or whipped. There probably were three mutually reinforcing factors at work: an unconscious response to overcontrol and absence of freedom, a conscious effort to sabotage the master's desires, and a conditioned response to the expectation of stereotypical behaviour. Some owners tried to overcome such behaviour by a system of incentives or by strict regimentation, such as the gang system, but historically they were in a minority. Less frequent was suicide. A number of slaves are known to have jumped overboard during the Middle Passage because they feared that the transatlantic voyage was taking them to be eaten by witches or barbarians, a fate that seemed worse than drowning.

Flight, either individually or in groups, was one of the most visible forms of protest against enslavement. The rates of flight usually depended less on individual slave-owner conduct than on the likelihood of success. Immediate conditions, such as the brutality of an overseer or master or a temporary lapse of supervision, often precipitated slave flight, but willingness to undertake such a form of rebellion was infrequent in the South because the refuge of freedom was often very distant. During the American Revolution, however, when the slave owners were occupied with fighting the British, fugitive slaves numbered in the tens of thousands.

The Underground Railroad

Moreover, in the 19th century a system came into being in the Northern states by which escaped slaves from the South were secretly helped by sympathetic Northerners, in defiance of the Fugitive Slave Acts, to reach places of safety in the North or in Canada. Though neither underground nor a railroad, the system was called the Underground Railroad because its activities had to be carried out in secret, using darkness or disguise, and because railway terms were used in reference to the conduct of the system. Various routes were lines, stopping places were called stations, those who aided along the way were conductors, and their charges were known as packages or freight. The network of routes extended in all directions throughout 14 Northern states and "the promised land" of Canada, which was beyond the reach of fugitive-slave hunters. Those who most actively assisted slaves to escape by way of the "railroad" were members of the free black community (including such former slaves as Harriet Tubman), Northern abolitionists, philanthropists, and such church leaders as Quaker Thomas Garrett. Harriet Beecher Stowe, famous for her novel

Uncle Tom's Cabin, gained firsthand knowledge of fugitive slaves through her contact with the Underground Railroad in Cincinnati, Ohio.

Estimates of the number of black people who reached freedom vary greatly, from 40,000 to 100,000. Although only a small minority of Northerners participated in the Underground Railroad, its existence did much to arouse Northern sympathy for the lot of the slave in the antebellum period, at the same time convincing many Southerners that the North as a whole would never peaceably allow the institution of slavery to remain unchallenged.

In Focus: Fugitive Slave Acts

Passed by Congress in 1793 and 1850 (and repealed in 1864), the Fugitive Slave Acts provided for the seizure and return of runaway slaves who escaped from one state into another or into a federal territory. The 1793 law enforced Article IV, Section 2, of the U.S. Constitution in authorizing any federal district judge or circuit court judge, or any state magistrate, to decide finally and without a jury trial the status of an alleged fugitive slave.

The measure met with strong opposition in the Northern states, some of which enacted personal-liberty laws to hamper the execution of the federal law; these laws provided that fugitives who appealed from an original decision against them were entitled to a jury trial. As early as 1810 individual dissatisfaction with the law of 1793 had taken the form of systematic assistance rendered to black slaves escaping from the South to New England or Canada—via the Underground Railroad.

The demand from the South for more effective legislation resulted in enactment of a second Fugitive Slave Act in 1850. Under this law, fugitives could not testify on their own behalf, nor were they permitted a trial by jury. Heavy penalties were imposed upon federal marshals who refused to enforce the law or from whom a fugitive escaped; penalties were also imposed on individuals who helped slaves to escape. Finally, under the 1850 act, special commissioners were to have concurrent jurisdiction with the U.S. courts in enforcing the law. The severity of the 1850 measure led to abuses and defeated its purpose. The number of abolitionists increased, the operations of the Underground Railroad became more efficient, and new personal-liberty laws were enacted in many Northern states. These state laws were among the grievances officially referred to by South Carolina in December 1860 as justification for its secession from the Union. Attempts to carry into effect the law of 1850 aroused much bitterness and probably had as much to do with inciting sectional hostility as did the controversy over slavery in the territories.

For some time during the Civil War, the Fugitive Slave Acts were considered to still hold in the case of blacks fleeing from masters in border states that were loyal to the Union government. It was not until June 28, 1864, that the acts were repealed.

Slave Revolts

Striking Back

Direct, personal attacks on slave owners often were determined by the nature of the slave regime. Where owners believed they enjoyed automatic sexual access to female slaves, both the women and their "husbands" were prone to respond by assaulting the owners or their agents. Where slaves were driven, assault on the drivers was not an uncommon response. As a result, overseers in the Mississippi Valley feared for their lives and constantly carried arms.

The most dramatic form of slave protest was outright rebellion, but slave rebellions in North America were noticeably few and involved only a handful of participants, including the New York revolt of 1712, the Stono rebellion of South Carolina (1739), and the Gabriel plot in Richmond, Va. (1800). Southern slave uprisings were so few and so small because of the absolute certainty that they would be brutally repressed. Nevertheless, three slave rebellions stand out; the Denmark Vesey conspiracy in Charleston, S.C. (1822), Nat Turner's uprising in Jerusalem, Va. (1831), and the *Amistad* mutiny (1839), the last of which occurred not in the South but at sea.

Denmark Vesey Conspiracy

In 1800, the self-educated slave Denmark Vesey was allowed to purchase his freedom with $600 he had won in a street lottery. He was already familiar with the great Haitian slave revolt of the 1790s, and while working as a carpenter he read antislavery literature. Dissatisfied with his second-class status as a freedman and determined to help relieve the far more oppressive conditions of bondsmen he knew, Vesey planned and organized an uprising of blacks in Charleston, S.C., and on nearby plantations. The plan reportedly called for the rebels to attack guardhouses and arsenals, seize their arms, kill all whites, burn and destroy the city, and free the slaves. As many as 9,000 blacks may have been involved, though some scholars dispute this figure.

Warned by a house servant, white authorities on the eve of the scheduled outbreak made massive military preparations, which forestalled the insurrection. During the ensuing two months, some 130 blacks were arrested. In the trials that followed, 67 were convicted of trying to raise an insurrection; of these, 35, including Vesey, were hanged, and 32 were condemned to exile. In addition, four white men were fined and imprisoned for encouraging the plot.

Nat Turner's Rebellion

Nat Turner—whose mother, an African native, transmitted a passionate hatred of slavery to her son—learned to read from one of his master's sons and eagerly absorbed intensive religious training. In the early 1820s, as his religious ardour tended to approach fanaticism, Turner saw himself called upon by God to lead his people out of bondage. He began to exert a powerful influence on many of the slaves in the area of Virginia in which he lived, earning the sobriquet "the Prophet."

In 1831, Turner interpreted an eclipse of the Sun as a sign that the hour to strike was near. His plan was to capture the armoury at the county seat, Jerusalem, and, having gathered many recruits, to press on to the Dismal Swamp, 30 miles (48 km) to the east, where capture would be difficult. On the night of August 21, together with seven fellow slaves in whom he had put his trust, he launched a campaign of total annihilation, murdering his owner and his family in their sleep and then setting forth on a bloody march toward Jerusalem. In two days and nights about 60 white people were ruthlessly slain. Doomed from the start, Turner's insurrection was handicapped by lack of discipline among his followers and by the fact that only 75 blacks rallied to his cause. Armed resistance from the local whites and the arrival of the state militia—a total force of 3,000 men—provided the final crushing blow. Only a few miles from the county seat the insurgents were dispersed and either killed or captured, and many innocent slaves were massacred in the hysteria that followed. Turner eluded his pursuers for six weeks but was finally captured, tried, and hanged.

Nat Turner's rebellion put an end to the white Southern myth that slaves were either contented with their lot or too servile to mount an armed revolt. In Southampton county black people came to measure time from "Nat's Fray," or "Old Nat's War." For many years in black churches throughout the country, the name Jerusalem referred not only to the Bible but also covertly to the place where the rebel slave had met his death. The Turner rebellion spread terror throughout the white South and set off a new wave of oppressive legislation prohibiting the education, movement, and assembly of slaves and stiffened proslavery, anti-abolitionist convictions.

The *Amistad* Mutiny

The slave rebellion that took place on the slave ship *Amistad* near the coast of Cuba on July 2, 1839, had important political and legal repercussions for the abolition movement in the United States, where the mutineers were captured and tried. The Spanish schooner *Amistad* was sailing from Havana to Puerto Príncipe, Cuba, when the ship's unwilling passengers, 53 slaves recently abducted from Africa, revolted. Led by Joseph Cinqué, they killed the captain and the cook but spared the life of a Spanish navigator, so that he could sail them home to Sierra Leone. The navigator managed instead to sail the *Amistad* generally northward. Two months later the U.S. Navy seized the ship off Long Island, N.Y, and towed it into New London, Conn. The mutineers were held in a jail in New Haven, Conn., a state in which slavery was legal.

The Spanish embassy's demand for the return of the Africans to Cuba led to an 1840 trial in a Hartford, Conn., federal court. New England abolitionist Lewis Tappan stirred public sympathy for the African captives, while the U.S. government took the pro-slavery side. U.S. Pres. Martin Van Buren ordered a Navy ship sent to Connecticut to return the Africans to Cuba immediately after the trial. A candidate for reelection that year, he anticipated a ruling against the defendants and hoped to gain pro-slavery votes by removing the Africans before abolitionists could appeal to a higher court.

Prosecutors argued that, as slaves, the mutineers were subject to the laws governing conduct between slaves and their masters. But trial testimony determined that while slavery was legal in Cuba, importation of slaves from Africa was not. Therefore, the judge ruled, rather than being merchandise, the Africans were victims of kidnapping and had the right to escape their captors in any way they could. When the U.S. government appealed the case before the U.S. Supreme Court the next year, congressman and former president John Quincy Adams argued eloquently for the *Amistad* rebels. The Supreme Court upheld the lower court, and private and missionary society donations helped the 35 surviving Africans secure passage home. They arrived in Sierra Leone in January 1842, along with five missionaries and teachers who intended to found a Christian mission.

Spain continued to insist that the United States pay indemnification for the Cuban vessel. The U.S. Congress intermittently debated the *Amistad* case, without resolution, for more than two decades, until the Civil War began in 1861. A committee formed to defend the slaves later developed into the American Missionary Association (incorporated 1846), one of the linchpins of the American abolition movement

CHAPTER 3

Abolitionism and Abolitionists

ABOLITIONISM

Passionately advocated and resisted with equal intensity, abolitionism, the antislavery movement, appeared as late as the 1850s to be a failure in American politics. Yet by 1865 it had succeeded in embedding its goal in the Constitution by amendment, though at the cost of a civil war. At its core lay the issue of "race," over which Americans have shown their best and worst faces for more than three centuries. When race became entangled in this period with the dynamics of American sectional conflict, its full explosive potential was released. If the reform impulse was a common one uniting the American people in the mid-19th century, its manifestation in abolitionism finally split them apart for four bloody years.

Despite its brutality and inhumanity, the slave system had aroused little protest throughout the world until the 18th century, when rationalist thinkers of the Enlightenment began to criticize it for its violation of the rights of man, and Quaker and other evangelical religious groups condemned it for its un-Christian qualities. By the late 18th century, moral disapproval of slavery was widespread, and antislavery reformers won a number of deceptively easy victories during this period. In Britain, Granville Sharp secured a legal decision in 1772 that West Indian planters could not hold slaves in Britain, since slavery was contrary to English law. In the United States, all of the states north of Maryland abolished slavery between 1777 (Vermont) and 1827 (New York). But antislavery sentiments had little effect on the centres of slavery themselves: the great plantations of the Deep South, the West Indies, and South America. Turning their attention to these areas, British and American abolitionists began working in the late 18th century to prohibit the importation of African slaves into the British colonies and the United States. Under the leadership of William Wilberforce and Thomas Clarkson, these forces succeeded in getting the slave trade to the British colonies abolished in 1807. The United States prohibited the importation of slaves that same year, though widespread smuggling continued until about 1862.

Antislavery forces then concentrated on winning the emancipation of those populations already in slavery. They were triumphant when slavery was abolished in the British West Indies by 1838 and in French possessions 10 years later.

The situation in the United States was more complex because slavery was a domestic rather than a colonial phenomenon, being the social and economic base of the plantations of 11 Southern states. Moreover, slavery had gained new vitality when an extremely profitable cotton-based agriculture developed in the South in the early 19th century. American abolitionism laboured under the handicap that it threatened the harmony of North and South in the Union, and it also ran counter to the U.S. Constitution, which left the question of slavery to the individual states. Consequently, the Northern public remained unwilling to adopt abolitionist policy and was distrustful of abolitionist extremism.

William Lloyd Garrsion and *The Liberator*

Abolition itself was a diverse phenomenon. At one end of its spectrum was William Lloyd Garrison, an "immediatist," advocating the immediate end of slavery, denouncing not only slavery but the Constitution of the United States for tolerating the evil. His weekly newspaper, *The Liberator*, founded Jan. 1, 1831, in Boston, was the most influential antislavery periodical in the pre-Civil War period. It claimed a paid circulation of only 3,000 but reached a much wider audience with its uncompromising advocacy of immediate emancipation for the millions of black Americans held in bondage throughout the South. In the North, Garrison's message of moral suasion challenged moderate reformers to apply the principles of the Declaration of Independence to all people, regardless of colour. Fearful slaveholders in the South, erroneously assuming that *The Liberator* represented the majority opinion of Northerners, reacted militantly by defending slavery as a "positive good" and by legislating ever more stringent measures to suppress all possible opposition to its "peculiar institution." Garrison's publication further altered the course of the American antislavery movement by insisting that abolition, rather than African colonization, was the answer to the problem of slavery.

The American Anti-Slavery Society

Founded in 1833, also under the leadership of Garrison, the American Anti-Slavery Society was the main activist arm of the Abolition Movement. By 1840 its auxiliary societies numbered 2,000, with a total membership ranging from 150,000 to 200,000. The societies sponsored meetings, adopted resolutions, signed antislavery petitions to be sent to Congress, published journals and enlisted subscriptions, printed and distributed propaganda in vast quantities, and sent out agents and lecturers (70 in 1836 alone) to carry the antislavery message to Northern audiences.

Participants in the societies were drawn mainly from religious circles and philanthropic backgrounds, as well as from the free black community, with six blacks serving on the first Board of Managers. The society's public meetings were most effective when featuring the eloquent testimony of former slaves such as Frederick Douglass or William Wells Brown. The society's antislavery activities frequently met with violent public opposition, with mobs invading meetings, attacking speakers, and burning presses.

Other Approaches

Garrison's uncompromising tone infuriated not only the South but many Northerners as well, and was long treated as though it were typical of abolitionism in general. Actually it was not. At the other end of the abolitionist spectrum and in between stood such men and women as Theodore Weld, James G. Birney, Gerrit Smith, Theodore Parker, Julia Ward Howe, Lewis and Arthur Tappan, Salmon P. Chase, John Greenleaf Whittier, and Lydia Maria Child, all of whom represented a variety of stances, all more conciliatory than Garrison's. James Russell Lowell, whose emotional balance was cited by a biographer as proof that abolitionists need not have been unstable, urged in contrast to Garrison that "the world must be healed by degrees." Also of importance was the work of free blacks such as David Walker and Robert Forten and ex-slaves such as Douglass and Brown, who had the clearest of all reasons to work for the cause but who shared some broader humanitarian motives with their white coworkers.

In 1839, the national organization of the American Anti-Slavery Society split over basic differences of approach. Less radical than Garrison and his followers (who not only denounced the Constitution

Primary Source: Harriet Beecher Stowe's *Uncle Tom's Cabin*

Few attacks upon slavery were as effective as Harriet Beecher Stowe's Uncle Tom's Cabin. *First written as a serial for the abolitionist journal,* National Era, *beginning in 1851, it appeared in book form in 1852. An immediate and enduring success, the book sold 300,000 copies during the first year and some 3,000,000 since. The portrayal of Uncle Tom, the first African American fictional hero created by an American author, elicited much sympathy for the plight of the slave. A portion of the novel is excerpted here.*

Source: Uncle Tom's Cabin, *Boston, 1883, pp. 419–423.*

Long after dusk, the whole weary train, with their baskets on their heads, defiled up to the building appropriated to the storing and weighing the cotton. Legree was there, busily conversing with the two drivers . . . Slowly, the weary, dispirited creatures wound their way into the room, and, with crouching reluctance, presented their baskets to be weighed.

Legree noted on a slate, on the side of which was pasted a list of names, the amount.

Tom's basket was weighed and approved; and he looked, with an anxious glance, for the success of the woman he had befriended.

Tottering with weakness, she came forward and delivered her basket. It was of full weight, as Legree well perceived; but, affecting anger, he said, "What, you lazy beast! Short again! Stand aside, you'll catch it, pretty soon!"

The woman gave a groan of utter despair and sat down on a board.

The person who had been called Misse Cassy now came forward and, with a haughty, negligent air, delivered her basket. As she delivered it, Legree looked in her eyes with a sneering yet inquiring glance.

She fixed her black eyes steadily on him, her lips moved slightly, and she said something in French. What it was, no one knew, but Legree's face became perfectly demoniacal in its expression as she spoke; he half raised his hand as if to strike—a gesture which she regarded with fierce disdain as she turned and walked away.

"And now," said Legree, "come here, you Tom. You see I telled ye I didn't buy ye jest for the common work; I mean to promote ye and make a driver of ye; and tonight ye may jest as well begin to get yer hand in. Now, ye jest take this yer gal and flog her; ye've seen enough on't to know how."

"I beg Mas'r's pardon," said Tom, "hopes Mas'r won't set me at that. It's what I an't used to—never did—and can't do, no way possible."

"Ye'll larn a pretty smart chance of things ye never did know before I've done with ye!" said Legree, taking up a cowhide and striking Tom a heavy blow across the cheek, and following up the infliction by a shower of blows.

"There!" he said, as he stopped to rest, "now will ye tell me ye can't do it?"

"Yes, Mas'r," said Tom, putting up his hand to wipe the blood that trickled down his face. "I'm willin' to work night and day, and work while there's life and breath in me; but this yer thing I can't feel it right to do; and, Mas'r, I *never* shall do it—*never*!"

Tom had a remarkably smooth, soft voice, and a habitually respectful manner that had given Legree an idea that he would be cowardly and easily subdued. When he spoke these last words, a thrill of amazement went through everyone; the poor woman clasped her hands and said, "O Lord!" and everyone involuntarily looked at each other and drew in their breath, as if to prepare for the storm that was about to burst.

Legree looked stupefied and confounded; but at last burst forth—

"What! ye blasted black beast! tell *me* ye don't think it *right* to do what I tell ye! What have any of you cussed cattle to do with thinking what's right? I'll put a stop to it! Why, what do ye think ye are? May be ye think ye're a gentleman, master Tom, to be a telling your master what's right and what an't! So you pretend it's wrong to flog the gal!"

"I think so, Mas'r," said Tom, "the poor crittur's sick and feeble; 't would be downright cruel, and it's what I never will do, not begin to. Mas'r, if you mean to kill me, kill me; but as to my raising my hand agin anyone here, I never shall—I'll die first!"

Tom spoke in a mild voice but with a decision that could not be mistaken. Legree shook with anger; his greenish eyes glared fiercely and his very whiskers seemed to curl with passion; but, like some ferocious beast that plays with its victim before he devours it, he kept back his strong impulse to proceed to immediate violence and broke out into bitter raillery.

"Well, here's a pious dog, at last, let down among us sinners!—a saint, a gentleman, and no less, to talk to us sinners about our sins! Powerful, holy crittur, he must be! Here, you rascal, you make believe to be so pious—didn't you never hear out of yer Bible, 'Servants, obey yer masters'? An't I yer master? Didn't I pay down $1,200 cash for all there is inside yer old cussed black shell? An't yer mine, now, body and soul?" he said, giving Tom a violent kick with his heavy boot. "Tell me!"

In the very depth of physical suffering, bowed by brutal oppression, this question shot a gleam of joy and triumph through Tom's soul. He suddenly stretched himself up, and, looking earnestly to heaven, while the tears and blood that flowed down his face mingled, he exclaimed—

"No! no! no! my soul an't yours, Mas'r! You haven't bought it—ye can't buy it! It's been bought and paid for by one that is able to keep it—no matter, no matter, you can't harm me!"

"I can't!" said Legree, with a sneer, "we'll see—we'll see! Here, Sambo, Quimbo, give this dog such a breakin' in as he won't get over this month!"

The two gigantic Negroes that now laid hold of Tom, with fiendish exultation in their faces, might have formed no unapt personification of the powers of darkness. The poor woman screamed with apprehension and all arose as by a general impulse while they dragged him unresisting from the place.

as supportive of slavery but insisted on sharing organizational responsibility with women), a more moderate wing, led by the Tappan brothers, formed the American and Foreign Anti-Slavery Society, which advocated moral suasion and political action and led directly to the birth of the Liberty Party in 1840. Because of this cleavage in national leadership, the bulk of the activity in the 1840s and '50s was carried on by state and local societies. However, a number of factors combined to give the movement increased momentum at this time. Chief among these was the question of permitting or outlawing slavery in new Western territories, with Northerners and Southerners taking increasingly adamant stands on opposite sides of that issue. There was also revulsion at the ruthlessness of slave hunters under the Fugitive Slave Law, and the far-reaching emotional response to Harriet Beecher Stowe's antislavery novel *Uncle Tom's Cabin* (1852) further strengthened the abolitionist cause. The antislavery issue entered the mainstream of American politics through the Free Soil Party (1848–54) and subsequently the Republican Party (founded in 1854).

Jolted by the raid of the abolitionist extremist John Brown on Harpers Ferry, Va., in 1859, the South became convinced that its entire way of life, based on the cheap labour provided by slaves, was irretrievably threatened by the election to the presidency of Abraham Lincoln (November 1860), who was opposed to the spread of slavery into the Western territories. The ensuing secession of the Southern states led to the Civil War.

ABOLITIONISTS

Anthony Benezet

(b. Jan. 31, 1713, Saint-Quentin, France—d. May 3, 1784, Philadelphia, Pa., U.S.)

An eminent teacher, the French-born Anthony Benezet was also an early abolitionist and an important social reformer in 18th-century America.

Escaping Huguenot persecution in France, the Benezet family fled first to Holland and then to London. Anthony was there apprenticed in a mercantile house, and he joined the Quaker sect. In 1731 he and his family immigrated to Philadelphia. Disliking the merchant's life, Benezet tried several other vocations before finally deciding to become a teacher. He taught at the Germantown Academy and then at the Friends' English Public School in Philadelphia. In 1755, distressed at the unequal educational opportunities afforded women, he established a school for girls. He devoted the remainder of his life to teaching. Convinced that personal kindness was the key to harmonious social relationships, Benezet made that principle the basis of his teaching methodology.

By the 1760s Benezet was an ardent abolitionist, writing and distributing pamphlets at his own expense to encourage opposition to slavery and the slave trade.

Late in his life he established and taught a school for blacks, and in his will he left his modest estate to endow the school. At various times during his long philanthropic career, Benezet came to the assistance of refugee French Acadians, American Indians, and other persecuted minorities. Pacifism, vegetarianism, and temperance were other causes he championed.

Among Benezet's many publications were *A Caution to Great Britain and Her Colonies, in a Short Representation of the Calamitous State of the Enslaved Negroes in the British Dominion* (1767) and *Some Historical Account of Guinea, with an Inquiry into the Rise and Progress of the Slave-Trade* (1772).

James G. Birney

(b. Feb. 4, 1792, Danville, Ky., U.S.—d. Nov. 25, 1857, Eagleswood, N.J.)

A prominent opponent of slavery, James Birney was twice the presidential candidate of the abolitionist Liberty Party.

Birney was trained in law and practiced in Danville. He won election to the Kentucky legislature in 1816, and in 1818 he moved to Alabama, where he was elected to the legislature in the following year. There he helped incorporate into the state constitution provisions that empowered the legislature to emancipate slaves and to prohibit selling slaves brought into the state.

In 1837 Birney was elected executive secretary of the American Anti-Slavery Society, which soon afterward split, one faction advocating the inflammatory approach of such abolitionists as William Lloyd Garrison and the other, which became the Liberty Party, emphasizing electoral activity. The party nominated Birney as its presidential candidate in 1840 and again in 1844. In 1840 he was a vice president of the World Anti-Slavery Convention in England, where he wrote *The American Churches, the Bulwarks of American Slavery* (1840). Birney's career was ended by an injury that invalided him in 1845.

John Brown

(b. May 9, 1800, Torrington, Conn., U.S.—d. Dec. 2, 1859, Charles Town, Va. [now in West Virginia])

Militant abolitionist John Brown led a raid on the federal arsenal at Harpers Ferry, Va. (now in West Virginia), in 1859 that made him a martyr to the antislavery cause and was instrumental in heightening sectional animosities that led to the Civil War.

Moving about restlessly through Ohio, Pennsylvania, Massachusetts, and New York, Brown was barely able to support his large family in any of several vocations at which he tried his hand: tanner, sheep drover, wool merchant, farmer, and land speculator. Though he was white, in 1849 Brown settled with his family in a black community founded at North Elba, N.Y., on land donated by the New York antislavery philanthropist Gerrit Smith. Long a foe of slavery, Brown became obsessed with the idea of taking overt action to help win justice for enslaved black people. In 1855 he followed five of his sons to the Kansas Territory to assist antislavery forces struggling for control there. With a wagon laden with guns and ammunition, Brown settled in Osawatomie and soon became the leader of antislavery guerrillas in the area.

Brooding over the sack of the town of Lawrence by a mob of slavery sympathizers (May 21, 1856), Brown concluded that he had a divine mission to take vengeance. Three days later he led a nighttime retaliatory raid on a proslavery settlement at Pottawatomie Creek, in which five men were dragged out of their cabins and hacked to death.

John Brown. Library of Congress, Washington, D.C.

After this raid, the name of "Old Osawatomie Brown" conjured up a fearful image among local slavery apologists.

In the spring of 1858, Brown convened a meeting of blacks and whites in Chatham, Ontario, at which he announced his intention of establishing in the Maryland and Virginia mountains a stronghold for escaping slaves. He proposed, and the convention adopted, a provisional constitution for the people of the United States. He was elected commander in chief of this paper government while gaining the moral and financial support of Gerrit Smith and several prominent Boston abolitionists.

In the summer of 1859, with an armed band of 16 whites and 5 blacks, Brown set up a headquarters in a rented farmhouse in Maryland, across the Potomac from Harpers Ferry, the site of a federal armoury. On the night of October 16, he quickly took the armoury and rounded up some 60 leading men of the area as hostages. Brown took this desperate action in the hope that escaped slaves would join his rebellion, forming an "army of emancipation" with which to liberate their fellow slaves. Throughout the next day and night he and his men held out against the local militia, but on the following morning he surrendered to a small force of U.S. Marines who had broken in and overpowered him. Brown himself was wounded, and 10 of his followers (including two sons) were killed. He was tried for murder, slave insurrection, and treason against the state and was convicted and hanged.

Primary Source: "John Brown's Body"

John Brown's execution brought together three of the most extraordinary figures in America's history. The colonel of marines who was in charge of the affair was Robert E. Lee, later to lead the Confederate armies against the Union. One of the militiamen was John Wilkes Booth, who would commit the last tragic act in the tragedy that was the Civil War by assassinating President Abraham Lincoln. And, of course, there was John Brown himself, who "never again," in Lloyd Lewis's words, "after that day's work, was . . . to be clearly a man any more in anybody's memory; thereafter he was to the South a gathering thunderhead on the Northern sky, promise of the hurricane to come. Thereafter he was to the North a song." The Union soldiers sang this "greatest of the world's war songs," as it has been called, throughout the war. They sang it quickly, lightly, as they marched into battle, and slowly, mournfully, after the many defeats.

John Brown's body lies a-moldering in the grave,
John Brown's body lies a-moldering in the grave,
John Brown's body lies a-moldering in the grave,
But his soul goes marching on.

Chorus:
Glory, glory, hallelujah!
Glory, glory, hallelujah!
Glory, glory, hallelujah!
His soul goes marching on!

John Brown died that the slaves might be free,
John Brown died that the slaves might be free,
John Brown died that the slaves might be free,
But his soul goes marching on.

He's gone to be a soldier in the army of the Lord,
He's gone to be a soldier in the army of the Lord,
He's gone to be a soldier in the army of the Lord,
And his soul is marching on.

The stars of heaven are looking kindly down,
The stars of heaven are looking kindly down,
The stars of heaven are looking kindly down,
On the grave of old John Brown.

Although Brown failed to spark a general slave revolt, the high moral tone of his defense helped to immortalize him and to hasten the war that would bring emancipation.

Maria Weston Chapman

(b. July 25, 1806, Weymouth, Mass., U.S.—d. July 12, 1885, Weymouth)

Abolitionist Maria Weston Chapman was the principal lieutenant of the radical antislavery leader William Lloyd Garrison.

Maria Weston spent several years of her youth living with the family of an uncle in England, where she received a good education. From 1828 to 1830 she was principal of the Young Ladies' High School in Boston. Her marriage in 1830 to Henry Grafton Chapman, a Boston merchant, brought her into abolitionist circles, and in 1832 with 12 other women, she founded the Boston Female Anti-Slavery Society. In 1835, as a violent mob was about to disrupt the group's meeting, Maria Chapman uttered a statement long quoted by abolitionists: "If this is the last bulwark of freedom, we may as well die here as anywhere."

Chapman became chief assistant to Garrison, helping him to run the Massachusetts Anti-Slavery Society and to edit *The Liberator*, a widely-circulated abolitionist publication. In 1839 she published *Right and Wrong in Massachusetts*, a pamphlet that argued that the deep divisions among abolitionists stemmed from their disagreements over women's rights. From 1839 to 1842 she also edited the *Non-Resistant*, the publication of Garrison's New England Non-Resistance Society. Chapman raised funds for the abolition movement by organizing antislavery fairs throughout New England.

In 1836 Chapman published a collection of *Songs of the Free and Hymns of Christian Freedom*. In May 1838 she addressed the Anti-Slavery Convention of American Women in Philadelphia in defiance of a threatening mob. (The mob returned the next day and burned down the hall.) In 1877 she published an edition of the autobiography of the English writer Harriet Martineau, an old friend, to which she appended a lengthy memoir. The essayist and poet John Jay Chapman was her grandson.

Lydia Maria Child

(b. Feb. 11, 1802, Medford, Mass., U.S.—d. Oct. 20, 1880, Wayland, Mass.)

Author Lydia Maria Child wrote antislavery works that had great influence in her time.

Born into an abolitionist family, Lydia Francis was primarily influenced in her education by her brother, a Unitarian clergyman and later a professor at the Harvard Divinity School. In the 1820s she taught, wrote historical novels, and founded a periodical for children, *Juvenile Miscellany* (1826). In 1828 she married David L. Child, an editor.

After meeting the abolitionist William Lloyd Garrison in 1831, she devoted her life to abolitionism.

Child's best-known antislavery work, *An Appeal in Favor of That Class of Americans Called Africans* (1833), related the history of slavery and denounced the inequality of education and employment for blacks; it was the first such work published in book form. As a result, Child was ostracized socially and her magazine failed in 1834. The book succeeded, however, in inducing many people to join the abolition movement. Child's further abolitionist efforts included editing the *National Anti-Slavery Standard* (1841–43) and later transcribing the recollections of slaves who had been freed.

In 1852 the Childs settled permanently on a farm in Wayland, Massachusetts. They continued to contribute liberally, from a small income, to the abolition movement. Child's other work included once-popular volumes of advice for women, such as *The Frugal Housewife* (1829), and books on behalf of the American Indian. Among her later books were three volumes of *Flowers for Children* (1844–47), *Fact and Fiction* (1846), *The Freedmen's Book* (1865), and *An Appeal for the Indians* (1868). Her letters have been compiled in *Lydia Maria Child, Selected Letters, 1817–1880* (1982). An ardent women's rights and antislavery activist, Childs may be best remembered for her poem "A Boy's Thanksgiving Day," popularly known as "Over the River and through the Woods."

Frederick Douglass

(b. February 1818?, Tuckahoe, Md., U.S.—d. Feb. 20, 1895, Washington, D.C.)

An African American who was one of the most eminent human-rights leaders of the 19th century, Frederick Douglass was thrust to the forefront of the abolition movement in the United States by virtue of his oratorical and literary brilliance. He became the first black

Frederick Douglass. Courtesy of the Holt-Messer Collection, Schlesinger Library, Radcliffe College, Cambridge, Massachusetts

citizen to hold high rank in the U.S. government.

Separated as an infant from his slave mother (he never knew his white father), Frederick lived with his grandmother on a Maryland plantation until, at age eight, his owner sent him to Baltimore to live as a house servant with the family of Hugh Auld, whose wife defied state law by teaching the boy to read. Auld, however, declared that learning would make him unfit for slavery, and Frederick was forced to continue his education surreptitiously with the aid of schoolboys in the street. Upon the death of his master, he was returned to the plantation as a field hand at 16. Later, he was hired out in Baltimore as a ship caulker. Frederick tried to escape with three others in 1833, but the plot was discovered before they could get away. Five years later, however, he fled to New York City and then to New Bedford, Mass., where he worked as a labourer for three years, eluding slave hunters by changing his surname to Douglass.

At a Nantucket, Mass., antislavery convention in 1841, Douglass was invited to describe his feelings and experiences under slavery. These extemporaneous remarks were so poignant and naturally eloquent that he was unexpectedly catapulted into a new career as agent for the Massachusetts Anti-Slavery Society. From then on, despite heckling and mockery, insult, and violent personal attack, Douglass never flagged in his devotion to the abolitionist cause.

To counter skeptics who doubted that such an articulate spokesman could ever have been a slave, Douglass felt impelled to write his autobiography in 1845, revised and completed in 1882 as *Life and Times of Frederick Douglass*. Douglass's account became a classic in American literature as well as a primary source about slavery from the bondsman's viewpoint. To avoid recapture by his former owner, whose name and location he had given in the narrative, Douglass left on a two-year speaking tour of Great Britain and Ireland. Abroad, Douglass helped to win many new friends for the abolition movement and to cement the bonds of humanitarian reform between the continents.

Douglass returned with funds to purchase his freedom and also to start his own antislavery newspaper, the *North Star* (later *Frederick Douglass's Paper*), which he published from 1847 to 1860 in Rochester, N.Y. The abolition leader William Lloyd Garrison disagreed with the need for a separate, black-oriented press, and the two men broke over this issue as well as over Douglass's support of political action to supplement moral suasion. Thus, after 1851 Douglass allied himself with the faction of the movement led by James G. Birney. He did not countenance violence, however, and specifically counseled against the raid on Harpers Ferry, Va. (October 1859).

During the Civil War Douglass became a consultant to Pres. Abraham Lincoln, advocating that former slaves be armed for the North and that the war be made a direct confrontation against slavery. Throughout Reconstruction, he fought for full civil rights for freedmen and vigorously supported the women's rights movement.

After Reconstruction, Douglass served as assistant secretary of the Santo Domingo Commission (1871), and in the District of Columbia he was marshal (1877–81) and recorder of deeds (1881–86); finally, he was appointed U.S. minister and consul general to Haiti (1889–91).

William Lloyd Garrison

(b. Dec. 10/12, 1805, Newburyport, Mass., U.S.—d. May 24, 1879, New York, N.Y.)

Arguably the leading American abolitionist, journalistic crusader William Lloyd Garrison published the abolition movement's most prominent newspaper, *The Liberator* (1831–65).

Garrison was the son of an itinerant seaman who subsequently deserted his family. The son grew up in an atmosphere of declining New England Federalism and lively Christian benevolence—twin sources of the abolition movement, which he joined at age 25. As editor of the *National Philanthropist* (Boston) in 1828 and the *Journal of the Times* (Bennington, Vermont) in 1828–29, he served his apprenticeship in the moral reform cause. In 1829, with a pioneer abolitionist, Benjamin Lundy, he became co-editor of the *Genius of Universal Emancipation* in Baltimore; he also served a short term in jail for libeling a Newburyport merchant who was engaged in the coastal slave trade. Released in June 1830, Garrison returned to Boston and, a year later, established *The Liberator,* which became known as the most uncompromising of American antislavery journals. In the first issue of *The Liberator* he stated his views on slavery vehemently: "I do not wish to think, or speak, or write, with moderation . . . I am in earnest—I will not equivocate—I will not excuse—I will not retreat a single inch—AND I WILL BE HEARD."

Like most of the abolitionists he recruited, Garrison was a convert from the American Colonization Society, which advocated the return of free blacks to Africa, to the principle of "immediate

William Lloyd Garrison. Library of Congress, Washington, D.C.

emancipation," borrowed from English abolitionists. "Immediatism," however variously it was interpreted by American reformers, condemned slavery as a national sin, called for emancipation at the earliest possible moment, and proposed schemes for incorporating the freedmen into American society. Through *The Liberator*, which circulated widely both in England and the United States, Garrison soon achieved recognition as the most radical of American antislavery advocates. In 1832 he founded the New England Anti-Slavery Society, the first immediatist society in the country. In 1833 he helped organize the American Anti-Slavery Society, writing its Declaration of Sentiments and serving as its first corresponding secretary. It was primarily as an editorialist, however, excoriating slave owners and their moderate opponents alike, that he became known and feared. "If those who deserve the lash feel it and wince at it," he wrote in explaining his refusal to alter his harsh tone, "I shall be assured that I am striking the right persons in the right place."

In 1837, in the wake of financial panic and the failure of abolitionist campaigns to gain support in the North, Garrison renounced church and state and embraced doctrines of Christian "perfectionism," which combined abolition, women's rights, and nonresistance, in the biblical injunction to "come out" from a corrupt society by refusing to obey its laws and support its institutions. From this blend of pacifism and anarchism came the Garrisonian principle of "No Union with Slaveholders," formulated in 1844 as a demand for peaceful Northern secession from a slaveholding South.

By 1840 Garrison's increasingly personal definition of the slavery problem had precipitated a crisis within the American Anti-Slavery Society, a majority of whose members disapproved of both the participation of women and Garrison's no-government theories. Dissension reached a climax in 1840, when the Garrisonians voted a series of resolutions admitting women and thus forced their conservative opponents to secede and form the rival American and Foreign Anti-Slavery Society. Later that year a group of politically minded abolitionists also deserted Garrison's standard and founded the Liberty Party. Thus, 1840 witnessed the disruption of the national organization and left Garrison in control of a relative handful of followers loyal to his "come-outer" doctrine but deprived of the support of new antislavery converts and of the Northern reform community at large.

In the two decades between the schism of 1840 and the Civil War, Garrison's influence waned as his radicalism increased. The decade before the war saw his opposition to slavery and to the federal government reach its peak: *The Liberator* denounced the Compromise of 1850, condemned the Kansas-Nebraska Act, damned the Dred Scott decision, and hailed John Brown's raid as "God's method of dealing retribution upon the head of the tyrant." In 1854 Garrison publicly burned a copy of the Constitution at an abolitionist rally in Framingham, Massachusetts. Three years later he held an abortive secessionist convention in Worcester, Massachusetts.

The Civil War forced Garrison to choose between his pacifist beliefs and emancipation. Placing freedom for the slave foremost, he supported Abraham Lincoln faithfully and in 1863 welcomed the Emancipation Proclamation as the fulfillment of all his hopes. Emancipation brought to the surface the latent conservatism in his program for the freedmen, whose political rights he was not prepared to guarantee immediately. In 1865 he attempted without success to dissolve the American Anti-Slavery Society and then resigned. In December 1865 he published the last issue of *The Liberator* and announced that "my vocation as an abolitionist is ended." He spent his last 14 years in retirement from public affairs, regularly supporting the Republican Party and continuing to champion temperance, women's rights, pacifism, and free trade. "It is enough for me," he explained in justifying his refusal to participate in radical egalitarian politics, "that every yoke is broken, and every bondman set free."

Thomas Wentworth Higginson

(b. Dec. 22, 1823, Cambridge, Mass., U.S.—d. May 9, 1911, Cambridge)

Minister and reformer Thomas Wentworth Higginson was dedicated to the abolition movement.

Ordained after graduating from Harvard Divinity School (1847), Higginson became pastor of the First Religious Society of Newburyport, Massachusetts, where he preached a social gospel too liberal even for Unitarians. Two years later his progressive views on temperance, women's rights, labour, and slavery caused him to lose his congregation.

On the passage of the Fugitive Slave Act (1850), Higginson joined the Boston Vigilance Committee to aid escaping slaves. While pastor of a "Free Church" in Worcester, Massachusetts (1852–61), he took a leading part in liberating the fugitive Anthony Burns (1854), and he supported John Brown both in Kansas (1856) and in his raid on Harpers Ferry, Virginia (1859). During the Civil War Higginson accepted command of the 1st South Carolina Volunteers, later the 33rd U.S. Colored Troops, the first black regiment in the U.S. armed forces. After 1864 he wrote a series of popular biographies and histories and a novel. Higginson discovered and encouraged the poet Emily Dickinson.

Elijah P. Lovejoy

(b. Nov. 9, 1802, Albion, Maine, U.S.—d. Nov. 7, 1837, Alton, Ill.)

Newspaper editor and abolitionist Elijah P. Lovejoy was martyred when he died in defense of his right to print antislavery material in the period leading up to the Civil War.

In 1827 Lovejoy moved to St. Louis, Missouri, where he established a school and entered journalism. Six years later he became editor of the *St. Louis Observer*, a Presbyterian weekly in which he strongly condemned slavery and supported gradual emancipation. Missouri was a slave state, and in 1835 a letter signed by a number of important men in St. Louis requested him to moderate the tone of his editorials. He replied in an editorial reiterating his views and his right to publish them. Threats of mob violence, however, forced him to move his press across the Mississippi River to Alton, in the free state of Illinois. Despite its new location, his press was destroyed by mobs several times in one year. Finally, on the night of Nov. 7, 1837, a mob attacked the building, and Lovejoy was killed in its defense. The news of his death stirred the people of the North profoundly and led to a great strengthening of abolitionist sentiment.

BENJAMIN LUNDY

(b. Jan. 4, 1789, Sussex County, N.J., U.S.—d. Aug. 22, 1839, Lowell, Ill.)

In the 1820s and 1830s, Benjamin Lundy was a prominent abolitionist and the publisher of some the era's leading antislavery periodicals.

Born to Quaker parents, Lundy was introduced early on to antislavery sentiment, as Quakers condemned the practice. His dedication to the abolitionist cause, however, did not begin until he was working as an apprentice saddlemaker in Wheeling, Virginia, where he was first exposed to the slave trade. In 1815 he organized the Union Humane Society, an antislavery association, in Ohio. In 1821 he founded a newspaper, the *Genius of Universal Emancipation*, which he edited at irregular intervals in various places until 1835, when he began publication of another newspaper, *The National Enquirer* (later the *Pennsylvania Freeman*), in Philadelphia. Much of his time was spent traveling in search of suitable places where freed slaves could settle, such as Canada and Haiti. From 1836 to 1838 he worked closely with U.S. Representative John Quincy Adams against the annexation of Texas, which would provide an opportunity for the extension of slavery. He moved to Illinois in 1839 and reestablished the *Genius*, which he published until his death.

WENDELL PHILLIPS

(b. Nov. 29, 1811, Boston, Mass., U.S.—d. Feb. 2, 1884, Boston)

One of the most eloquent abolitionist crusaders, orator Wendell Phillips helped energize the antislavery cause during the period leading up to the Civil War.

After opening a law office in Boston, Phillips, a wealthy Harvard Law School graduate, sacrificed social status and a prospective political career in order to join the antislavery movement. He became a close associate of the abolitionist leader William Lloyd Garrison and began lecturing for antislavery societies, writing pamphlets and editorials for Garrison's *The Liberator*, and contributing financially to the abolition movement.

Phillips's reputation as an orator was established at Faneuil Hall, Boston (Dec. 8, 1837), at a meeting called to protest the murder of abolitionist Elijah Lovejoy at Alton, Illinois, the previous month. When Phillips spontaneously delivered a stirring and passionate denunciation of the mob action against the martyred editor, he was recognized as one of the most brilliant orators of his day.

As a reform crusader, Phillips allied himself with Garrison in refusing to link abolition with political action; together they condemned the federal Constitution for its compromises over slavery and advocated national disunion rather than continued association with the slave states. During the Civil War he assailed Pres. Abraham Lincoln's reluctance to uproot slavery at once, and after the Emancipation Proclamation (January 1863) he threw his support to full civil liberties for freedmen. In 1865 he became president of the American Anti-Slavery Society after Garrison resigned.

After the Civil War, Phillips also devoted himself to temperance, women's rights, universal suffrage, and the Greenback Party (a minor political movement). He was an unsuccessful Massachusetts gubernatorial candidate of the Labor Reform and Prohibition parties in 1870. He continued to lecture on the lyceum circuits until the 1880s.

Gerrit Smith

(b. March 6, 1797, Utica, N.Y., U.S.—d. Dec. 28, 1874, New York, N.Y.)

Reformer and philanthropist Gerrit Smith was among those who provided financial backing for the antislavery crusader John Brown.

Smith was born into a wealthy family. In about 1828 he became an active worker in the cause of temperance, and in his home village, Peterboro, he built one of the first temperance hotels in the country. He became an abolitionist in 1835, after witnessing the disruption of an antislavery meeting by a mob in Utica. In 1840 he took a leading part in the organization of the antislavery Liberty Party, and in 1848 and 1852 he was nominated for the presidency by the remnant of this organization that had not been absorbed by the Free Soil Party. In 1852 he was elected to the U.S. House of Representatives as an independent. At the end of the first session in 1854 he resigned his seat.

After becoming an opponent of land monopoly, Smith gave numerous farms of 50 acres each to indigent families, and he also attempted to colonize tracts in northern New York with free blacks, but this experiment was a failure. Peterboro became a station on the Underground Railroad, and after 1850 Smith furnished money for the legal expenses of persons charged with infractions of the Fugitive Slave Law. He became very close to John Brown, to whom he gave a farm in

Essex County (New York), and from time to time supplied him with funds, though it seems without knowing that any of the money would be employed in an attempt to incite a slave insurrection. Under the excitement following the raid on Harpers Ferry in October 1859, he became temporarily insane, and for several weeks was confined in an asylum in Utica.

Smith favoured a vigorous prosecution of the Civil War but at its close advocated a mild policy toward the late Confederate states, declaring that part of the guilt of slavery lay upon the North. He even became one of the securities for Jefferson Davis, thereby incurring the resentment of Northern radical leaders.

Harriet Beecher Stowe

(b. June 14, 1811, Litchfield, Conn., U.S.—d. July 1, 1896, Hartford, Conn.)

Harriet Beecher Stowe's novel *Uncle Tom's Cabin* contributed so much to popular feeling against slavery that it is cited among the causes of the Civil War.

Harriet Beecher was a member of one of the 19th century's most remarkable families. The daughter of the prominent Congregationalist minister Lyman Beecher and the sister of Catharine, Henry Ward, and Edward, she grew up in an atmosphere of learning and moral earnestness. She attended her sister Catharine's school in Hartford, Conn., in 1824–27, thereafter teaching at the school. In 1832 she accompanied Catharine and their father to Cincinnati, Ohio, where he became president of Lane Theological Seminary and she taught at another school founded by her sister.

In Cincinnati she took an active part in the literary and school life, contributing stories and sketches to local journals and compiling a school geography, until the school closed in 1836. That same year she married Calvin Ellis Stowe, a clergyman and seminary professor, who encouraged her literary activity and was himself an eminent biblical scholar. She wrote continually and in 1843 published *The Mayflower; or, Sketches of Scenes and Characters Among the Descendants of the Pilgrims.*

Stowe lived for 18 years in Cincinnati, separated only by the Ohio River from a slave-holding community; she came in contact with fugitive slaves and learned about life in the South from friends and from her own visits there. In 1850 her husband became professor at Bowdoin College and the family moved to Brunswick, Maine.

There Harriet Stowe began to write a long tale of slavery, based on her reading of abolitionist literature and on her personal observations in Ohio and Kentucky. Her tale was published serially (1851–52) in the *National Era,* an antislavery paper of Washington, D.C.; in 1852 it appeared in book form as *Uncle Tom's Cabin; or, Life Among the Lowly.* The book was an immediate sensation and was taken up eagerly by abolitionists while, along with its author, it was vehemently denounced in the South, where reading or possessing the book became an extremely dangerous enterprise. With sales of 300,000 in the first year, the book exerted an influence equaled by few other novels in history, helping to solidify both pro- and antislavery sentiment. The book was translated widely and several times dramatized (the first time, in 1852, without Stowe's permission), where it played to capacity audiences. Stowe was enthusiastically received on a visit to England in 1853, and there she formed friendships with many leading literary figures. In that same year she published *A Key to Uncle Tom's Cabin*, a compilation of documents and testimonies in support of disputed details of her indictment of slavery.

In 1856 she published *Dred: A Tale of the Great Dismal Swamp*, in which she depicted the deterioration of a society resting on a slave basis. When *The Atlantic Monthly* was established the following year, she found a ready vehicle for her writings; she also found outlets in the *Independent* of New York City and later the *Christian Union*, of which papers her brother Henry Ward Beecher was editor.

She thereafter led the life of a woman of letters, writing novels, of which *The Minister's Wooing* (1859) is best known, many studies of social life in both fiction and essay, and a small volume of religious poems. An article she published in *The Atlantic* in 1869, in which she alleged that Lord Byron had had an incestuous affair with his half-sister, created an uproar in England and cost her much of her popularity there, but she remained a leading author and lyceum lecturer in the United States. Late in her life she assisted her son Charles E. Stowe on a biography of her, which appeared in 1889. Stowe had moved to Hartford in 1864, and she largely remained there until her death.

Charles Sumner

(b. Jan. 6, 1811, Boston, Mass., U.S.—d. March 11, 1874, Washington, D.C.)

Dedicated to human equality, Sen. Charles Sumner was a persistent advocate of abolition during the lead-up to the Civil War.

A graduate of Harvard Law School (1833), Sumner crusaded for many causes, including prison reform, world peace, and Horace Mann's educational reforms. It was in his long service as a U.S. senator from Massachusetts (1852–74), however, that he exercised his major influence on history. He bitterly attacked the Compromise of 1850, which attempted to balance the demands of North against South. On May 19/20, 1856, he denounced the "Crime against Kansas" (the Kansas-Nebraska Act) as "in every respect a swindle" and characterized its authors, Senators Andrew P. Butler and Stephen A. Douglas, as myrmidons (followers) of slavery. Two days later Congressman Preston S. Brooks of South Carolina invaded the Senate, labelled the speech a libel on his state and on his uncle, Senator Butler, and then severely beat Sumner with a cane. It took three years for Sumner to recover from the beating.

Sumner was chairman of the Senate Foreign Relations Committee from March

1861 to March 1871. Close acquaintanceships with prominent Englishmen such as Richard Cobden, John Bright, William Ewart Gladstone, and other European leaders—gained during his several European sojourns (1837–40)—afforded him unusual understanding of and influence in international affairs. He helped preserve peace between Britain and the United States by persuading President Lincoln to give up Confederate commissioners James M. Mason and John Slidell after their capture aboard the *Trent* in November 1861. (See page 65.)

Sumner opposed President Lincoln and later Pres. Andrew Johnson on postwar Reconstruction policy. He took the position that the defeated South was a conquered province outside the protection of the Constitution, and that the Confederate states should provide constitutional guarantees of equal voting rights to blacks before those states could be readmitted to the Union.

In 1870 Sumner helped defeat Pres. Ulysses S. Grant's proposal to annex Santo Domingo. As a result, Grant apparently brought about Sumner's removal from the chairmanship of the Foreign Relations Committee, a blow that almost broke Sumner.

In a move for magnanimity toward the defeated South, Sumner introduced a Senate resolution (1872) providing that the names of battles between fellow citizens should not be placed on the regimental colours of the U.S. Army. Reaction in his home state was immediate and bitter. The Massachusetts legislature censured the resolution as "an insult to the loyal soldiery of the nation" and as meeting "the unqualified condemnation of the people of the Commonwealth." Two years later, however, the legislature rescinded its action. Shortly after receiving news that he had been exonerated, Sumner suffered a fatal heart attack.

Arthur Tappan

(b. May 22, 1786, Northampton, Mass., U.S.—d. July 23, 1865, New Haven, Conn.)

Philanthropist Arthur Tappan used much of his energy and his fortune in the struggle to end slavery.

After a devoutly religious upbringing, Tappan moved to Boston at age 15 to enter the dry goods business. Six years later, he launched his own firm in Portland, Maine, and then in 1809 moved the business to Montreal. Tappan struggled with the business both in Canada and, after the outbreak of the War of 1812, back in the United States. But in 1826 he started a new company in New York City. This business, a silk-importing firm, was successful, and Arthur and his brother Lewis became wealthy. The Panic of 1837 forced the Tappans to close their doors, but the brothers founded another lucrative enterprise when they opened the first commercial credit-rating service in the 1840s.

Arthur Tappan early and consistently used his wealth to support missionary societies, colleges, and theological seminaries. Conservative in his moral outlook, he founded the *New York Journal of Commerce* in 1827 to provide a newspaper free of "immoral advertisements." He also backed movements for temperance and stricter observance of the Sabbath and against the use of tobacco.

It was the abolition movement, however, to which Tappan devoted himself during the latter part of his life. He helped found several abolitionist journals, and he was founder and first president (1833–40) of the American Anti-Slavery Society. Tappan at first backed the efforts of the abolitionist William Lloyd Garrison but broke with him and the American Anti-Slavery Society when Garrison insisted upon linking abolition with other reforms.

Tappan then created a new organization, the American and Foreign Anti-Slavery Society. He advocated trying to achieve abolition through the political process and backed the Liberty Party in the 1840s. With the passage of the Fugitive Slave Law of 1850, however, both of the Tappan brothers became more radical. Arthur Tappan openly declared his determination to disobey the law, and he supported the Underground Railroad.

Old age limited Tappan's activities as the slavery controversy heated during the 1850s, but he did live to see the Emancipation Proclamation fulfill much of his life's work.

David Walker

(b. Sept. 28, 1785, Wilmington, N.C., U.S.—d. June 28, 1830, Boston, Mass.)

African American abolitionist David Walker wrote one of the most radical documents of the antislavery movement, the pamphlet *Appeal . . . to the Colored Citizens of the World . . .* (1829), which urged slaves to fight for their freedom.

Born of a slave father and a free mother, Walker grew up free, obtained an education, and traveled throughout the country, settling in Boston. There he became involved in the abolition movement and was a frequent contributor to *Freedom's Journal,* an antislavery weekly. Sometime in the 1820s he opened a secondhand clothing store on the Boston waterfront. Through this business he could purchase clothes taken from sailors in barter for drink and then resell them to seamen about to embark. In the copious pockets of these garments, he concealed copies of his *Appeal,* which he reasoned would reach Southern ports and pass through the hands of other used-clothes dealers who would know what to do with them. He also used sympathetic black seamen to distribute pamphlets directly.

When the smuggled pamphlets began to appear in the South, the states reacted with legislation prohibiting circulation of abolitionist literature and forbidding slaves to learn to read and write. Warned that his life was in danger, Walker refused to flee to Canada. His

Frontispiece from the 1830 edition of David Walker's Appeal . . . to the Colored Citizens of the World . . . *first published in 1829.*

body was found soon afterward near his shop, and many believed he had been poisoned.

Walker's *Appeal* for a slave revolt, widely reprinted after his death, was accepted by a small minority of abolitionists, but most antislavery leaders and free blacks rejected his call for violence at the time.

Walker's only son, Edwin G. Walker, was elected to the Massachusetts legislature in 1866.

Theodore Dwight Weld

(b. Nov. 23, 1803, Hampton, Conn., U.S.—d. Feb. 3, 1895, Hyde Park, Mass.)

Theodore Dwight Weld was a prominent antislavery crusader in the pre-Civil War period.

While a ministerial student at Lane Seminary, Cincinnati, Ohio, Weld participated in antislavery debates and led a group of students who withdrew from Lane to enroll at Oberlin (Ohio) College. Weld left his studies in 1834 to become an agent for the American Anti-Slavery Society, recruiting and training people to work for the cause. His converts included such well-known abolitionists as James G. Birney, Harriet Beecher Stowe, and Henry Ward Beecher.

Weld wrote pamphlets (largely anonymous), notably *The Bible Against Slavery* (1837) and *Slavery As It Is* (1839). The latter was said to be the work on which Harriet Beecher Stowe partly based her *Uncle Tom's Cabin.*

Soon after his marriage (1838) to Angelina Grimké, a coworker in the antislavery crusade, Weld withdrew to private life on a farm in Belleville, New Jersey. He ventured back into public life in 1841–43, when he went to Washington, D.C., to head an antislavery reference bureau for the group of insurgents in Congress who broke with the Whigs on the slavery issue and were seeking the repeal of the "gag rule" restricting the consideration of antislavery petitions in Congress. Having demonstrated the value of an antislavery lobby in Washington, Weld returned to private life. He and his wife spent the remainder of their lives directing schools and teaching in New Jersey and Massachusetts.

John Greenleaf Whittier

(b. Dec. 17, 1807, near Haverhill, Mass., U.S.—d. Sept. 7, 1892, Hampton Falls, Mass.)

In addition to sharing with Henry Wadsworth Longfellow the distinction of being a household name in both England and the United States, poet John Greenleaf Whittier was a dedicated abolitionist.

Born on a farm into a Quaker family, Whittier had only a limited formal education. He became an avid reader of British poetry, however, and was especially influenced by the Scot Robert Burns, whose lyrical treatment of everyday rural life reinforced his own inclination to be a writer.

Whittier's career naturally divides into four periods: poet and journalist (1826–32), abolitionist (1833–42), writer and humanitarian (1843–65), and Quaker poet (1866–92). At age 19 he submitted his poem "The Exile's Departure" to the abolitionist William Lloyd Garrison for publication in the *Newburyport Free Press*, and it was accepted. Garrison encouraged other poetic contributions from Whittier, and the two men became friends and associates in the abolitionist cause. Whittier soon turned to journalism. He edited newspapers in Boston and Haverhill and by 1830 had become editor of the *New England Weekly Review* in Hartford, Connecticut, the most important Whig journal in New England. He also continued writing verse, sketches, and tales, and he published his first volume of poems, *Legends of New England*, in 1831. In 1832, however, a failed romance, ill health, and the discouragement he felt over his lack of literary recognition caused him to resign and return to Haverhill.

Deciding that his rebuffs had been caused by personal vanity, Whittier resolved to devote himself to more altruistic activities, and he soon embraced Garrisonian abolitionism. His fiery antislavery pamphlet *Justice and Expediency* made him prominent in the abolition movement, and for a decade he was probably its most influential writer. He served a term in the Massachusetts legislature, spoke at antislavery meetings, and edited the *Pennsylvania Freeman*

(1838–40) in Philadelphia. In 1840 he returned to live in Amesbury with his mother, aunt, and sister.

By 1843 Whittier had broken with Garrison, having decided that abolitionist goals could be better accomplished through regular political channels. He became more active in literature, in which new avenues of publication were now open to him. In the next two decades he matured as a poet, publishing numerous volumes of verse, among them *Lays of My Home* (1843), *Voices of Freedom* (1846), *Songs of Labor* (1850), *The Panorama* (1856), and *Home Ballads and Poems* (1860). Among his best-known poems of this period is "Maud Muller" (1854), with its lines "Of all sad words of tongue and pen/The saddest are these, 'It might have been.' " Most of his literary prose, including his one novel, *Leaves from Margaret Smith's Journal* (1849), was also published during this time, along with numerous articles and reviews.

Whittier's mother and his beloved younger sister died in the period from 1857 to 1864, but his personal grief, combined with the larger national grief of the Civil War, furthered his literary maturity. The publication in 1866 of his best-known poem, the winter idyll "Snow-Bound", was followed by other triumphs in the verse collections *The Tent on the Beach* (1867), *Among the Hills* (1868), and *The Pennsylvania Pilgrim* (1872). Whittier's 70th birthday was celebrated at a dinner attended by almost every prominent American writer, and his 80th birthday became an occasion for national celebration.

After outgrowing the romantic verse he wrote in imitation of Robert Burns, Whittier became an eloquent advocate of justice, tolerance, and liberal humanitarianism. The lofty spiritual and moral values he proclaimed earned him the title of "America's finest religious poet," and many of his poems are still sung as church hymns by various denominations. After the Civil War he changed his focus, depicting nature and homely incidents in rural life. Whittier's verse is often marred by sentimentality, poor technique, or excessive preaching, but his best poems are still read for their moral beauty and simple sentiments. He was not a literary figure of the highest stature but was nevertheless an important voice of his age.

CHAPTER 4

Secession and the Politics of the Civil War

A HOUSE DIVIDING

On Nov. 6, 1860, Abraham Lincoln was elected as the 16th president of the United States. Little over a month later, on Dec. 20, a special convention called in South Carolina unanimously passed an ordinance of secession, making that state the first to withdraw from the Union. Mississippi, Florida, Alabama, Georgia, and Louisiana followed in January, while Texas voted to secede on Feb. 1, 1861. Pres. James Buchanan and his administration feebly denied the right of secession, but he also denied the right of the federal government to use force against the seceded states.

Secession had a long history in the United States—but as a threat rather than as an actual dissolution of the Union. Pro-secessionists found philosophical justification for altering or abolishing a government and instituting a new one in the Declaration of Independence. More specifically, those who held that the Union was simply a compact among the states argued that states could secede from that compact just as they had earlier acceded to it.

While never counseling secession, James Madison and Thomas Jefferson had clearly enunciated the states' rights-compact doctrine in the Virginia and Kentucky Resolutions of 1798. Their political opponents, New England Federalists, briefly considered withdrawing from the Union at the Hartford Convention in 1814. The Mississippi question elicited hints of secession from pro-slavery states, but the Missouri Compromise (1820) temporarily quieted the agitation. South Carolinians, however, went to the very brink of secession in the 1830s over the tariff question.

From the 1840s to 1860, Southerners frequently threatened to withdraw from the Union as antislavery sentiment in the North grew stronger. The Compromise of 1850 eased some of the sectional strife, but the problem of permitting or prohibiting slavery in the western territories continued to inflame opinion on both sides throughout the 1850s.

THE CONFEDERATE STATES OF AMERICA

In the wake of the 1860 election, neither Southerners, now intent upon secession, nor Republicans, intent upon reaping the rewards of their hard-won election victory, were really interested in conciliation. In addition to the ineffectual efforts by the Buchanan administration, more strenuous attempts were made by others in Washington to work out a compromise. (The most promising plan was John J. Crittenden's proposal to extend the Missouri Compromise line, dividing free from slave states, to the Pacific.) All of these efforts failed, too.

On Feb. 4, 1861—a month before Lincoln would be inaugurated in Washington—six Southern states (South Carolina, Georgia, Alabama, Florida, Mississippi, Louisiana) sent representatives to Montgomery, Ala., to set up a new independent government. Delegates from Texas soon joined them. A provisional government was established in Montgomery. The Confederacy, operating under a structure similar to that of the United States, was headed by Pres. Jefferson Davis and Vice Pres. Alexander H. Stephens. The new country soon acquired other symbols of sovereignty, such as its own stamps and currency and a flag known as the Stars and Bars.

Lincoln waited a month after his inauguration before deciding to send provisions to Fort Sumter in the harbour of Charleston, S.C. On April 12, 1861, Confederate guns opened fire on the fort. The Civil War had begun. Forced now to make a choice between the Union and the Confederacy, the states of the upper South—Virginia, North Carolina, Arkansas, and Tennessee—voted to secede. Not until May, after hostilities had broken out did the new government transfer its capital to Richmond, Va.

The main concern of the Confederate States was raising and equipping an army. The Southern Congress first voted to permit direct volunteering up to 400,000, but conscription was begun in April 1862. The total number of Confederate soldiers is estimated at 750,000, as opposed to twice that many

Primary Source: Jefferson Davis's Inaugural Address

As a senator from Mississippi in the pre–Civil War period and the secretary of war for Democrat Franklin Pierce between 1853 and 1857, Jefferson Davis was one of the influential politicians of his time. Between 1858 and 1860 he delivered speeches in both the North and the South urging the preservation of the Union. During the presidential campaign of 1860 he attempted to discourage secessionist sentiment. Yet when secession came Davis was elected president of the Confederate States of America. Unlike most of the Southern leaders, Davis had expected war and hoped to become the commander in chief of the Southern armies. Nevertheless, his first act as president of the Confederacy was to send a commission to Washington to negotiate a peaceful settlement with the government. Abraham Lincoln refused to receive his commission. On Feb. 18, 1861, in a state of poor health and with grave doubts about both his ability to serve as president as well as the South's ability to fight a war, Davis delivered his Inaugural Address, which is excerpted here.

Source: The Rebellion Record: A Diary of American Events, with Documents, Narratives, Illustrative Incidents, Poetry, etc., *Frank Moore, ed., New York, 1861–1868, I, Document 37.*

> . . . Our present condition, achieved in a manner unprecedented in the history of nations, illustrates the American idea that governments rest upon the consent of the governed, and that it is the right of the people to alter or abolish governments whenever they become destructive to the ends for which they were established. The declared compact of the Union from which we have withdrawn was to establish justice, insure domestic tranquillity, provide for the common defense, promote the general welfare, and secure the blessings of liberty to ourselves and our posterity; and when, in the judgment of the sovereign states now composing this Confederacy, it has been perverted from the purposes for which it was ordained, and ceased to answer the ends for which it was established, a peaceful appeal to the ballot box declared that, so far as they are concerned, the government created by that compact should cease to exist.
>
> In this they merely asserted the right which the Declaration of Independence of 1776 defined to be "inalienable." Of the time and occasion of its exercise, they, as sovereigns, were the final judges, each for itself. The impartial, enlightened verdict of mankind will vindicate the rectitude of our conduct; and He who knows the hearts of men will judge of the sincerity with which we labored to preserve the government of our fathers in its spirit.
>
> The right solemnly proclaimed at the birth of the States, and which has been affirmed and reaffirmed in the bills of rights of the states subsequently admitted into the Union of 1789, undeniably recognizes in the people the power to resume the authority delegated for the purposes of government. Thus the sovereign states here represented proceeded to form this Confederacy . . .
>
> An agricultural people, whose chief interest is the export of a commodity required in every manufacturing country, our true policy is peace and the freest trade which our

necessities will permit. It is alike our interest and that of all those to whom we would sell, and from whom we would buy, that there should be the fewest practicable restrictions upon the interchange of commodities. There can be but little rivalry between ours and any manufacturing or navigating community, such as the Northeastern states of the American Union. It must follow, therefore, that mutual interest would invite to goodwill and kind offices. If, however, passion or lust of dominion should cloud the judgment or inflame the ambition of those states, we must prepare to meet the emergency and maintain by the final arbitrament of the sword the position which we have assumed among the nations of the earth.

We have entered upon a career of independence, and it must be inflexibly pursued through many years of controversy with our late associates of the Northern states. We have vainly endeavored to secure tranquillity and obtain respect for the rights to which we were entitled. As a necessity, not a choice, we have resorted to the remedy of separation, and henceforth our energies must be directed to the conduct of our own affairs and the perpetuity of the Confederacy which we have formed. If a just perception of mutual interest shall permit us peaceably to pursue our separate political career, my most earnest desire will have been fulfilled. But if this be denied us, and the integrity of our territory and jurisdiction be assailed, it will but remain for us with firm resolve to appeal to arms and invoke the blessing of Providence on a just cause . . .

With a constitution differing only from that of our fathers insofar as it is explanatory of their well-known intent, freed from sectional conflicts, which have interfered with the pursuit of the general welfare, it is not unreasonable to expect that states from which we have recently parted may seek to unite their fortunes to ours under the government which we have instituted. For this your constitution makes adequate provision; but beyond this, if I mistake not, the judgment and will of the people are that reunion with the states from which they have separated is neither practicable nor desirable. To increase the power, develop the resources, and promote the happiness of the Confederacy, it is requisite that there should be so much homogeneity that the welfare of every portion would be the aim of the whole. Where this does not exist, antagonisms are engendered which must and should result in separation . . .

We have changed the constituent parts but not the system of government. The Constitution formed by our fathers is that of these Confederate States.

It is joyous in the midst of perilous times to look around upon a people united in heart, when one purpose of high resolve animates and actuates the whole; where the sacrifices to be made are not weighed in the balance against honor, right, liberty, and equality. Obstacles may retard, but they cannot long prevent the progress of a movement sanctioned by its justice and sustained by a virtuous people. Reverently let us invoke the God of our fathers to guide and protect us in our efforts to perpetuate the principles which by His blessing they were able to vindicate, establish, and transmit to their posterity. And with a continuance of His favor ever gratefully acknowledged, we may hopefully look forward to success, to peace, to prosperity.

Federal troops. (Confederate population stood at about 5,500,000 whites and 3,500,000 black slaves, as against 21,000,000 Northerners.) In railroads, the South had only 9,000 miles, the industrial North 22,000.

The Confederacy's early attempts to raise funds centred on printing money, which proved highly inflationary, and issuing bonds that could be paid for in kind. Because of the Federal blockade of Southern ports, tariff revenues proved inadequate. In 1863 a general tax bill was passed, imposing license and occupational taxes, a profits tax, and a 10 percent tax on farm products, collected in kind. Profitable private blockade running was put under strict supervision in 1864. Prices of farm products for the army were eventually fixed to check profiteering.

In foreign affairs, the South had been initially confident of the power and influence of "King Cotton," the crop that accounted for more than half the value of U.S. exports before the war. Confederates felt that the importance of cotton would force diplomatic recognition from the Federal government and European countries. Neither the commissioners sent abroad in 1861 nor the permanent envoys who replaced them were able to secure recognition from Great Britain, France, or any other European power. The South was able, however, to buy considerable war matériel and several fast ships.

THE COMING OF THE WAR

Faced with a fait accompli, Lincoln when inaugurated was prepared to conciliate the South in every way but one: he would not recognize that the Union could be divided. The test of his determination came early in his administration, when he learned that the Federal troops under Major Robert Anderson in Fort Sumter, South Carolina—then one of the few military installations in the South still in Federal hands—had to be promptly supplied or withdrawn. After agonized

In Focus: *Trent* Affair

On Nov. 8, 1861, Capt. Charles Wilkes, commanding the Union frigate San Jacinto, *seized from the neutral British ship* Trent *two Confederate commissioners, James Murray Mason and John Slidell, who were seeking the support of England and France for the cause of the Confederacy.*

Despite initial rejoicing by the Northern populace and Congress, this unauthorized seizure aroused a storm of indignant protest and demands for war throughout Britain. The British government sent an ultimatum demanding an American apology and the release of Mason and Slidell. To avert armed conflict, Secretary of State William Seward, on December 26, replied that Wilkes had erred in failing to bring the Trent *into port for adjudication, thus violating America's policy of freedom of the seas. The Confederate commissioners were released shortly thereafter.*

Primary Source: Daniel Decatur Emmett's and Albert Pike's "Dixie"

Dan Emmett wrote Dixie *for Bryant's Minstrels, who first performed it in New York, probably in the late fall of 1859. The song soon reverberated through the land: people clapped their hands to it; soldiers in both the North and the South sang it merrily; Abraham Lincoln loved it. And many wrote lyrics for it. Albert Pike, a Southern poet, produced an "improved" version, eliminating the dialect and the "vulgarisms"; but it is Emmett's version that is remembered. (Both versions are reprinted here.) During the war,* Dixie *became the favourite Confederate marching song. After Appomattox, President Lincoln was heard to remark that "the song is federal property now."*

Source: Heart Songs, *Cleveland, 1909.* War Songs and Poems of the Southern Confederacy 1861–1865, *H. M. Wharton, ed., n.p., 1904.*

I wish I was in de land ob cotton,
Old times dar am not forgotten;
Look away, look away, look away,
Dixie land!
In Dixie land whar I was born in,
Early on one frosty mornin',
Look away, look away, look away,
Dixie land!

Chorus:
Den I wish I was in Dixie!
Hooray! hooray!
In Dixie's land I'll take my stand
To lib an' die in Dixie,
Away, away, away down south in Dixie!
Away, away, away down south in Dixie!

Old missus marry Will de weaber,
Willium was a gay deceaber;
Look away, look away, look away,
Dixie land!
When he put his arm around 'er,
He look as fierce as a forty-pounder,
Look away, look away, look away,
Dixie land!

His face was sharp as a butcher cleaber,
But dat did not seem to greab 'er;
Look away, look away, look away,
Dixie land!
Will run away, missus took a decline, O,
Her face was the color of bacon rhine, O,
Look away, look away, look away,
Dixie land!

While missus lib, she lib in clover,
When she die, she die all over;
Look away, look away, look away,
Dixie land!
How could she act de foolish part
An' marry a man to break her heart?
Look away, look away, look away,
Dixie land!

Now here's a health to de nex' old missus,
An' all de gals dat want to kiss us;
Look away, look away, look away,
Dixie land!
An' if you want to dribe away sorrow,
Come an' hear dis song tomorrow,
Look away, look away, look away,
Dixie land!

—Daniel Decatur Emmett

Southrons, hear your country call you!
Up, lest worse than death befall you!
To arms! To arms! To arms, in Dixie!
Lo! all the beacon-fires are lighted—
Let all hearts be now united!
To arms! To arms! To arms, in Dixie!
Advance the flag of Dixie!
Hurrah! Hurrah!
For Dixie's land we take our stand,
And live or die for Dixie!
To arms! To arms!
And conquer peace for Dixie!
To arms! To arms!
And conquer peace for Dixie!

Northern thunders mutter!
Northern flags in South winds flutter!
Send them back your fierce defiance!
Stamp upon the accursed alliance!

Fear no danger! Shun no labor!
Lift up rifle, pike, and saber!
Shoulder pressing close to shoulder,
Let the odds make each heart bolder!

How the South's great heart rejoices
At your cannons' ringing voices!
For faith betrayed and pledges broken,
Wrongs inflicted, insults spoken.

Strong as lions, swift as eagles,
Back to their kennels hunt these beagles!
Cut the unequal bonds asunder!
Let them hence each other plunder!

Swear upon your country's altar
Never to submit or falter,
Till the spoilers are defeated,
Till the Lord's work is completed.

Halt not till our Federation
Secures among earth's powers its station!
Then at peace, and crowned with glory,
Hear your children tell the story!

If the loved ones weep in sadness,
Victory soon shall bring them gladness—
To arms! To arms! To arms, in Dixie!
Exultant pride soon banish sorrow,
Smiles chase tears away tomorrow.
To arms! To arms! To arms, in Dixie!
Advance the flag of Dixie!
Hurrah! Hurrah!
For Dixie's land we take our stand,
And live or die for Dixie!
To arms! To arms!
And conquer peace for Dixie!
To arms! To arms!
And conquer peace for Dixie!

—Albert Pike

consultation with his cabinet, Lincoln determined that supplies must be sent even if doing so provoked the Confederates into firing the first shot. On April 12, 1861, just before Federal supply ships could reach the beleaguered Anderson, the flash and dull roar of a 10-inch Confederate mortar directed at Fort Sumter announced the opening of the Civil War. After a 34-hour bloodless bombardment, Anderson, in command of a Federal garrison of about 85 soldiers, surrendered Fort Sumter to some 5,500 besieging Confederate troops under P. G. T. Beauregard.

Primary Source: Robert E. Lee's Resignation from the United States Army

Robert E. Lee was a colonel in the U.S. Army when Confederate soldiers fired on Fort Sumter. Lee was devoted to the Union and could not rationally justify secession. But stronger than his commitments to the Union were the emotional ties to his home state, born out of his family's deep roots in Virginia. On April 18, 1861, he was offered the field command of the U.S. Army but declined the offer. General Winfield Scott, a close friend, advised him either to resign his commission or to accept the assignment. The following day the Virginia convention voted to secede. Lee was torn between his conscience, which would not allow him to bear arms against his homeland, and his devotion to the Union. Even on April 20, when he resigned from the U.S. Army, Lee had hoped he would not have to participate in a war he detested. That day he wrote the following letter to General Scott. Three days later Virginia named him commander of its army.

Source: Personal Reminiscences, Anecdotes, and Letters of Gen. Robert E. Lee, *J. William Jones, ed., New York, 1875, pp. 138–140. Keep here.*

General:

Since my interview with you on the 18th instant, I have felt that I ought no longer to retain my commission in the Army. I, therefore, tender my resignation, which I request you will recommend for acceptance. It would have been presented at once but for the struggle it has cost me to separate myself from a service to which I have devoted the best years of my life and all the ability I possessed.

During the whole of that time—more than a quarter of a century—I have experienced nothing but kindness from my superiors and the most cordial friendship from my comrades. To no one, General, have I been as much indebted as to yourself for uniform kindness and consideration; and it has always been my ardent desire to meet your approbation. I shall carry to the grave the most grateful recollections of your kind consideration, and your name and fame will always be dear to me.

Save in defense of my native state, I never desire again to draw my sword.

Be pleased to accept my most earnest wishes for the continuance of your happiness and prosperity.

THE POLITICAL COURSE OF THE WAR

For the next four years the Union and the Confederacy were locked in conflict—by far the most titanic waged in the Western Hemisphere.

The war management policies pursued by the governments of Abraham Lincoln and Jefferson Davis were astonishingly similar. Both presidents at first relied on volunteers to man the armies, and both administrations were poorly prepared to arm and equip the hordes of young men who flocked to the colours in the initial stages of the war. As the fighting progressed, both governments reluctantly resorted to conscription—the Confederates first, in early 1862, and the Federal government more slowly, with an ineffective measure of late 1862 followed by a more stringent law in 1863. Both governments pursued an essentially laissez-faire policy in economic matters, with little effort to control prices, wages, or profits. Only the railroads were subject to close government regulation in both regions; and the Confederacy, in constructing some of its own powder mills, made a few experiments in "state socialism." Neither Lincoln's nor Davis's administration knew how to cope with financing the war; neither developed an effective system of taxation until late in the conflict, and both relied heavily upon borrowing. Faced with a shortage of funds, both governments were obliged to turn to the printing press and to issue fiat money; the U.S. government issued $432,000,000 in "greenbacks" (as this irredeemable, non-interest-bearing paper money was called), while the Confederacy printed over $1,554,000,000 in such paper currency. In consequence, both sections experienced runaway inflation, which was much more drastic in the South, where, by the end of the war, flour sold at $1,000 a barrel.

Even toward slavery, the root cause of the war, the policies of the two warring governments were surprisingly similar. The Confederate constitution, which was in most other ways similar to that of the United States, expressly guaranteed the institution of slavery. Despite pressure from abolitionists, Lincoln's administration was not initially disposed to disturb the "peculiar institution," if only because any move toward emancipation would upset the loyalty of Delaware, Maryland, Kentucky, and Missouri—the four slave states that remained in the Union.

Moves Toward Emancipation

Gradually, however, under the pressure of war, both governments moved to end slavery. Lincoln came to see that emancipation of African Americans would favourably influence European opinion toward the Northern cause, might deprive the Confederates of their productive labour force on the farms, and would add much-needed recruits to the Federal armies. In September 1862, he issued his preliminary proclamation of emancipation, promising to free all slaves in rebel territory by Jan. 1, 1863, unless those states returned to the Union; and when the Confederates remained obdurate, he followed it with his promised final proclamation. A natural accompaniment of emancipation was the use of African American troops, and by the end of the war the number of blacks who served in the Federal armies totaled 178,895. Uncertain of the constitutionality of his Emancipation Proclamation,

In Focus: Emancipation Proclamation

Issued by U.S. Pres. Abraham Lincoln on Jan. 1, 1863, the Emancipation Proclamation freed the slaves of the Confederate states in rebellion against the Union.

Before the start of the Civil War, many people and leaders of the North had been primarily concerned merely with stopping the extension of slavery into western territories that would eventually achieve statehood within the Union. With the secession of the Southern states and the consequent start of the Civil War, however, the continued tolerance of Southern slavery by Northerners seemed no longer to serve any constructive political purpose. Emancipation thus quickly changed from a distant possibility to an imminent and feasible eventuality. Lincoln had declared that he meant to save the Union as best he could—by preserving slavery, by destroying it, or by destroying part and preserving part. Just after the Battle of Antietam (Sept. 17, 1862) he issued his proclamation calling on the revolted states to return to their allegiance before the next year, otherwise their slaves would be declared free men. No state returned, and the threatened declaration was issued on Jan. 1, 1863.

As president, Lincoln could issue no such declaration; as commander in chief of the armies and navies of the United States, he could issue directions only as to the territory within his lines; but the Emancipation Proclamation applied only to territory outside of his lines. It has therefore been debated whether the proclamation was in reality of any force. It may fairly be taken as an announcement of the policy that was to guide the army, and as a declaration of freedom taking effect as the lines advanced. At all events, this was its exact effect.

Its international importance was far greater. The locking up of the world's source of cotton supply had been a general calamity, and the Confederate government and people had steadily expected that the English and French governments would intervene in the war. The conversion of the struggle into a crusade against slavery made European intervention impossible.

The Emancipation Proclamation did more than lift the war to the level of a crusade for human freedom. It brought some substantial practical results because it allowed the Union to recruit black soldiers. Blacks responded to this invitation to join the army in considerable numbers, nearly 180,000 of them enlisting during the remainder of the war. By Aug. 26, 1863, Lincoln could report, in a letter to James C. Conkling, that "the emancipation policy, and the use of colored troops, constitute the heaviest blow yet dealt to the rebellion."

Two months before the war ended—in February 1865—Lincoln told portrait painter Francis B. Carpenter that the Emancipation Proclamation was "the central act of my administration, and the greatest event of the nineteenth century." To Lincoln and to his countrymen it had become evident that the proclamation had dealt a deathblow to slavery in the United States, a fate that was officially sealed by the ratification of the Thirteenth Amendment in December 1865.

Meanwhile the Confederacy, though much more slowly, was also inexorably drifting in the direction of emancipation. The South's desperate need for troops caused many military men, including Robert E. Lee, to demand the recruitment of blacks; finally, in March 1865 the Confederate congress authorized the raising of African American regiments. Though a few blacks were recruited for the Confederate armies, none actually served in battle because surrender was at hand. In yet another way Davis's government showed its awareness of slavery's inevitable end when, in a belated diplomatic mission to seek assistance from Europe, the Confederacy in March 1865 promised to emancipate the slaves in return for diplomatic recognition. Nothing came of the proposal, but it is further evidence that by the end of the war both North and South realized that slavery was doomed.

Lincoln urged Congress to abolish slavery by constitutional amendment; but this was not done until Jan. 31, 1865, with the Thirteenth Amendment, and the actual ratification did not take place until after the war.

Sectional Dissatisfaction

As war leaders, both Lincoln and Davis came under severe attack in their own sections. Both had to face problems of disloyalty. In Lincoln's case, the Irish immigrants to the eastern cities and the Southern-born settlers of the northwestern states were especially hostile to African Americans and, therefore, to emancipation, while many other Northerners became tired and disaffected as the war dragged on interminably. Residents of the Southern hill country, where slavery never had much of a foothold, were similarly hostile toward Davis. Furthermore, in order to wage war, both presidents had to strengthen the powers of their respective central governments, thus further accelerating the process of national integration that had brought on the war. Both administrations were, in consequence, vigorously attacked by state governors, who resented the encroachment upon their authority and who strongly favoured local autonomy.

The extent of Northern dissatisfaction was indicated in the congressional elections of 1862, when Lincoln and his party sustained a severe rebuff at the polls and the Republican majority in the House of Representatives was drastically reduced. Similarly in the Confederacy the congressional elections of 1863 went so strongly against the administration that Davis was able to command a majority for his measures only through the continued support of representatives and senators from the states of the upper South, which were under control of the Federal army and consequently unable to hold new elections.

As late as August 1864, Lincoln despaired of his reelection to the presidency and fully expected that the Democratic candidate, Gen. George B. McClellan, would defeat him. Davis, at about the same time, was openly attacked by Alexander H. Stephens, the vice president of the Confederacy. But Federal military victories, especially William Tecumseh Sherman's capture of Atlanta, greatly strengthened Lincoln; and, as the war came to a triumphant close for the North, he attained new heights of

President Abraham Lincoln and General George B. McClellan in the general's tent, Antietam, Maryland, October 3, 1862. Photograph by Alexander Gardner. Library of Congress, Washington, D.C. (LC-B8171-0602 DLC)

popularity. Davis's administration, on the other hand, lost support with each successive defeat, and in January 1865, the Confederate congress insisted that Davis make Robert E. Lee the supreme commander of all Southern forces.

With war upon the land, Abraham Lincoln called for 75,000 militiamen to serve for three months. He proclaimed a naval blockade of the Confederate States, directed the secretary of the treasury to advance $2 million to assist in the raising of troops, and suspended the writ of habeas corpus. The Confederate government had previously authorized a call for 100,000 soldiers for at least six months' service, and this figure was soon increased to 400,000. As the fighting progressed, both governments reluctantly resorted to

In Focus: Draft Riot of 1863

Although labouring people in general supported the Northern war effort, they had no voice in Republican policy and occasionally deserted from the army or refused reenlistment. Because of their low wages, often less than $500 a year, they were particularly antagonized by the federal provision allowing more affluent draftees to buy their way out of the Federal Army for $300. Minor riots occurred in several cities, and when the drawing of names began in New York on July 11, 1863, mobs (mostly of foreign-born, especially Irish, workers) surged onto the streets assaulting residents, defying police, attacking draft headquarters, and burning buildings. Property damage eventually totalled $1,500,000. It is estimated that 120 people were killed.

The New York draft riot was also closely associated with racial competition for jobs. Northern labour feared that emancipation of slaves would cause an influx of African American workers from the South, and employers did in fact use black workers as strikebreakers during this period. Thus the white rioters eventually vented their wrath on the homes and businesses of innocent African Americans—including the Colored Orphan Asylum on Fifth Avenue—and Civil War freedmen's associations were forced to send aid to their brethren in New York. (This racial ill feeling in the ranks of urban labour persisted into the second half of the 20th century.) The four-day draft riot—the worst urban violence in the young nation's history—was finally quelled by police cooperating with the 7th N.Y. Regiment, which had been hastily recalled from Gettysburg; the drawing of names proceeded on August 19 without incident.

conscription—the Confederates first, in early 1862, and the Federal government more slowly, with ineffective measures in late 1862 followed by a more stringent law in 1863. However, it was common for wealthy men to hire substitutes to fulfill their service obligation. In addition to employing conscription, the Union sought troops by offering cash rewards to enlistees through the bounty system. Both substitution and enticed enlistment led to widespread abuse, and "bounty jumpers" were a persistent drain on Northern manpower and finances. Support for conscription was far from universal in the North, and public resistance culminated in the Draft Riot of 1863, a racially charged four-day melee in which white rioters attacked federal buildings and African American workers in the streets of New York City.

CHAPTER 5

The War: The Big Picture

THE MILITARY BACKGROUND OF THE WAR

Comparison of North and South

At first glance it seemed that the 23 states of the Union were more than a match for the 11 seceding Southern states. There were approximately 21 million people in the North compared with some 9 million in the South (of whom about 3.5 million were slaves). In addition, the Union possessed over 100,000 manufacturing plants as against 18,000 south of the Potomac River, and more than 70 percent of the railroads were in the North. Furthermore, the Union had at its command a 30-to-1 superiority in arms production, a 2-to-1 edge in available manpower, and a great preponderance of commercial and financial resources. It had a functioning government and a small but efficient regular army and navy.

The Confederacy was not predestined to defeat, however. The Southern armies had the advantage of fighting on interior lines, and their military tradition had bulked large in the history of the United States before 1860. The long Confederate coastline of 3,500 miles (5,600 km) seemed to defy blockade. Moreover, the Confederate president, Jefferson Davis, hoped to receive decisive foreign aid and intervention.

Confederate soldiers were fighting to achieve a separate and independent nation based on what they called "Southern institutions," the chief of which was the institution of slavery. So the Southern cause was not a lost one; indeed, other nations had won independence against equally heavy odds.

The High Commands

Command problems plagued both sides. Of the two rival commanders in chief, most people in 1861 thought Davis to be abler than Lincoln. Davis was a West Point graduate, a hero of the Mexican War, a capable secretary of war under Pres. Franklin Pierce, and a U.S. representative and senator from Mississippi. Lincoln, however, who had served in the Illinois state legislature and as an undistinguished one-term member of the U.S. House of Representatives, could boast of only a brief period of military service in the Black Hawk War, in which he did not perform well.

As president and commander in chief of the Confederate forces, Davis revealed many fine qualities, including patience, courage, dignity, restraint, firmness, energy, determination, and honesty; but he was flawed by his excessive pride, hypersensitivity to criticism, and inability to delegate minor details to his subordinates. To a large extent Davis was his own secretary of war, although five different men served in that post during the lifetime of the Confederacy. Davis himself also filled the position of general in chief of the Confederate armies until he named Robert E. Lee to that position on Feb. 6, 1865, when the Confederacy was near collapse. In naval affairs—an area about which he knew little—the Confederate president seldom intervened directly, allowing the competent secretary of the navy, Stephen Mallory, to handle the Southern naval buildup and operations on the water. Although his position was onerous and perhaps could not have been filled so well by any other Southern political leader, Davis's overall performance in office left something to be desired.

To the astonishment of many, Lincoln grew in stature with time and experience, and by 1864 he had become a consummate war director. But he had much to learn at first, especially in strategic and tactical matters and in his choices of army commanders. With an ineffective first secretary of war—Simon Cameron—Lincoln unhesitatingly insinuated himself directly into the planning of military movements. Edwin M. Stanton, appointed to the secretaryship on Jan. 20, 1862, was equally untutored in military affairs but was fully as active a participant as his superior.

Winfield Scott was the Federal general in chief when Lincoln took office. The 75-year-old Scott—a hero of the War of 1812 and of the Mexican War—was a magnificent and distinguished soldier whose mind was still keen but was physically incapacitated and had to be retired from the service on Nov. 1, 1861. Scott was replaced by young George B. McClellan, an able and imaginative general in chief but one who had trouble in establishing harmonious and effective relations with Lincoln, as well as difficulties implementing his plans on the field of battle. For these reasons, and because he had to campaign with his own Army of the Potomac, McClellan was relieved as general in chief on March 11, 1862. He was eventually succeeded on July 11 by the limited Henry W. Halleck, who held the position until replaced by Ulysses S. Grant on March 9, 1864. Halleck then became chief of staff under Grant in a long-needed streamlining of the Federal high command. Grant served efficaciously as general in chief throughout the remainder of the war.

Strategic Plans

In the area of grand strategy, Davis persistently adhered to the defensive, permitting only occasional "spoiling" forays into Northern territory. Yet perhaps the Confederates' best chance of winning would have been an early grand offensive into the Union states before the Lincoln administration could find its ablest generals and bring the preponderant resources of the North to bear against the South.

Lincoln, on the other hand, in order to crush the rebellion and reestablish the authority of the Federal government, had to direct his blue-clad armies to invade, capture, and hold most of the vital areas of the Confederacy. His grand strategy was based on Scott's so-called Anaconda plan, a design that evolved from strategic ideas discussed in messages between Scott and McClellan on April 27, May 3, and May 21, 1861. It called for a Union blockade of the Confederacy's littoral as well as a decisive thrust down the Mississippi River and an ensuing strangulation of the South by Federal land and naval forces. But it was to take four years of grim, unrelenting warfare and enormous casualties and devastation before the Confederates could be defeated and the Union preserved.

The Land War

The War in 1861

The first military operations took place in northwestern Virginia, where nonslaveholding pro-Unionists sought to secede from the Confederacy. McClellan, in command of Federal forces in southern Ohio, advanced on his own initiative in the early summer of 1861 into western Virginia with about 20,000 men. He encountered smaller forces sent there by Lee, then in Richmond in command of all Virginia troops. Although showing signs of occasional hesitation, McClellan quickly won three small but significant battles: on June 3 at Philippi, on July 11 at Rich Mountain, and on July 13 at Carrick's (or Corrick's) Ford (all now in West Virginia). McClellan's casualties were light, and his victories went far toward eliminating Confederate resistance in northwestern Virginia, which had refused to recognize secession, and toward paving the way for the admittance into the Union of the new state of West Virginia in 1863.

Meanwhile, sizable armies were gathering around the Federal capital of Washington, D.C., and the Confederate capital of Richmond, Virginia. Federal forces abandoned positions in Virginia, including, on April 18, Harpers Ferry (now West Virginia), which was quickly occupied by Southern forces, who held it for a time, and the naval base at Norfolk, which was prematurely abandoned to the enemy on April 20. On May 6 Lee ordered a Confederate force—soon to be commanded by P. G. T. Beauregard—northward to hold the rail hub of Manassas Junction, Virginia, some 26 miles (42 km) southwest of Washington. With

Catharpin Run, Sudley Church, and the remains of the Sudley Sulpher Spring house, Bull Run, Virginia, photograph by George N. Barnard. Library of Congress, Washington, D.C. (LC-B8171-0314 DLC)

Lincoln's approval, Scott appointed Irvin McDowell to command the main Federal army that was being hastily collected near Washington. But political pressure and Northern public opinion impelled Lincoln, against Scott's advice, to order McDowell's still-untrained army forward to push the enemy back from Manassas. Meanwhile, Federal forces were to hold Confederate soldiers under Joseph E. Johnston in the Shenandoah Valley near Winchester, Virginia, thus preventing them from reinforcing Beauregard along the Bull Run near Manassas.

McDowell advanced from Washington on July 16 with some 32,000 men and moved slowly toward Bull Run. Two days later a reconnaissance in force was repulsed by the Confederates at Mitchell's and Blackburn's Fords, and when McDowell attacked on July 21 in the First Battle of Bull Run (in the South, First Manassas), he discovered that Johnston had escaped the Federals in the valley and had joined Beauregard near Manassas just in time, bringing the total Confederate force to around 28,000. McDowell's sharp attacks with green troops forced the equally untrained Southerners back a bit, but a strong defensive stand by Thomas Jonathan Jackson (who thereby gained the nickname "Stonewall") enabled the Confederates to check and finally throw back the Federals in the afternoon. The Federal retreat to Washington soon became a rout. McDowell lost 2,708 men—killed, wounded, and missing (including prisoners)—against a Southern loss of 1,981. Both sides now settled down to a long war.

The War in the East in 1862

Fresh from his victories in western Virginia, McClellan was called to Washington to replace Scott. There he began to mold the Army of the Potomac into a resolute, effective shield and sword of the Union. But personality clashes and unrelenting opposition to McClellan from the Radical Republicans in Congress hampered the sometimes tactless, conservative, Democratic general. It took time to drill, discipline, and equip this force of considerably more than 100,000 men, but as fall blended into winter, loud demands arose that McClellan advance against Johnston's Confederate forces at Centreville and Manassas in Virginia. McClellan fell seriously ill with typhoid fever in December, and when he had recovered weeks later he found that Lincoln, desperately eager for action, had ordered him to advance on Feb. 22, 1862. Long debates ensued between president and commander. When in March McClellan finally began his Peninsular Campaign, he discovered that Lincoln and Stanton had withheld large numbers of his command in front of Washington for the defense of the capital—forces that were actually not needed there. Upon taking command of the army in the field, McClellan was relieved of his duties as general in chief.

The Peninsular Campaign

Advancing up the historic peninsula between the York and James rivers in Virginia, McClellan began a month-long siege of Yorktown and captured that stronghold on May 4, 1862. A Confederate rearguard action at Williamsburg the next day delayed the blue-clads, who then slowly moved up through heavy rain to within 4 miles (6 km) of Richmond. Striving to seize the initiative, Johnston attacked McClellan's left wing at Seven Pines (Fair Oaks) on May 31 and, after scoring initial gains, was checked;

Union forces passing the Trent House, between Fair Oaks Station and Chickahomin, Virginia, drawing by Alfred R. Waud, June 1862. Library of Congress, Washington, D.C. (262-14325)

Johnston was severely wounded, and Lee, who had been serving as Davis's military adviser, succeeded Johnston in command of the Army of Northern Virginia. McClellan counterattacked on June 1 and forced the Southerners back into the environs of Richmond. The Federals suffered a total of 5,031 casualties out of a force of nearly 100,000, while the Confederates lost 6,134 of about 74,000 men.

As McClellan inched forward toward Richmond in June, Lee prepared a counterstroke. He recalled from the Shenandoah Valley Jackson's forces—which had threatened Harpers Ferry and had brilliantly defeated several scattered Federal armies—and, with about 90,000 soldiers, attacked McClellan on June 26 to begin the fighting of the Seven Days' Battles (usually dated June 25–July 1). In the ensuing days at Mechanicsville,

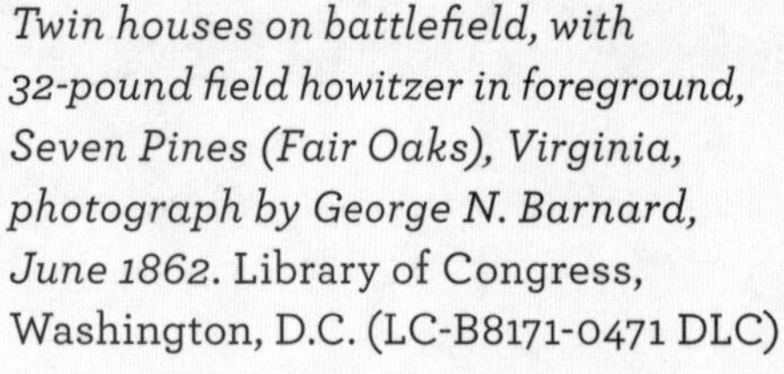

Twin houses on battlefield, with 32-pound field howitzer in foreground, Seven Pines (Fair Oaks), Virginia, photograph by George N. Barnard, June 1862. Library of Congress, Washington, D.C. (LC-B8171-0471 DLC)

Ruins of Gaines's Mill, near Cold Harbor, Virginia, photograph by John Reekie, April 1865. Library of Congress, Washington, D.C. (LC-B8171-0932 DLC)

Gaines's Mill, Savage's Station, Frayser's Farm (Glendale), and Malvern Hill, Lee tried unsuccessfully to crush the Army of the Potomac, which McClellan was moving to another base on the James River; but the Confederate commander had at least saved Richmond. McClellan inflicted 20,614 casualties on Lee while suffering 15,849 himself. McClellan felt he could not move upon Richmond without considerable reinforcement, and against his protests his army was withdrawn from the peninsula to Washington by Lincoln and the new general in chief, Halleck. Many of McClellan's units were given to a new Federal army commander,

Union field hospital, Savage's Station, Virginia, photograph by James F. Gibson, June 30, 1862. Library of Congress, Washington, D.C. (LC-B8171-0491 DLC)

John Pope, who was directed to move overland against Richmond.

Second Battle of Bull Run (Manassas) and Antietam

Pope advanced confidently toward the Rappahannock River with his Army of Virginia, while Lee, once McClellan had been pulled back from near Richmond, moved northward to confront Pope before he could be joined by all of McClellan's troops. Daringly splitting his army, Lee sent Jackson to destroy Pope's base at Manassas, while he himself advanced via another route with

Confederate dead by a fence on the Hagerstown road, Antietam, Maryland, photo by Alexander Gardner, September 1862. The Battle of Antietam was one of the most costly of the Civil War in terms of lives lost. Library of Congress, Washington, D.C. (LC-B8171-0560 DLC)

James Longstreet's half of the army. Pope opened the Second Battle of Bull Run (in the South, Second Manassas) on August 29 with heavy but futile attacks on Jackson. The next day Lee arrived and crushed the Federal left with a massive flank assault by Longstreet, which, combined with Jackson's counterattacks, drove the Northerners back in rout upon Washington. Pope lost 16,054 men out of a force of about 70,000, while Lee lost 9,197 out of about 55,000. With the Federal soldiers now lacking confidence in Pope, Lincoln relieved him and merged his forces into McClellan's Army of the Potomac.

Lee followed up his advantage with his first invasion of the North, pushing as far as Frederick, Maryland. McClellan had to reorganize his army on the march, a task that he performed capably. But he was beset by contradictory orders: Lincoln urged him to pursue Lee more swiftly; Halleck directed him to slow down and to stay closer to Washington. Biding his time, McClellan pressed forward and wrested the initiative from Lee by attacking and defeating a Confederate force at three gaps of the South Mountain between Frederick and Hagerstown on September 14. Lee fell back into a cramped defensive position along the Antietam Creek, near Sharpsburg, Maryland, where he was reinforced by Jackson, who had just captured about 11,500 Federals at Harpers Ferry. After a delay, McClellan struck the Confederates on September 17 in the bloodiest single day's battle of the war. Although gaining some ground, the Federals were unable to drive the Confederate army into the Potomac, but Lee was compelled to retreat back into Virginia. At Antietam, McClellan lost 12,410 of some 69,000 engaged, while Lee lost 13,724 of perhaps 52,000. When McClellan did not pursue Lee as quickly as Lincoln and Halleck thought he should, he was replaced in command by Ambrose E. Burnside, who had been an ineffective corps commander at Antietam.

Fredericksburg

Burnside delayed for a number of weeks before marching his reinforced army of 120,281 men to a point across the Rappahannock River from Fredericksburg, Virginia. On December 13 he ordered a series of 16 hopeless, piecemeal frontal assaults across open ground against Lee's army of 78,513 troops, drawn up in an impregnable position atop high ground and behind a stone wall. The Federals were repelled with staggering losses; Burnside had lost 12,653 men, compared to Lee's 5,309. The plunging Federal morale was reflected in an increasing number of desertions. Therefore, on Jan. 25, 1863, Lincoln replaced Burnside with a proficient corps commander, Joseph ("Fighting Joe") Hooker, who was a harsh critic of other generals and even of the president. Both armies went into winter quarters near Fredericksburg.

Union engineers constructing a pontoon bridge across the Rappahannock River during the Battle of Fredericksburg, Virginia. Confederate forces can be seen in the distance firing on the engineers. Drawing by Alfred R. Waud, December 1862. Library of Congress, Washington, D.C. (LC-USZ62-7023)

The War in the West in 1862

Military events, meanwhile, were transpiring in other arenas.

Trans-Mississippi Theatre and Missouri

In the Trans-Mississippi theatre covetous Confederate eyes were cast on California, where ports for privateers could be seized, as could gold and silver to buttress a sagging treasury. Led by Henry Sibley, a Confederate force of some 2,600 invaded the Union's Department of New Mexico, where the Federal commander, Edward Canby, had but 3,810 men to defend the entire vast territory. Although plagued by pneumonia and smallpox, Sibley bettered a Federal force on Feb. 21, 1862, at Valverde, and captured Albuquerque and Santa Fe on March 23. But at the crucial engagement of La Glorieta Pass (known also as Apache Canyon, Johnson's Ranch, or Pigeon's Ranch) a few days later, Sibley was checked and lost most of his wagon train. He had to retreat into Texas, where he reached safety in April but with only 900 men and seven of 337 supply wagons left.

Farther eastward, in the more vital Mississippi valley, operations were unfolding as large and as important as those on the Atlantic seaboard. Missouri and Kentucky were key border states that Lincoln had to retain within the Union orbit. Commanders there—especially on the Federal side— had greater autonomy than those in Virginia. Affairs began inauspiciously for the Federals in Missouri when Union General Nathaniel Lyon's 5,000 troops were defeated at Wilson's Creek on Aug. 10, 1861, by a Confederate force of more than 10,000 under Sterling Price and Benjamin McCulloch, each side losing some 1,200 men. But the Federals under Samuel Curtis decisively set back a gray-clad army under Earl Van Dorn at Pea Ridge (Elkhorn Tavern), Arkansas, on March 7–8, 1862, saving Missouri for the Union and threatening Arkansas.

Operations in Kentucky and Tennessee

The Confederates to the east of Missouri had established a unified command under Albert Sidney Johnston, who manned, with only 40,000 men, a long line in Kentucky running from near Cumberland Gap on the east through Bowling Green to Columbus on the Mississippi River.

Numerically superior Federal forces cracked this line in early 1862. First, George H. Thomas smashed Johnston's right flank at Mill Springs (Somerset), Kentucky, on January 19. Then, in February, Grant, assisted by Federal gunboats commanded by Andrew H. Foote and acting under Halleck's orders, ruptured the centre of the Southern line in Kentucky by capturing Fort Henry on the Tennessee River and Fort Donelson, 11 miles (18 km) to the east on the Cumberland River (both forts located in Tennessee). The Confederates suffered more than 16,000 casualties at the latter stronghold—most of them taken prisoner—as against Federal losses of less than 3,000. Johnston's left anchor fell when Pope seized New Madrid, Missouri, and Island Number Ten in the Mississippi River in March and April.

This forced Johnston to withdraw his remnants quickly from Kentucky through Tennessee and to reorganize them for a counterstroke. This seemingly impossible task he performed splendidly.

The Confederate onslaught came at Shiloh, Tennessee, near Pittsburg Landing, a point on the west bank of the Tennessee River to which Grant and William T. Sherman had incautiously advanced. In a herculean effort, Johnston had pulled his forces together and, with 40,000 men, suddenly struck a like number of unsuspecting Federals on April 6. Johnston hoped to crush Grant before the arrival of Don Carlos Buell's 20,000 Federal troops, approaching from Nashville, Tennessee. A desperate combat ensued, with Confederate assaults driving the Unionists perilously close to the river. But at the height of success, Johnston was mortally wounded; the Southern attack then lost momentum, and Grant held on until reinforced by Buell. On the following day the Federals counterattacked and drove the Confederates, now under Beauregard, steadily from the field, forcing them to fall back to Corinth, in northern Mississippi. Grant's victory cost him 13,047 casualties, compared to Southern losses of 10,694. Halleck then assumed personal command of the combined forces of Grant, Buell, and Pope and inched forward to Corinth, which the Confederates evacuated on May 30.

Beauregard, never popular with Davis, was superseded by Braxton Bragg, one of the president's favourites. Bragg was a creative strategist and an effective drillmaster and organizer; but he was also a weak tactician and a martinet who was disliked by a number of his principal subordinates. Leaving 22,000 men in Mississippi under Price and Van Dorn, Bragg moved through Chattanooga, Tennessee, with 30,000, hoping to reconquer the state and carry the war into Kentucky. Some 18,000 other Confederate soldiers under Edmund Kirby-Smith were at Knoxville, Tennessee. Buell led his Federal force northward to save Louisville, Kentucky, and to force Bragg to fight. Occupying Frankfort, Kentucky, Bragg failed to move promptly against Louisville. In the ensuing Battle of Perryville on October 8, Bragg, after an early advantage, was halted by Buell and impelled to fall back to a point south of Nashville. Meanwhile, Federal General William S. Rosecrans had checked Price and Van Dorn at Iuka, Mississippi, on September 19 and had repelled their attack on Corinth on October 3–4.

Buell—like McClellan a cautious, conservative, Democratic general—was slow in his pursuit of the retreating Confederates and, despite his success at Perryville, was relieved of his command by Lincoln on October 24. His successor, Rosecrans, was able to safeguard Nashville and then to move southeastward against Bragg's army at Murfreesboro, Tennessee. He scored a partial success by bringing on the bloody Battle of Stones River (or

Murfreesboro, Dec. 31, 1862–Jan. 2, 1863). Again, after first having the better of the combat, Bragg was finally contained and forced to retreat. Of some 41,400 men, Rosecrans lost 12,906, while Bragg suffered 11,739 casualties out of about 34,700 effectives. Although it was a strategic victory for Rosecrans, his army was so shaken that he felt unable to advance again for five months, despite the urgings of Lincoln and Halleck.

The War in the East in 1863

In the east, after both armies had spent the winter in camp, the arrival of the active 1863 campaign season was eagerly awaited—especially by Hooker. "Fighting Joe" had capably reorganized and refitted his army, the morale of which was high once again. This massive host numbered around 132,000—the largest formed during the war—and was termed by Hooker "the finest army on the planet." It was opposed by Lee with about 62,000. Hooker decided to move most of his army up the Rappahannock, cross, and come in upon the Confederate rear at Fredericksburg, while John Sedgwick's smaller force would press Lee in front.

Chancellorsville

Beginning his turning movement on April 27, 1863, Hooker masterfully swung around toward the west of the Confederate army. Thus far he had outmaneuvered Lee; but Hooker was astonished on May 1 when the Confederate commander suddenly moved the bulk of his army directly against him. "Fighting Joe" lost his nerve and pulled back to Chancellorsville, Virginia, in the Wilderness, where the superior Federal artillery could not be used effectively.

Lee followed up on May 2 by sending Jackson on a brilliant flanking movement against Hooker's exposed right flank. Bursting like a thunderbolt upon Oliver O. Howard's 11th Corps late in the afternoon, Jackson crushed this wing; while continuing his advance, however, Jackson was accidentally wounded by his own men and died of complications shortly thereafter. This event helped stall the Confederate advance. Lee then resumed the attack on the morning of May 3 and slowly pushed Hooker back; the latter was wounded by Southern artillery fire. That afternoon Sedgwick drove Jubal Early's Southerners from Marye's Heights at Fredericksburg, but Lee countermarched his weary troops, fell upon Sedgwick at Salem Church, and forced him back to the north bank of the Rappahannock. Lee then returned to Chancellorsville to resume the main engagement; but Hooker, though he had 37,000 fresh troops available, gave up the contest on May 5 and retreated across the river to his old position opposite Fredericksburg. The Federals suffered 17,278 casualties at Chancellorsville, while the Confederates lost 12,764.

Gettysburg

While both armies were licking their wounds and reorganizing, Hooker, Lincoln, and Halleck debated Union strategy. They were thus engaged when Lee launched his second invasion of the North on June 5, 1863. His advance elements moved down the Shenandoah Valley toward Harpers Ferry, brushing aside small Federal forces near Winchester. Marching through Maryland into Pennsylvania, the Confederates reached Chambersburg and turned eastward. They occupied York and Carlisle and menaced Harrisburg. Meanwhile, the dashing Confederate cavalryman J.E.B. ("Jeb") Stuart set off on a questionable ride around the Federal army and was unable to join Lee's main army until the second day at Gettysburg.

Hooker—on unfriendly terms with Lincoln and especially Halleck—ably moved the Federal forces northward, keeping between Lee's army and Washington. Reaching Frederick, Hooker requested that the nearly 10,000-man Federal garrison at Harpers Ferry be added to his field army. When Halleck refused, Hooker resigned his command and was succeeded by the steady George Gordon Meade, the commander of the 5th Corps. Meade was granted a greater degree of freedom of movement than Hooker had enjoyed, and he carefully felt his way northward, looking for the enemy.

Learning to his surprise on June 28 that the Federal army was north of the Potomac, Lee hastened to concentrate his far-flung legions. Hostile forces came together unexpectedly at the important crossroads town of Gettysburg, in southern Pennsylvania, bringing on the greatest battle ever fought in the Western Hemisphere. Attacking on July 1 from the west and north with 28,000 men, Confederate forces finally prevailed after nine hours of desperate fighting against 18,000 Federal soldiers under John F. Reynolds. When Reynolds was killed, Abner Doubleday ably handled the outnumbered Federal troops, and only the sheer weight of Confederate numbers forced him back through the streets of Gettysburg to strategic Cemetery Ridge south of town, where Meade assembled the rest of the army that night.

On the second day of battle, Meade's 93,000 troops were ensconced in a strong, fishhook-shaped defensive position running northward from the Round Top hills along Cemetery Ridge and thence eastward to Culp's Hill. Lee, with 75,000 troops, ordered Longstreet to attack the Federals diagonally from Little Round Top northward and Richard S. Ewell to assail Cemetery Hill and Culp's Hill. The Confederate attack, coming in the late afternoon and evening, saw Longstreet capture the positions known as the Peach Orchard, Wheat Field, and Devil's Den on the Federal left in furious fighting but fail to seize the vital Little Round Top. Ewell's later assaults on Cemetery Hill were repulsed, and he could capture only a part of Culp's Hill.

Breastworks on Little Round Top, with Big Round Top in the distance, Gettysburg, Pennsylvania, July 1863. Library of Congress, Washington, D.C. (LC-B8171-7491 DLC)

On the morning of the third day, Meade's right wing drove the Confederates from the lower slopes of Culp's Hill and checked Stuart's cavalry sweep to the east of Gettysburg in mid-afternoon. Then, in what has been called the greatest infantry charge in American history, Lee—against Longstreet's advice—hurled nearly 15,000 soldiers, under the immediate command of George E. Pickett, against the centre of Meade's lines on Cemetery Ridge, following a fearful artillery duel of two hours. Despite heroic efforts, only several hundred Southerners temporarily cracked the Federal centre at the so-called High-Water Mark; the rest were shot down by Federal cannoneers and musketry men, captured, or thrown back, suffering casualties of almost 60 percent. Meade felt

Primary Source: Gettysburg Address

On Nov. 19, 1863, at the dedication of the National Cemetery at Gettysburg, Pa., on the site of the Battle of Gettysburg, President Abraham Lincoln delivered one of the world's most famous speeches.

The main address at the dedication ceremony was one of two hours, delivered by Edward Everett, the best-known orator of the time. In the wake of such a performance, Lincoln's brief speech would hardly seem to have drawn notice. However, despite some criticism from his opposition, it was widely quoted and praised and soon came to be recognized as one of the classic utterances of all time, a masterpiece of prose poetry. On the day following the ceremony, Everett himself wrote to Lincoln, "I wish that I could flatter myself that I had come as near to the central idea of the occasion in two hours as you did in two minutes."

The text quoted in full below represents the fifth of five extant copies of the address in Lincoln's handwriting; it differs slightly from earlier versions and may reflect, in addition to afterthought, interpolations made during the delivery.

> Four score and seven years ago our fathers brought forth on this continent a new nation, conceived in Liberty, and dedicated to the proposition that all men are created equal. Now we are engaged in a great civil war, testing whether that nation or any nation so conceived and so dedicated, can long endure. We are met on a great battle-field of that war. We have come to dedicate a portion of that field, as a final resting place for those who here gave their lives that that nation might live. It is altogether fitting and proper that we should do this. But, in a larger sense, we can not dedicate—we can not consecrate—we can not hallow—this ground. The brave men, living and dead, who struggled here, have consecrated it, far above our poor power to add or detract. The world will little note, nor long remember what we say here, but it can never forget what they did here. It is for us the living, rather, to be dedicated here to the unfinished work which they who fought here have thus far so nobly advanced. It is rather for us to be here dedicated to the great task remaining before us—that from these honored dead we take increased devotion to that cause for which they gave the last full measure of devotion—that we here highly resolve that these dead shall not have died in vain— that this nation, under God, shall have a new birth of freedom—and that government of the people, by the people, for the people, shall not perish from the earth.

unable to counterattack, and Lee conducted an adroit retreat into Virginia. The Confederates had lost 28,063 men at Gettysburg, and the Federals, 23,049. After indecisive maneuvering and light actions in northern Virginia in the fall of 1863, the two armies went into winter quarters. Never again was Lee able to mount a full-scale invasion of the North with his entire army.

The War in the West in 1863

Arkansas and Vicksburg

In Arkansas, Federal troops under Frederick Steele moved upon the Confederates and defeated them at Prairie Grove, near Fayetteville, on Dec. 7, 1862—a victory that paved the way for Steele's eventual capture of Little Rock the next September.

More important, Grant, back in good graces following his undistinguished performance at Shiloh, was authorized to move against the Confederate "Gibraltar of the West"—Vicksburg, Mississippi. This bastion was difficult to approach: Admiral David G. Farragut, Grant, and Sherman had failed to capture it in 1862. In the early months of 1863, in the so-called Bayou Expeditions, Grant was again frustrated in his efforts to get at Vicksburg from the north. Finally, escorted by Admiral David Dixon Porter's gunboats, which ran the Confederate batteries at Vicksburg, Grant landed his army to the south at Bruinsburg, Mississippi, on April 30, 1863, and pressed northeastward. He won small but sharp actions at Port Gibson, Raymond, and Jackson, while the circumspect Confederate defender of Vicksburg, John C. Pemberton, was unable to link up with a smaller Southern force under Joseph E. Johnston near Jackson.

Turning due westward toward the rear of Vicksburg's defenses, Grant smashed Pemberton's army at Champion's Hill and the Big Black River and invested the fortress. During his 47-day siege, Grant eventually had an army of 71,000; Pemberton's command numbered 31,000, of whom 18,500 were effectives. After a courageous stand, the outnumbered Confederates were forced to capitulate on July 4. Five days later, 6,000 Confederates yielded to Nathaniel P. Banks at Port Hudson, Louisiana, to the south of Vicksburg, and Lincoln could say, in relief, "The Father of Waters again goes unvexed to the sea."

Chickamauga and Chattanooga

Meanwhile, 60,000 Federal soldiers under Rosecrans sought to move southeastward from central Tennessee against the important Confederate rail and industrial centre of Chattanooga, then held by Bragg with some 43,000 troops. In a series of brilliantly conceived movements, Rosecrans maneuvered Bragg out of Chattanooga without having to

Site of the second day of battle, along the banks of Chickamauga Creek, near Chattanooga, Tennessee. Library of Congress, Washington, D.C. (B8184-10260)

fight a battle. Bragg was then bolstered by troops from Longstreet's veteran corps, sent swiftly by rail from Lee's army in Virginia. With this reinforcement, Bragg turned on Rosecrans and, in a vicious two-day battle (September 19–20) at Chickamauga Creek, Georgia, just southeast of Chattanooga, gained one of the few Confederate victories in the west. Bragg lost 18,454 of his 66,326 men; Rosecrans, 16,170 out of 53,919 engaged. Rosecrans fell back into Chattanooga, where he was almost encircled by Bragg.

But the Southern success was short-lived. Instead of pressing the siege of Chattanooga, Bragg unwisely sent Longstreet off in a futile attempt to capture Knoxville, then being held by Burnside. When Rosecrans showed signs of disintegration, Lincoln replaced him with Grant and strengthened the hard-pressed Federal army at Chattanooga by sending, by rail, the remnants of the Army of the Potomac's 11th and 12th Corps, under Hooker's command. Outnumbering Bragg now 56,359 to 46,165, Grant attacked on November 23–25, capturing Lookout Mountain and Missionary Ridge, defeating Bragg's army, and driving it southward toward Dalton, Georgia. Grant sustained 5,824 casualties at Chattanooga and Bragg, 6,667. Confidence having been lost in Bragg by most of his top generals, Davis replaced him with Joseph E. Johnston. Both armies remained quiescent until the following spring.

The War in 1864–65

Finally dissatisfied with Halleck as general in chief and impressed with Grant's victories, Lincoln appointed Grant to supersede Halleck and to assume the rank of lieutenant general, which Congress had re-created. Leaving Sherman in command in the west, Grant arrived in Washington on March 8, 1864. He was given largely a free hand in developing his grand strategy. He retained Meade in technical command of the Army of the Potomac but in effect assumed direct control by establishing his own headquarters with it. He sought to move this army against Lee in northern Virginia while Sherman marched against Johnston and Atlanta. Several lesser Federal armies were also to advance in May.

Grant's Overland Campaign

Grant surged across the Rapidan and Rappahannock rivers in Virginia on May 4, hoping to get through the

In Focus: Saint Albans Raid

On Oct. 19, 1864, about 25 Confederate soldiers based in Canada raided the town of St. Albans, Vt., killed one man, robbed three banks, and then retreated to Canadian territory. A Union posse pursued the raiders and captured several of them, but it was forced to surrender them to the Canadian authorities. On October 21 about half the Confederates were arrested by the Canadians, but they were released again on December 13, and the $200,000 they had stolen was returned.

Although the Canadian government reimbursed the plundered banks, the release of the raiders led to strong protests in the United States. Consequently, five of the raiders were rearrested and remained in custody for a time for violating Canadian neutrality. In 1872 a claims commission established under the Anglo-American Treaty of Washington (1871) ruled against further American claims to compensation.

General Ulysses S. Grant, Cold Harbor, Virginia; photograph by Mathew Brady, 1864. National Archives, Brady Collection, Civil War Photographs

tangled Wilderness before Lee could move. But the Confederate leader reacted instantly and, on May 5, attacked Grant from the west in the Battle of the Wilderness. Two days of bitter, indecisive combat ensued. Although Grant had 115,000 men available against Lee's 62,000, he found both Federal flanks endangered. Moreover, Grant lost 17,666 soldiers compared to a probable Southern loss of about 8,000. Pulling away from the Wilderness battlefield, Grant tried to hasten southeastward to the crossroads point of Spotsylvania Court House, only to have the Confederates get there first. In savage action (May 8–19), including hand-to-hand fighting at the famous "Bloody Angle," Grant, although gaining a little ground, was essentially thrown back. He had lost 18,399 men at Spotsylvania. Lee's combined losses at the Wilderness and Spotsylvania were an estimated 17,250.

Again Grant withdrew, only to move forward in another series of attempts to get past Lee's right flank; again, at the North Anna River and at the Totopotomoy Creek, he found Lee confronting him. Finally at Cold Harbor, just northeast of Richmond, Grant launched several heavy attacks, including a frontal, near-suicidal one on June 3, only to be repelled with grievous total losses of 12,737. Lee's casualties are unknown but were much lighter.

Grant, with the vital rail centre of Petersburg—the southern key to Richmond—as his objective, made one final effort to swing around Lee's right and finally outguessed his opponent and stole a march on him. But several blunders by Federal officers, swift action by Beauregard, and Lee's belated though rapid reaction enabled the Confederates to hold Petersburg. Grant attacked on June 15 and 18, hoping to break through before Lee could consolidate the Confederate lines east of the city, but he was contained with 8,150 losses.

Unable to admit defeat but having failed to destroy Lee's army and capture Richmond, Grant settled down to a nine-month active siege of Petersburg. The summer and fall of 1864 were highlighted by the Federal failure with a mine explosion under the gray lines at Petersburg on July 30, the near capture of Washington by the Confederate Jubal Early in July, and Early's later setbacks in the Shenandoah Valley at the hands of Philip H. Sheridan.

Sherman's Georgia Campaigns

Meanwhile, Sherman was pushing off toward Atlanta from Dalton, Georgia, on May 7, 1864, with 110,123 men against Johnston's 55,000. This masterly campaign comprised a series of cat-and-mouse moves by the rival commanders. Nine successive defensive positions were taken up by Johnston. Trying to outguess his opponent, Sherman attempted to swing around the Confederate right flank twice and around the left flank the other times, but each time Johnston divined which way Sherman was moving and each time pulled back in time to thwart him. At one point Sherman's patience snapped and he frontally assaulted the Southerners at Kennesaw Mountain, Georgia, on June 27; Johnston threw him back with heavy losses. All the while Sherman's lines of communication in his rear were being menaced by audacious Confederate cavalry raids conducted by Nathan Bedford Forrest and Joseph Wheeler. Forrest administered a crushing defeat to Federal troops under Samuel D. Sturgis at Brice's Cross Roads, Mississippi, on June 10. But these Confederate forays were more annoying than decisive, and Sherman pressed forward.

When Johnston finally informed Davis that he could not realistically hope to annihilate Sherman's mighty army, the Confederate president replaced him with John B. Hood, who had already lost two limbs in the war. Hood inaugurated a series of premature offensive battles at Peachtree Creek, Atlanta, Ezra Church, and Jonesboro, but he was repulsed in each of them. With his communications threatened, Hood evacuated Atlanta on the night of August 31–September 1. Sherman pursued only at first. Then, on November 15, he commenced his great March to the Sea with more than 60,000 men, laying waste to the economic resources of Georgia in a 50-mile- (80-km-) wide swath of destruction. He captured Savannah on December 21.

Hood had sought unsuccessfully to lure Sherman out of Georgia and back into Tennessee by marching northwestward with nearly 40,000 men toward the key city of Nashville, the defense of which had been entrusted by Sherman to George H. Thomas. At Franklin, Hood was checked for a day with severe casualties by a Federal holding force under John M. Schofield. This helped Thomas

Covered cannon on the steps of the capitol, Nashville, Tennessee, photograph by George N. Barnard, 1864. Library of Congress, Washington, D.C. (LC B8171-2629 LC)

to retain Nashville, where, on December 15–16, he delivered a crushing counterstroke against Hood's besieging army, cutting it up so badly that it was of little use thereafter.

Western Campaigns

Sherman's force might have been larger and his Atlanta-Savannah Campaign consummated much sooner had not Lincoln approved the Red River Campaign in Louisiana led by Banks in the spring of 1864. Accompanied by Porter's warships, Banks moved up the Red River with some 40,000 men. He had two objectives: to capture cotton and to defeat Southern forces under Kirby-Smith and Richard Taylor. Not only did he fail to net much cotton but he was also checked with loss on April 8 at Sabine Cross Roads, Louisiana, and forced to retreat. Porter lost several gunboats, and the campaign amounted to a costly debacle.

That fall Kirby-Smith ordered the reconquest of Missouri. Sterling Price's Confederate army advanced on a broad front into Missouri but was set back temporarily by Thomas Ewing at Pilot Knob on September 27. Resuming the advance toward St. Louis, Price was forced westward along the south bank of the Missouri River by pursuing Federal troops under A.J. Smith, Alfred Pleasonton, and Samuel Curtis. Finally, on October 23, at Westport, near Kansas City, Price was decisively defeated and forced to retreat along a circuitous route, arriving back in Arkansas on December 2. This ill-fated raid cost Price most of his artillery as well as the greater part of his army, which numbered about 12,000.

Sherman's Carolina Campaigns

On Jan. 10, 1865, with Tennessee and Georgia now securely in Federal hands, Sherman's 60,000-man force began to march northward into the Carolinas. It was only lightly opposed by much smaller Confederate forces. Sherman captured Columbia, South Carolina, on February 17 and compelled the Confederates to evacuate Charleston (including Fort Sumter). When Lee was finally named Confederate general in chief, he promptly reinstated Johnston as commander of the small forces striving to oppose the Federal advance. Nonetheless, Sherman pushed on into North Carolina, capturing Fayetteville on March 11 and, after an initial setback, repulsing the counterattacking Johnston at Bentonville on March 19–20. Goldsboro fell to the Federals on March 23, and Raleigh on April 13. Finally, perceiving that he no longer had any reasonable chance of containing the relentless Federal advance, Johnston surrendered to Sherman at the Bennett House near Durham Station on April 18. When Sherman's generous terms proved unacceptable to Secretary of War Stanton (Lincoln had been assassinated on April 14), the former submitted new terms that Johnston signed on April 26.

The Final Land Operations

Grant and Meade were continuing their siege of Petersburg and Richmond early in 1865. For months the Federals had been lengthening their left (southern) flank while operating against several important railroads supplying the two Confederate cities. This stretched Lee's dwindling forces very thin. The Southern leader briefly threatened to break the siege when he attacked and captured Fort Stedman on March 25. But an immediate Federal counterattack regained the strongpoint, and Lee, when his lines were subsequently pierced, evacuated both Petersburg and Richmond on the night of April 2–3.

An 88-mile (142-km) pursuit west-southwestward along the Appomattox River in Virginia ensued, with Grant and Meade straining every nerve to bring Lee to bay. The Confederates were detained at Amelia Court House, awaiting delayed food supplies, and were badly cut up at Five Forks and Sayler's Creek, with their only avenue of escape now cut off by Sheridan and George A. Custer. When Lee's final attempt to break out failed, he surrendered the remnants of his gallant Army of Northern Virginia at the McLean house at Appomattox Court House on April 9. The lamp of magnanimity was reflected in Grant's unselfish terms.

On the periphery of the Confederacy, 43,000 gray-clad soldiers in Louisiana under Kirby-Smith surrendered to Canby on May 26. The port of Galveston, Texas, yielded to the Federals on June 2, and the greatest war on American soil was over.

THE NAVAL WAR

While the Federal armies actually stamped out Confederate land resistance, the increasingly effective Federal naval effort must not be overlooked. If Union sea power did not win the war, it enabled the war to be won. When hostilities opened, the U.S. Navy numbered 90 warships, of which only 42 were in commission, and many of these were on foreign stations. Fortunately for the Federals, Lincoln had, in the person of Gideon Welles, a wise secretary of the navy and one of his most competent cabinet members. Welles was ably seconded by his assistant, Gustavus Vasa Fox.

By the time of Lee's surrender, Lincoln's navy numbered 626 warships, of which 65 were ironclads. From a tiny force of nearly 9,000 seamen in 1861, the Union navy increased by war's end to about 59,000 sailors, whereas naval appropriations per year leaped from approximately $12 million to perhaps $123 million. The blockade of about 3,500 miles (5,600 km) of Confederate coastline was a factor of incalculable value in the final defeat of the Davis government, although the blockade did not become truly effective before the end of 1863.

The Confederates, on the other hand, had to start from almost nothing in building a navy. That they did so well was largely because of untiring efforts by the capable secretary of the navy, Stephen Mallory. He dispatched agents to Europe to purchase warships, sought to refurbish captured or scuttled Federal vessels, and made every effort to arm and employ Southern-owned ships then in Confederate ports. Mallory's only major omission was his delay in seeing the advantage of Confederate government control of blockade runners bringing in strategic supplies; not until later in the war did the government begin closer supervision of blockade-running vessels. Eventually, the government commandeered space on all privately owned blockade runners and even built and operated some of its own late in the war.

The naval side of the Civil War was a revolutionary one. In addition to their increasing use of steam power, the screw propeller, shell guns, and rifled ordnance, both sides built and employed ironclad warships. The notable clash on March 9, 1862, between the North's *Monitor* and the South's *Virginia* (formerly the *Merrimack*) was the first battle ever waged between ironclads. Also, the first sinking of a warship by a submarine occurred on Feb. 17, 1864, when the Confederate submersible *Hunley* sank the blockader USS *Housatonic*.

Daring Confederate sea raiders preyed upon Union commerce. Especially successful were the *Sumter*, commanded by Raphael Semmes, which captured 18 Northern merchantmen early in the war; the *Florida*, captained by John Maffit, which, in 1863, seized 37 Federal prizes in the North and South Atlantic; and the *Shenandoah*, with James Waddell as skipper, which took 38 Union merchant ships, mostly in the Pacific. But the most famous of all the Confederate cruisers was the *Alabama*, commanded by Semmes, which captured 69 Federal ships in two years; not until June 19, 1864, was the *Alabama* intercepted and sunk off Cherbourg, France, by the Federal warship *Kearsarge*, captained by John Winslow. A great many other Federal ships were captured, and marine insurance rates were driven to a prohibitive high by these Southern depredations. This led to a serious deterioration of the American merchant marine, the effects of which lasted into the 20th century.

In Focus: *Alabama* Claims

The Alabama *claims are significant in international law for furthering the use of arbitration to settle disputes peacefully and for delineating certain responsibilities of neutrals toward belligerents. The dispute centred on the Confederate cruiser* Alabama, *built in England and used against the Union as a commerce destroyer, which captured, sank, or burned 68 ships in 22 months before being sunk by the USS* Kearsarge *off Cherbourg, France (June 1864).*

At the outset of the war, a Federal blockade of Southern ports and coasts automatically extended belligerent status to the Confederacy. To protect its own interests, Britain took the lead among European countries in proclaiming its neutrality (May 14, 1861). The Confederacy immediately set about building a navy to engage the Union's naval power and to destroy its merchant marine. Along with several other ships, the Alabama *was built or fitted out privately on British territory and put to sea despite the belated intervention of the British government.*

As early as October 1863, the U.S. minister to Great Britain, Charles Francis Adams, protested that the British must take responsibility for the damages caused by British-built Confederate raiders, but he conceded that his government would be willing to submit the matter to arbitration. Amid bombastic U.S. threats of annexing Canada, Anglo-American misunderstanding was exacerbated after the end of the Civil War by unsettled disputes over Canadian fisheries and the northwestern boundary. A proposed settlement in the Johnson-Clarendon Convention was angrily rejected by the United States. To avoid further deterioration of Anglo-American relations, a joint high commission was set up, and on May 8, 1871, the parties signed the Treaty of Washington, which, by establishing four separate arbitrations, afforded the most ambitious arbitral undertaking the world had experienced up to that time. In addition, Great Britain expressed official regret over the matter.

Certain wartime maritime obligations of neutrals, already agreed to in article 6 of the treaty, were outlined in the principal arbitration of the Alabama claims, meeting at Geneva, as follows: that a neutral government must use "due diligence" to prevent the fitting out, arming, or equipping, within its jurisdiction, of any vessel believed to be intended to carry a war against a power with which it was at peace and to prevent the departure of such a vessel (the substance of this clause was included in article 8 of the 1907 Hague Convention) and that a neutral must not permit its ports or waters to be used as a base of naval operations for similar purposes. In addition, on Sept. 14, 1872, the tribunal voted unanimously that Britain was legally liable for direct losses caused by the Alabama and other ships and awarded the United States damages of $15,500,000 in gold.

This settlement gave new impetus to the process of arbitration, which had been latent for many years.

Besides fighting efficaciously with ironclads on the inland rivers, Lincoln's navy also played an important role in a series of coastal and amphibious operations, some in conjunction with the Federal army. As early as Nov. 7, 1861, a Federal flotilla under Samuel Francis du Pont seized Port Royal, S.C., and another squadron under Louis M. Goldsborough assisted Burnside's army in capturing Roanoke Island and New Bern on the North Carolina littoral in February–March 1862. One month later, Savannah, Ga., was closed to Confederate blockade runners when the Federal navy reduced Fort Pulaski guarding the city; and on April 25 David Glasgow Farragut, running the forts near the mouth of the Mississippi, took New Orleans, which was subsequently occupied by Benjamin F. Butler's army.

But in April 1863 and again in July and August, Federal warships were repelled at Fort Sumter when they descended upon Charleston, and a Federal army under Quincy A. Gillmore fared little better when it tried to assist. Farragut had better luck, however, when he rendered Mobile, Ala., useless by reducing Fort Morgan and destroying several defending Confederate ships on Aug. 5, 1864, in the hardest-fought naval action of the war. The Confederacy's last open Atlantic port, Wilmington, N.C., successfully withstood a Federal naval attack by Porter on defending Fort Fisher when Butler's army failed to coordinate its attack properly in December 1864, but it fell one month later to Porter and to an ably conducted army assault led by Alfred H. Terry. Only Galveston remained open to the Confederates in the last months of the war. In short, "Uncle Sam's web feet," as Lincoln termed the Union navy, played a decisive role in helping to crush the Confederacy.

THE COST AND SIGNIFICANCE OF THE CIVIL WAR

The triumph of the North, above and beyond its superior naval forces, numbers, and industrial and financial resources, was due in part to the statesmanship of Lincoln, who by 1864 had become a masterful war leader, to the pervading valour of Federal soldiers, and to the increasing skill of their officers. The victory can also be attributed in part to failures of Confederate transportation, resources, and political leadership. Only praise can be extended to the continuing bravery of Confederate soldiers and to the strategic and tactical dexterity of such generals as Lee, Jackson, and Joseph E. Johnston.

While there were some desertions on both sides, the personal valour and enormous casualties—both in absolute numbers and in percentage of numbers engaged—have not yet ceased to astound scholars and military historians. Based on the three-year standard of enlistment, about 1,556,000 soldiers served in the Federal armies, which suffered a total of 634,703 casualties (359,528 dead and 275,175 wounded). There were probably about 800,000 men serving in the Confederate forces, which sustained approximately 483,000 casualties (about 258,000 dead and perhaps 225,000 wounded).

The Civil War has been called by some the last of the old-fashioned wars; others have termed it the first of the modern wars of history. Actually it was a transitional war, and it had a profound impact, technologically, on the development of modern weapons and techniques. There were many innovations. It was the first war in history in which ironclad warships clashed; the first in which the telegraph and railroad played significant roles; the first to use, extensively, rifled ordnance and shell guns and to introduce a machine gun; the first to have widespread newspaper coverage, voting by servicemen in national elections, and photographic recordings; the first to organize medical care of troops systematically; and the first to use land and water mines and to employ a submarine that could sink a warship. It was also the first war in which armies widely employed aerial reconnaissance (by means of balloons).

The Civil War has been written about as have few other wars in history. More than 60,000 books and articles give eloquent testimony to the accuracy of Walt Whitman's prediction that "a great literature will . . . arise out of the era of those four years." The events of the war left a rich heritage for future generations, and that legacy was summed up by the martyred Lincoln as showing that the reunited sections of the United States constituted "the last best hope of earth."

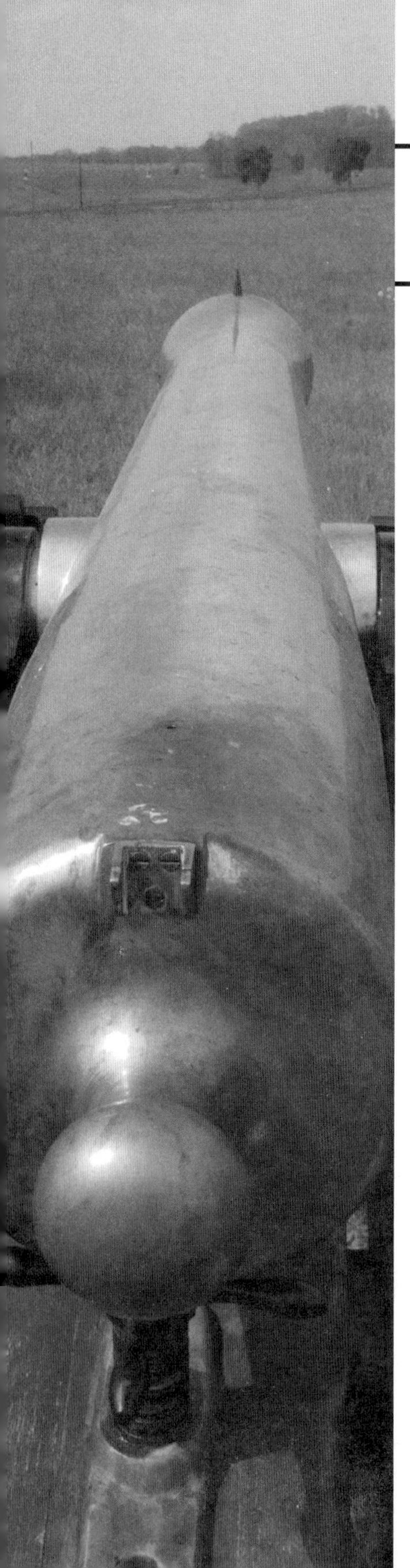

CHAPTER 6

THE WAR: BATTLES UP CLOSE

Here, in chronological order, is a look at the battles, campaigns, and sieges of the Civil War.

SIEGE OF FORT SUMTER

By early 1861 the seven Southern states that had already seceded from the Union claimed possession of all U.S. forts and arsenals within their territory. Only two forts remained under federal jurisdiction: Fort Pickens, Florida, and Fort Sumter, which was garrisoned by U.S. troops under Major Robert Anderson. Situated on a man-made island at the entrance to the harbour of Charleston, S. C., Sumter was of no strategic value to the Union. Construction of it, which had begun in 1829, was still incomplete and its 60 guns pointed out to sea; however, it assumed critical value as a symbol of national union. When Pres. Abraham Lincoln took office in March, he was faced with the Confederate demand for evacuation of the fort, which was threatened by other fortifications erected by South Carolina in the harbour area. Lincoln had either to attempt resupplying the fort, then in danger of being starved out, or to abandon it and accede to disunion. The president determined to prepare relief expeditions to both forts, but, before the arrival of supplies, Confederate authorities demanded Fort Sumter's immediate evacuation. When this order was refused, the South's batteries opened fire at 4:30 AM on April 12, initiating the Civil

War. Anderson was forced to surrender after 34 hours of shelling. On April 14 Fort Sumter was evacuated by federal troops, who marched out waving the American flag to a gun salute; on the 50th round of a 100-gun salute, an explosion occurred, causing the only death of the engagement. The shelling of U.S. property aroused and united the North. During the war the Confederates manning the fort withstood almost constant bombardment from July 1863 to February 1865. The fort itself was largely reduced to rubble.

FIRST BATTLE OF BULL RUN

Two significant engagements were fought in the summers of 1861 and 1862 at a small stream named Bull Run, near Manassas in northern Virginia. Both

Federal cavalry at Sudley Ford, Bull Run, Va., photograph by George N. Barnard. Library of Congress, Washington, D.C. (LC-B8171-0313 DLC)

battles gave military advantage to the Confederacy. The strategic significance of the location lay in the fact that Manassas was an important railroad junction.

The First Battle of Bull Run (called First Manassas, by the South) was fought on July 21, 1861. Although neither army was adequately prepared at this early stage of the war, political considerations and popular pressures caused the Federal government to order Gen. Irvin McDowell to advance southwest of Washington to Bull Run in a move against Richmond, Virginia. The 22,000 Confederates under Gen. P. G. T. Beauregard, after initial skirmishing, had retired behind Bull Run in defensive positions three days earlier. To counter a Union flanking movement, the Confederates swiftly moved in 10,000 additional troops from the Shenandoah under Gen. Joseph E. Johnston. On July 21 the Union army assaulted the Confederates. The battle raged back and forth, but finally the arrival of Johnston's last brigade forced the Federals into a disorganized retreat to Washington. The victors were also exhausted and did not pursue them. From among 37,000 Northern men, casualties numbered about 3,000; of 35,000 Southern troops, between 1,700 and 2,000 were wounded or lost.

BATTLE OF WILSON'S CREEK

On Aug. 10, 1861, the South triumphed in an engagement fought between 5,400 Union troops under Gen. Nathaniel Lyon and a combined force of more than 10,000 Confederate troops and Missouri Militia commanded by Gen. Benjamin McCulloch and Gen. Sterling Price. Ten miles (16 km) southwest of Springfield, Mo., Union General Franz Sigel attacked the rear of the Confederate forces with 1,200 men while Lyon led a frontal attack with the main Union force. Sigel was repulsed, and after several hours of fighting Lyon was killed. With casualties heavy on both sides, the Union forces retreated toward Springfield.

BATTLE OF FORT HENRY

Fought along the Tennessee River in early February 1862, the Battle of Fort Henry helped the Union regain western and middle Tennessee as well as most of Kentucky.

Fort Henry, situated on the Tennessee River, was a linchpin in Confederate General Albert Sidney Johnston's defense lines. Along with Fort Donelson on the Cumberland River, Fort Henry bisected Southern lines and guarded rich mineral deposits and agricultural lands as well as the important city of Nashville, Tennessee. Union General Henry Halleck hoped to regain control of western rivers as a means of piercing Confederate defenses, and in early February 1862 he sent Gen. Ulysses S. Grant and Commodore Andrew Foote on a joint endeavour to capture Forts Henry and Donelson. A Union force of 15,000 men and seven gunboats traveled along the Tennessee to Fort Henry, whose meagre defenses they overcame on February 6. About 2,500 Confederate defenders under Gen. Lloyd Tilghman fought briefly, then retreated 12 miles (19 km) overland to nearby Fort Donelson to prepare a stronger defensive line.

The Union victory was largely the result of a fierce gunboat bombardment, as Grant's men had arrived too late to see action. The victory cost the North 11 killed and 31 wounded; Southern losses totaled 5 killed, 11 wounded, and 78 prisoners of war. The battle's consequences were greater than its size, however. Navigation on the upper Tennessee fell to the Union, and Fort Donelson on the Cumberland River then stood alone guarding the Confederacy's western heartland and population centres.

BATTLE OF FORT DONELSON

Fought in February 1862, the Battle of Fort Donelson resulted in the collapse of Southern defenses in the Mid-South and forced the evacuations of Columbus, Kentucky, and Nashville, Tennessee, as well as a general Confederate retreat in Kentucky.

Fort Donelson, on the Cumberland River, and Fort Henry, on the Tennessee River, guarded the positions where those rivers bisected Confederate lines. After Fort Henry fell to Union forces on Feb. 6, 1862, Fort Donelson stood as a lone sentry protecting important Southern agricultural lands and the city of Nashville, the capital of Tennessee and a munitions centre. Confederate General Albert Sidney Johnston dispatched four generals and rushed 18,000 troops to meet the Union forces commanded by Gen. Ulysses S. Grant, who were marching from Fort Henry, and a Union gunboat flotilla steaming downriver under the command of Commodore Andrew Foote. The battle began on February 13 as Grant's soldiers prodded Confederate lines; this early action suggested the ensuing battle would be costly. When the Union gunboats arrived the next day, they met determined fire from shore batteries that severely damaged the flotilla and left Foote's flagship a shambles. The following day the Confederates had a fleeting chance to turn the battle in their favour, but poor coordination among their generals, as well as vague instructions from Johnston, conspired to cheat them of the opportunity.

On February 16 Southern General Simon B. Buckner asked for an armistice and surrender terms from his old friend Grant. Grant replied, "No terms except unconditional and immediate surrender can be accepted. I propose to move immediately upon your works." This was probably the war's first demand for unconditional surrender; although Buckner was appalled, he saw no option but to quit. He turned over about 15,000 men, 20,000 rifles, 48 pieces of artillery, 17 heavy guns, about 3,000 horses, and large commissary stores. The battle was bloody: the South lost 1,500 to 3,500 men; Union losses were 500 killed and 2,100 wounded. Although 3,000 Confederates managed to escape, the defeat demoralized Southern society; citizens in Nashville rioted, Southern hopes of help from England diminished, Johnston's reputation was destroyed, and the Union now owned a deep wedge into the Southern lines. With the fall of Fort Henry 10 days earlier, the South was compelled to retreat along a wide front, and Grant, whose first and middle names were transformed to the nickname "Unconditional Surrender," came to the favourable attention of Union Pres. Abraham Lincoln.

BATTLE OF PEA RIDGE

In the Battle of Pea Ridge (also called the Battle of Elkhorn Tavern), fought from March 7 to March 8, 1862, in Arkansas, 11,000 Union troops under Gen. Samuel Curtis defeated 16,000 attacking Confederate troops led by Generals Earl Van Dorn, Sterling Price, and Ben McCulloch. Following a fierce opening assault from the rear that almost overwhelmed Curtis' forces, the outnumbered Union troops rallied. After a desperate struggle with severe losses on both sides, Union forces counterattacked on March 8. The Confederates were forced to retreat, thus thwarting their hopes of regaining control of Arkansas.

BATTLE OF THE *MONITOR* AND *MERRIMACK*

The Battle of the *Monitor* and *Merrimack* (also called the Battle of Hampton Roads), was notable as history's first duel between ironclad warships and the beginning of a new era of naval warfare.

The Northern-built *Merrimack*, a conventional steam frigate, had been salvaged by the Confederates from the Norfolk navy yard and rechristened the *Virginia*. With her upper hull cut away and armoured with iron, this 263-foot (80.2-metre) masterpiece of improvisation resembled, according to one contemporary source, "a floating barn roof." Commanded by Commodore Franklin Buchanan and supported by several other Confederate vessels, the *Virginia* virtually decimated a Union fleet of wooden warships off Newport News, Virginia, on March 8th—destroying the sloop *Cumberland* and the 50-gun frigate *Congress*, while the frigate *Minnesota* ran aground.

The Union ironclad *Monitor*, under the command of Lieutenant John Worden, arrived the same night. This 172-foot "Yankee Cheese Box on a raft," with its water-level decks and armoured revolving gun turret, represented an entirely new concept of naval design. Thus the stage was set for the dramatic naval battle of March 9, 1862, with crowds of Union and Confederate supporters watching from the decks of nearby vessels and the shores on either side. Soon after 8:00 AM the *Virginia* opened fire on the *Minnesota*, and the *Monitor* appeared. They passed back and forth on opposite courses. Both crews lacked training; firing was ineffective. The *Monitor* could fire only once in seven or eight minutes but was faster and more maneuverable than her larger opponent. After additional action and reloading, the *Monitor*'s pilothouse was hit, driving iron splinters into Worden's eyes. The ship sheered into shallow water, and the *Virginia*, concluding that the enemy was disabled, turned again to attack the *Minnesota*. But her officers reported low ammunition, a leak in the bow, and difficulty in keeping up steam. At about 12:30 PM the *Virginia* headed for its navy yard; the battle was over.

The *Virginia*'s spectacular success on March 8 had not only marked an end to the day of wooden navies but had also thrilled the South and raised the false hope that the Union blockade might be broken. The subsequent battle between the two ironclads was generally interpreted as a victory for the *Monitor*, however, and produced feelings of combined relief and exultation in the North. While the battle was indecisive, it is difficult to exaggerate the profound effect on morale that was produced in both regions.

On May 9, 1862, following the Confederate evacuation of Norfolk, the *Virginia* was destroyed by its crew. The *Monitor*—with 16 crewmen—was lost during a gale off Cape Hatteras, North Carolina, on Dec. 31, 1862. The wreck of the *Monitor* was located in 1973, and in 2002 marine salvagers raised the ship's gun turret and other artifacts from the wreckage.

SHENANDOAH VALLEY CAMPAIGNS

For four years (July 1861–March 1865) the Union and Confederacy waged a military struggle for control of the strategic Shenandoah Valley in Virginia, running roughly north and south between the Blue Ridge and the Allegheny Mountains. The South used the transportation advantages of the valley so effectively that it often became the "valley of humiliation" for the North. For most of the war, Confederate armies were able to move north through the valley and toward Washington, D.C., whereas Union armies advancing south found themselves pushed farther away from Richmond, the Confederate capital. When a Southern army crossed the Potomac at its confluence with the Shenandoah River, it cut across the Baltimore and Ohio Railroad and was only 60 miles (100 km) northwest of Washington. Hence the presence of a Confederate army in the northern part of the Shenandoah Valley was often considered a sufficient menace to justify calling back Union troops from campaigns elsewhere to ensure the security of the capital. Late in the war, Union forces finally took undisputed control of the region.

During the first several years of the war, the valley was the arena for a series of Confederate attacks and maneuvers under such generals as P. G. T. Beauregard, Thomas J. "Stonewall" Jackson, Richard S. Ewell, and Wade Hampton. From

March to June 1862, Jackson led his famous "foot cavalry" on a campaign that ranged more than 650 miles (1,050 km) and fought five battles (Kernstown, March 23; Front Royal, May 23; Winchester, May 25; Cross Keys, June 8; Port Republic, June 9) in a brilliant action that pinned down much larger Union forces and posed a continual threat to Washington, D.C. Besides catapulting Jackson to fame, these actions drew thousands of Federal troops away from a drive on Richmond; Jackson's diversions may well have saved the Southern capital from early capture.

The valley hosted another intense period of campaigning late in the war, when in August 1864 Union General Ulysses S. Grant dispatched Gen. Philip H. Sheridan to clear the Shenandoah once and for all, partly to rid the Federals of a continual menace and partly to deny the South the valley's rich agricultural produce. Like Jackson before him, Sheridan's aggressive and mobile campaign made him famous. From late September to late October 1864, Sheridan's forces won three major battles: the Third Battle of Winchester (September 19), the Battle of Fishers Hill (September 22), and the Battle of Cedar Creek (October 19). These victories gave the Federals an upper hand in the valley they never relinquished. Although Sheridan's campaign was essentially over, the Southern position was not to be eliminated until a cavalry division led by Gen. George Custer defeated Gen. Jubal Early's troops at Waynesboro on March 2, 1865. A month later the Confederacy collapsed, and Robert E. Lee surrendered the South's last field army.

MISSISSIPPI VALLEY CAMPAIGN

Western waterways were major arteries of communication and commerce for the South, as well as a vital link to the Confederate states of Louisiana and Texas. Early in the war, Union strategists settled on the Mississippi River and tributary rivers such as the Cumberland and Tennessee as proper avenues of attack. In addition to the fighting along the Richmond, Virginia–Washington, D.C., axis, the campaign for Atlanta, Georgia, and Gen. William Sherman's March to the Sea, the struggles for western rivers constituted the major battles of the Civil War.

The West's vast expanse complicated Confederate defense of the region, a problem first obvious at the Battles of Fort Henry and Fort Donelson in February 1862. After these forts fell to Union troops, Nashville, Tenn., was evacuated, and the way to Atlanta was clearer for Federal troops later in the war. The Battle of Shiloh, fought on April 6 and 7, 1862, farther down the Tennessee River from Fort Henry, was up to that point the biggest battle in American history. It pitted more than 100,000 men in armed struggle near a steamboat docking point called Pittsburg Landing, presenting a preview of the terrible carnage that was to come at places such as Antietam and Gettysburg; after the North won the battle, each side counted more than 1,700 dead and 8,000 wounded. The Battle of Shiloh preserved an important Union flank along the Mississippi River and opened the way to split the Confederacy along the river. In May and June of 1863, Union General Ulysses S. Grant marched on Vicksburg, Mississippi, trapping a Southern army led by Gen. John Pemberton. After a brilliant joint operation using land and naval forces, Vicksburg fell to the Federals on July 4. With the capture of the city, the Union not only gained control of the lower Mississippi, its outlet to the Gulf of Mexico, but also effectively cut the South in two.

Later in the war a smaller campaign along a western tributary, the Red River, consolidated Union control of the Mississippi basin and helped seal the Confederate fate. Altogether, Americans fought at least 26 named battles and innumerable skirmishes along western waterways. The contests for these rivers were a critical cog in Northern strategy and helped produce some of the war's greatest personalities, including Generals Grant and Sherman.

PENINSULAR CAMPAIGN

Conducted from April 4 to July 1, 1862, the Peninsular Campaign was a large-scale but unsuccessful Union effort to capture the Confederate capital at Richmond, Va., by way of the peninsula formed by the York and the James rivers. Following the engagement between the ironclads *Monitor* and *Merrimack* at nearby Hampton Roads (March 9), Federal supplies and 100,000 troops were disembarked at Fort Monroe under Major General George B. McClellan. The first phase of the campaign, during which the North reached the town of White House, within striking distance of Richmond, concluded with the indecisive Battle of Seven Pines (May 31–June 1), in which Confederate General Joseph E. Johnston was seriously wounded and field command passed to Robert E. Lee. A second phase was characterized by three weeks of inactivity. The final phase ended triumphantly for the Confederate forces of General Lee, who forced the withdrawal of the Federal Army of the Potomac after the Seven Days' Battles (June 25–July 1).

BATTLE OF SHILOH

A Northern victory that resulted in large casualties for both sides, the Battle of Shiloh (also called the Battle of Pittsburg Landing) was fought in southwestern Tennessee from April 6 to April 7, 1862. In February, Union General Ulysses S. Grant had taken Fort Henry on the Tennessee River and Fort Donelson on the Cumberland. The Confederates had acknowledged the importance of these forts by abandoning their strong position at Columbus,

Ky., and by evacuating Nashville. Grant's next aim was to attack the Memphis and Charleston Railroad, and to this end he encamped his troops on the Tennessee at Pittsburg Landing. At this point Gen. A.S. Johnston, commanding Confederate forces in the West, along with Gen. P. G. T. Beauregard, were collecting a force aimed at recovering some of their recent losses. Since Union troops were planning an offensive, they had not fortified their camps. To their surprise, General Johnston seized the initiative and attacked Grant before reinforcements could arrive. The battle was fought in the woods by inexperienced troops on both sides. Johnston was mortally wounded on the first afternoon. Despite a rallying of Northern troops and reinforcements for the South, the battle ended the next day with the Union army doing little more than reoccupying the camp it had lost the day before while the Confederates returned to Corinth, Mississippi. Although both sides claimed victory, it was a Confederate failure; both sides were immobilized for the next three weeks because of the heavy casualties—about 10,000 men on each side.

BATTLE OF NEW ORLEANS

A Union naval squadron of 43 ships under Admiral David Farragut entered the lower Mississippi near New Orleans and soon breached the heavy chain cables that were stretched across the river as a prime defense. Realizing that resistance was useless, Confederate General Mansfield Lovell withdrew his 3,000 troops northward, and the city fell on April 25, 1862. On May 1 Gen. B. F. Butler led 15,000 Union troops into the city to take command for the remainder of the war. The permanent loss of New Orleans was considered one of the worst disasters suffered by the Confederacy in the western theatre of the war.

BATTLE OF SEVEN PINES

Part of the Peninsular Campaign, the Battle of Seven Pines (also called the Battle of Fair Oaks) was fought May 31–June 1, 1862, 6 miles (10 km) east of the Confederate capital at Richmond, Va. The Union Army of the Potomac, commanded by Major General George B. McClellan, repulsed attacks by the Confederates led by Gen. Joseph E. Johnston, who was severely wounded in the first day of fighting. Northern casualties numbered more than 5,000, Southern more than 6,000.

SEVEN DAYS' BATTLES

The Confederate army under Gen. Robert E. Lee drove back Gen. George B. McClellan's Union forces and thwarted the Northern attempt to capture the Confederate capital of Richmond, Va., in the Seven Days' Battles, fought from June 25 to July 1, 1862. McClellan was forced to retreat from a position 4 miles (6 km) east of the Confederate capital to a new base of operations at Harrison's Landing on the James River.

After the indecisive Battle of Oak Grove (June 25), Lee's attack on the Union right at Mechanicsville (June 26) was repulsed with great losses, but Lee and Gen. Thomas J. "Stonewall" Jackson combined to defeat Gen. Fitz-John Porter's V Corps in a bloody encounter at Gaines's Mill (June 27). In the battles of Peach Orchard and Savage's Station (June 29) and Frayser's Farm (Glendale; June 30), the retreating Union forces inflicted heavy casualties on the pursuing Confederates. Reaching the James River, and supported by Union gunboats, the Northern troops turned back Lee's final assaults at Malvern Hill (July 1). Lee later stated in his official report that "Under ordinary circumstances the Federal Army should have been destroyed."

McClellan's failure to capture Richmond, and the subsequent withdrawal of the Union's Army of the Potomac from the Yorktown Peninsula, signified the end of the Peninsular Campaign. Northern casualties were estimated at 16,000 men and Southern at 20,000.

FIRST BATTLE OF COLD HARBOR

Two engagements of the Civil War were fought at Cold Harbor, 10 miles (16 km) northeast of the Confederate capital of Richmond.

The first battle (June 27, 1862), sometimes called the Battle of Gaines's Mill, was part of the Seven Days' Battles (June 25–July 1), which ended the Peninsular Campaign (April 4–July 1), the large-scale Union effort to take Richmond. After fighting at Mechanicsville and Beaver Dam Creek, Gen. George B. McClellan ordered Union troops to high ground between Gaines's Mill and Cold Harbor.

When Confederate General Robert E. Lee attacked on June 27, the Union troops were driven back in disorder and withdrew to the south side of the Chickahominy River.

SECOND BATTLE OF BULL RUN

The Second Battle of Bull Run (Second Manassas) took place more than a year after the first Battle of Bull Run, on Aug. 29–30, 1862, between a Confederate army of more than 56,000 men under Gen. Robert E. Lee and a newly formed Federal force of 70,000 troops under Major General John Pope. It had become Pope's responsibility to cover Washington until his army could be joined with the Army of the Potomac. To prevent the achievement of this goal, Lee split his forces and ordered Gen. Thomas J. "Stonewall" Jackson to march around Pope's right flank; in two days Jackson had captured Pope's supply depot at Manassas and had safely hidden his three divisions in a nearby wood. August 27–29 saw considerable maneuvering and fighting while Lee rushed forward the main body of his army to join Jackson. On the afternoon of August 30, Confederate artillery fire prevented the success of a Union assault on Jackson's positions, after which Lee ordered his entire army forward in a grand counterattack. The Confederate victory was not complete because the Union forces withstood repeated assaults on certain defensive positions. Finally, however, Pope withdrew his defeated army across Bull Run and eventually retreated to the fortifications of the capital. Casualties on both sides were high: 15,000 for the North, 9,000 for the South.

BATTLE OF ANTIETAM

Fought on Sept. 17, 1862, the Battle of Antietam (also called the Battle of Sharpsburg) was a decisive engagement in which Union forces halted the Confederate advance on Maryland undertaken for the purpose of gaining military supplies. The advance was also regarded as one of the greatest Confederate threats to Washington, D.C. The battle took its name from Antietam Creek, which flows south from Gettysburg, Pa., to the Potomac River near Harpers Ferry, W.V.

Following the Union defeat at the Second Battle of Bull Run, Confederate General Robert E. Lee advanced into Maryland with some hope of capturing the Federal capital of Washington to the southeast. On Sept. 17, 1862, his forces were met at Antietam by the reorganized Federal army under Gen. George B. McClellan, who blocked Lee's advances but allowed him to retire to Virginia. Most military historians have strongly criticized McClellan's conduct of the battle, which proved to be one of the bloodiest single days of the war. The South lost 13,724 troops and the North suffered casualties of 12,410.

In addition to protecting the Federal capital, the battle is sometimes cited as having influenced Great Britain not to recognize the Confederacy. Pres. Abraham Lincoln used the occasion of the Antietam victory to issue his preliminary Emancipation Proclamation (Sept. 22, 1862), announcing that unless the Confederates laid down their arms by Jan. 1, 1863, he would free all slaves not residing in Union-controlled territory.

BATTLE OF CORINTH

A decisive victory of Union forces over Confederate forces in northeastern Mississippi, the Battle of Corinth was fought Oct. 3–4, 1862. Believing that the capture of the strategically important town of Corinth would break the Union hold on the Corinth-Memphis railroad and drive Union General Ulysses S. Grant from western Tennessee, the Confederate generals Earl Van Dorn and Sterling Price attacked with 22,000 men. After indecisive fighting on October 3, a furious hour-long battle was fought near Corinth on October 4, during which Union forces under Gen. William S. Rosecrans repulsed the Confederates and sent them into full retreat. During this brief but bloody clash, Union casualties totaled 2,520; the Confederates lost 4,233.

BATTLE OF PERRYVILLE

Union troops, under Gen. Don Carlos Buell, were marching from Louisville, Ky., when they unexpectedly encountered the Confederate army, whom Braxton Bragg was leading in an advance on Louisville from Chattanooga, Tenn. A bloody but indecisive battle ensued at Perryville, near Danville, Ky., on Oct. 8, 1862. Bragg's forces held the field, though, and continued to control the area until forced to withdraw three months later following the Battle of Stones River.

BATTLE OF FREDERICKSBURG

A crushing Union defeat, the Battle of Fredericksburg, fought in Virginia on Dec. 13, 1862, immeasurably strengthened the

Fredericksburg, Virginia, from the east bank of the Rappahannock River. Photograph by Timothy H. O'Sullivan, March 1863. Library of Congress, Washington, D.C. (LC-B8171-7927 DLC)

Confederate cause. Gen. A.E. Burnside, newly appointed commander of the Northern forces, planned to cross the Rappahannock River with an army of more than 120,000 troops and advance on the Southern capital at Richmond. Confederate General Robert E. Lee countered by taking a strong position on high ground behind Fredericksburg with a force of about 78,000. The attack on December 13 proved a complete failure, and Burnside's casualties totaled more than 12,500, compared to only about 5,000 for the carefully entrenched Confederates. General Burnside was relieved of his command the following month and has been severely criticized by historians for his conduct of this battle.

Once again the Union had failed in what should have been its main objective—destruction of the Army of Northern Virginia. Richmond seemed as far away as ever. For the South, the victory restored morale lost after Lee's retreat from Maryland following his unsuccessful Antietam campaign in September.

VICKSBURG CAMPAIGN

From 1862 to 1863 Union forces fought to take the Confederate stronghold of Vicksburg, Miss., which lay on the east bank of the Mississippi River, halfway between Memphis (north) and New Orleans (south). The capture of Vicksburg divided the Confederacy and proved the military genius of Union General Ulysses S. Grant.

After the spring of 1862, when the Confederates lost Fort Henry, Fort Donelson, and Memphis in Tennessee and New Orleans in Louisiana, Vicksburg became the key remaining point of their defense of the Mississippi River. The capture of Vicksburg would yield the North control of the entire course of the river, and thus enable it to isolate those Confederate states that lay west of the river from those in the east. Vicksburg was ideally suited for defensive purposes, however; it was situated on high bluffs along the river and was protected on the north by a maze of swampy bayous. The Confederates' batteries on the bluffs could outgun any Union ships on the river.

A Union naval expedition using ironclads (May–June 1862) to subdue the Confederate batteries failed, as did an attempt to take the city by land from the north by Gen. William Tecumseh Sherman (December 1862) and an attempt by Grant to cut a canal around Vicksburg that would divert the river (February–March 1863). After this string of frustrating failures, Grant conceived a bold move that would enable him to take the city using the high-ground approaches from the east, well behind Confederate lines. Moving his army of 40,000 troops to the west bank of the Mississippi, he marched south along it for a considerable distance until he could recross the river at Bruinsburg, which lay about 30 miles (48 km) south of Vicksburg. His army recrossed to the east bank of the river by means of a Union fleet, which, under the command of Admiral David D. Porter, had run south past the batteries at Vicksburg. Once across the river, Grant quickly began moving northeast, though this meant abandoning his already tenuous supply lines and feeding his troops off the surrounding enemy countryside. His forces took Port Gibson on May 2, reached Grand Gulf on May 3, and prevented the small Confederate army of Gen. Joseph E. Johnston near Jackson from linking up with the Vicksburg forces.

Vicksburg's commander, Gen. John C. Pemberton, led his forces out in an effort to link up with Johnston but met Grant moving westward and was forced to return to the city. On May 18 Grant arrived in the rear of Vicksburg, within which Pemberton's 30,000 troops were isolated. After two assaults in mid-May failed, Grant settled down to methodical siege tactics while augmenting his forces. He controlled all the approaches to the city, and by early June the Confederate garrison was desperately short of ammunition and on the brink of starvation. Pemberton surrendered the city on July 4.

The surrender of Vicksburg, with the victory at the Battle of Gettysburg the previous day (July 3), greatly heartened the North and in fact marked the turning point of the war.

BATTLE OF STONES RIVER

Bloody but indecisive, the Battle of Stones River (also called the Battle of Murfreesboro) was a psychological victory for the Union forces. It was fought in Tennessee from Dec. 31, 1862 to Jan. 2, 1863. Gen. Braxton Bragg's 34,700-man Confederate army was confronted on Stones River near Murfreesboro by 41,400 Union troops under Gen. William S. Rosecrans, who had orders to drive Bragg out of eastern Tennessee. After the first day's bitter, seesaw battle, the battered Union army was on the verge of retreating, but Rosecrans decided to hold fast. On January 3, Bragg's equally exhausted Confederate forces withdrew southward. Rosecrans's tenacity thus averted a potentially serious Union defeat. Union casualties numbered 12,906; Confederate losses totaled 11,739. Stones River National Battlefield (established 1927) commemorates the battle.

BATTLE OF CHANCELLORSVILLE

Fought from May 1 to May 5, 1863, the Battle of Chancellorsville was a bloody assault by the Union army in Virginia that failed to encircle and destroy the Confederate Army of Northern Virginia. Following the "horror of Fredericksburg" (Dec. 13, 1862), the Confederate army of Gen. Robert E. Lee and the Union force under Gen. Joseph Hooker had spent the winter facing each other across the Rappahannock River in Virginia. On April 27 Hooker dispatched his cavalry behind Lee's army, intending to cut off a retreat. Two days later he sent a small diversionary force across the Rappahannock below Fredericksburg and crossed upriver with the main body of his army. By May 1 his superior forces were massed near Chancellorsville, a crossroads in a densely forested lowland called the Wilderness. Deprived of his cavalry, however, Hooker was blind to Lee's movements, and on May 2, when Lee ordered Gen. Thomas J. "Stonewall" Jackson's "foot cavalry" to swing around and attack the Union right, Hooker's surprised flank was routed. The Union general withdrew, and Lee's pressure over the next three days forced a Union retreat north of the river. The South's greatest casualty was the loss of Jackson, who died May 10 of battle wounds. Of 130,000 Union soldiers engaged at Chancellorsville, more than 17,000 were lost; of 60,000 Confederates, more than 12,000 were lost.

BATTLE OF BIG BLACK RIVER

Union forces under Gen. Ulysses S. Grant, who were pursuing Confederate troops under Gen. John C. Pemberton toward Vicksburg, Miss., won an important victory in Battle of Big Black River on May 17, 1863. After his defeat at Champion's Hill (May 16), Pemberton left 5,000 troops to make a stand on both sides of the Big Black River, while he withdrew with his main command to nearby Vicksburg. Ten thousand attacking Union troops led by Grant routed the demoralized Confederate defenders, inflicting heavy losses and capturing over 1,700 prisoners. The survivors began a disorderly flight and retreated within the entrenched lines of Vicksburg, which was soon besieged by Grant's army.

BATTLE OF GETTYSBURG

A crushing defeat for the South that is considered by most the turning point of the Civil War, the Battle of Gettysburg was fought from July 1 to July 3, 1863, in and around the small town of Gettysburg, Pa., roughly 35 miles (56 km) southwest of Harrisburg. After defeating the Union forces of Gen. Joseph Hooker at Chancellorsville, Virginia, in May, Confederate General Robert E. Lee decided to invade the North in hopes of further discouraging the enemy and possibly inducing European countries to recognize the Confederacy. His invasion army numbered 75,000 troops. When he learned that the Union Army of the Potomac had a new commander, Gen. George G. Meade, Lee ordered Gen. R.S. Ewell to move to Cashtown or Gettysburg. However, the commander of Meade's advance cavalry, Gen. John Buford, recognized the strategic importance of Gettysburg as a road centre and was prepared to hold this site until reinforcements arrived.

The first day of battle saw considerable fighting in the area, Union use of newly issued Spencer repeating carbines, heavy casualties on each side, and the simultaneous conclusion by both

The battlefield at Gettysburg, Pa., photograph by Timothy O'Sullivan, July 1863. Library of Congress, Washington, D.C. (LC-B8184-7964-A DLC)

commanders that Gettysburg was the place to fight. On the second day there were a great number of desperate attacks and counterattacks in an attempt to gain control of such locations as Little Round Top, Cemetery Hill, Devil's Den, the Wheatfield, and the Peach Orchard. There were again heavy losses on both sides. On the third day Lee was determined to attack. Some 15,000 Confederate troops assaulted Cemetery Ridge, held by about 10,000 Federal infantrymen. The Southern spearhead broke through and penetrated the ridge, but there it could do no more. Critically weakened by artillery during their approach, formations hopelessly tangled, lacking reinforcement, and under savage attack from three sides, the Southerners retreated, leaving 19 battle flags and hundreds of prisoners. On

July 4 Lee waited to meet an attack that never came. That night, taking advantage of a heavy rain, he started retreating toward Virginia. His defeat stemmed from overconfidence in his troops, Ewell's inability to fill the boots of Gen. Thomas J. "Stonewall" Jackson, and faulty reconnaissance. Though Meade has been criticized for not destroying the enemy by a vigorous pursuit, he had stopped the Confederate invasion and won a critical three-day battle.

Losses were among the war's heaviest: of 88,000 Northern troops, casualties numbered about 23,000; out of 75,000 Southerners, more than 20,000.

Dedication of the National Cemetery at the site in November 1863 was the occasion of Pres. Abraham Lincoln's Gettysburg Address. The battlefield became a national military park in 1895, and jurisdiction passed to the National Park Service in 1933.

BATTLE OF CHICKAMAUGA CREEK

The Battle of Chickamauga Creek, fought Sept. 19–20, 1863, was a vital part of the maneuvering and fighting to control the railroad centre at nearby Chattanooga, Tenn. Union General William S. Rosecrans had established his army at Chickamauga, Georgia, 12 miles (19 km) southeast of Chattanooga. Confederate General Braxton Bragg collected reinforcements and prepared to do battle, assisted by Gen. James Longstreet. For two days the conflict raged in a tangled forest along Chickamauga Creek.

Dazed by the ferocious Confederate assault, the main body of the Union army gave way and retreated in disorder. Union General George H. Thomas, the "Rock of Chickamauga," skillfully organized the defenses and withstood the attack until the assistance of a reserve corps made possible an orderly withdrawal to Chattanooga. Of 120,000 troops participating, casualties numbered 16,000 Union troops and 18,000 Confederate troops, making this one of the bloodiest engagements of the Civil War.

Chickamauga was considered a decisive victory for the South, but General Bragg did not choose to follow it up, and two months later the results were completely nullified at the Battle of Chattanooga. In 1890 an Act of Congress created a national military park at the two battlegrounds.

BATTLE OF CHATTANOOGA

A decisive engagement fought at Chattanooga on the Tennessee River from Nov. 23 to Nov. 25, 1863, the Battle of Chattanooga contributed significantly to the victory of the North. Chattanooga had strategic importance as a vital railroad junction for the Confederacy.

In September 1863 a Federal army led by Gen. William S. Rosecrans was besieged there by a Southern army commanded by Gen. Braxton Bragg. The following month Gen. Ulysses S. Grant took over the campaign to relieve the Union troops and seize the offensive. With the help of reinforcements from Gen. Joseph Hooker and Gen. William Tecumseh Sherman, the Federal forces defeated the Confederates in the Battles of Lookout Mountain and Missionary Ridge and lifted the siege; by the end of the month the Confederate army was in retreat into Georgia. Losses of men were less than at Chickamauga (about 6,000 Union and 7,000 Confederate), but the result was completely decisive, ranking in importance with Vicksburg and Gettysburg the same year. The way had been opened for Sherman's march to Atlanta and Savannah the following year.

RED RIVER CAMPAIGN

Conducted from March 10 to May 22, 1864, the Red River Campaign was an unsuccessful Union effort to seize control of the important cotton-growing states of Louisiana, Arkansas, and Texas. In the spring of 1864, Union General Nathaniel Banks led an expedition up the Red River and, with the support of a river fleet commanded by Admiral David Dixon Porter, took Fort DeRussy and the town of Alexandria, La. However, Confederate troops under Gen. Richard Taylor confronted the Union forces at Sabine Crossroads, near Mansfield, and defeated them on April 8. Shortly afterward the Union withdrew from the area, though the fleet barely escaped capture by the Confederates and destruction in the rapids. The failure of the Red River Campaign ended any significant trans-Mississippi Union operations, and the Confederates, under Gen. Edmund Kirby-Smith, succeeded in holding the area until the end of the war.

FORT PILLOW MASSACRE

The Confederate slaughter of black Federal troops stationed at Fort Pillow, Tenn., on April 12, 1864, stemmed from Southern outrage at the North's use of black soldiers.

From the beginning of hostilities, the Confederate leadership was faced with the question of whether to treat black soldiers captured in battle as slaves in insurrection or, as the Union insisted, as prisoners of war. In what proved the ugliest racial incident of the war, Confederate forces under Gen. Nathan B. Forrest captured Fort Pillow on April 12, 1864, and proceeded to kill all the black troops within; some were burned or buried alive. A Federal congressional investigating committee subsequently verified that more than 300 blacks, including women and children, had been slain after the fort surrendered. After the incident, black soldiers going into battle used the cry "Remember Fort Pillow!"

BATTLE OF THE WILDERNESS

The first stage of a carefully planned Union campaign to capture the Confederate capital at Richmond, Va., the Battle of the Wilderness was fought from May 5 to May 7, 1864. Crossing the Rappahannock River near Fredericksburg, Va., early in May, Gen. Ulysses S. Grant advanced with a Union army of 115,000 men. On May 5 he met a Confederate army of 62,000 troops under Gen. Robert E. Lee. The confrontation occurred in dense thickets, called the Wilderness, where orderly movement was impossible and cavalry and artillery were almost useless. Burning brush killed many of the wounded. After indecisive but intense fighting for two days, Grant saw the futility of further hostilities in this area and moved on to do battle at Spotsylvania Court House, nearer Richmond.

BATTLE OF SPOTSYLVANIA COURT HOUSE

A Union failure to smash or outflank Confederate forces defending Richmond, Va., the Battle of Spotsylvania Court House was fought from May 8 to May 19, 1964. Following the Battle of the Wilderness (May 5–6), Union General Ulysses S. Grant moved his left flank forward, engaging the Confederate forces of Gen. Robert E. Lee at Spotsylvania Court House, Va.. The battle raged for about a week and a half, and on May 20 Grant continued his march southeastward in a flanking movement toward the Confederate capital. His casualties were 18,000; Lee's, 11,000.

ATLANTA CAMPAIGN

An important series of battles fought in Georgia from May to September 1864, the Atlanta Campaign eventually cut off a main Confederate supply centre and influenced the Federal presidential election of 1864. By the end of 1863, with Chattanooga, Tenn., and Vicksburg, Miss., firmly under the control of the North, Atlanta, an important Confederate railroad, supply, and manufacturing centre and a gateway to the lower South, became the logical point for Union forces to attack in their western campaign. The Union commander, Gen. William Sherman, also believed a sustained campaign deep into Confederate territory would bring the entire war to an end. Southern defenders were under the strategic direction of Gen. Joseph E. Johnston, until he was replaced by Lieutenant General John Bell Hood in July. The Atlanta Campaign itself consisted of nine individual battles as well as nearly five months of unbroken skirmishes and small actions. The fighting foreshadowed Sherman's March to the Sea later in the year and introduced many Southern civilians to the horrors and ravages of "total war," working to undermine Confederate morale. After a series of seesaw battles, Sherman forced Confederate evacuation of Atlanta (August 31–September 1). This Union victory presented Pres. Abraham Lincoln with the key to reelection in the fall of 1864. It also greatly complicated the Confederate position near the Southern capital of Richmond, Va., as troops there now had to contend with Union forces to the north and south.

SECOND BATTLE OF COLD HARBOR

The second Battle of Cold Harbor (June 3–12, 1864) is considered one of the worst tactical defeats suffered by the North in the Civil War, though its subsequent effect was negligible. Following the Battle of Spotsylvania Court House (May 8–19), Union General Ulysses S. Grant advanced southward toward Richmond in a series of flanking movements. Confederate troops under Lee at Cold Harbor entrenched themselves in

Federal earthwork defenses, near Point of Rocks, Bermuda Hundred, Va., 1864. Library of Congress, Washington, D.C. (LC-B8171-2606 DLC)

defensive positions behind earthworks. From these, Union assaults were repulsed with heavy losses. Because of Grant's vast numbers (more than 100,000 men), his losses of about 7,000 (compared with fewer than 1,500 for Lee) did not deter him from continuing to Petersburg later that month in his drive toward Richmond.

PETERSBURG CAMPAIGN

Petersburg, Va., an important rail centre 23 miles (37 km) south of Richmond, was a strategic point for the defense of the Confederate capital. In June 1864 the Union army began a siege of the two cities, with both sides rapidly constructing fortifications 35 miles (56 km) long. In a

Skeletal remains of soldiers being collected on the battlefield, Cold Harbor, Va., photograph by John Reekie, April 1865. Library of Congress, Washington, D.C. (LC-B8171-7926 DLC)

series of battles that summer, Union losses were heavy, but, by the end of August, Gen. Ulysses S. Grant had crossed the Petersburg–Weldon Railroad; he captured Fort Harrison on September 29. By year's end, however, Gen. Robert E. Lee still held Richmond and Petersburg. But, mostly owing to mismanagement and inefficiency, Southern railroads had broken down or been destroyed. Thus the Confederates were ill-fed to the point of physical exhaustion, and the lack of draft animals and cavalry mounts nearly immobilized the troops. Hunger, exposure, and the apparent hopelessness of further resistance led to increasing desertion, especially among recent conscripts.

BATTLE OF MOBILE BAY

By 1864, Mobile Bay in Alabama was the most important Confederate port left on the Gulf of Mexico. It was protected by Fort Morgan, the ironclad *Tennessee*, and a string of mines (called torpedoes) in the narrow entrance passage to the bay.

Admiral David Farragut's Union fleet sailed into Mobile Bay on the morning of Aug. 5, 1864. The Union ship *Tecumseh* hit a mine and sank. Farragut then climbed into the rigging of his flagship *Hartford* and cried out, "Damn the torpedoes: Full speed ahead!"

With the *Hartford* in the lead, the fleet sailed on into Mobile Bay, where for two hours it fought the *Tennessee* while coming under shelling from the guns at Fort Morgan. With the surrender of the *Tennessee*, Mobile Bay was in Union hands. On August 23, Fort Morgan surrendered, thereby sealing the Gulf coast from further blockade running.

BATTLE OF NASHVILLE

The Union victory over the Confederates at the Battle of Nashville, fought Dec. 15–16, 1864, ended organized Southern resistance in Tennessee for the remainder of the war. Hoping to cut the supply lines of the Union Gen. William Tecumseh Sherman and perhaps to threaten Cincinnati, Ohio, and other Northern cities, Confederate General John B. Hood moved back into Tennessee in late 1864, incurring heavy losses in an engagement with Gen. John M. Schofield's Union troops at Franklin, Tennessee, on November 30. As Hood approached Nashville in early December, a Union force of quickly assembled heterogeneous troops under Gen. George H. Thomas marched out of the city and administered a resounding defeat to the South on December 15–16.

The Confederate army retreated in near disorder to Alabama, and, though Hood escaped, his army virtually ceased to exist as a fighting force.

LAST BATTLES OF THE PETERSBURG CAMPAIGN

In March 1865, the Confederates were driven back at the Battle of Fort Stedman, leaving Lee with 50,000 troops as opposed to Grant's 120,000. Soon after, Grant crushed a main Southern force

Union troops behind the lines, Nashville, Tenn., December 16, 1864. Photograph by George N. Barnard. Library of Congress, Washington, D.C. (LC B8171-2639 LC)

under Gen. George E. Pickett and Gen. Fitzhugh Lee at the Battle of Five Forks (April 1); the next day the defenders were driven back within the Petersburg inner defenses. Lee immediately informed Pres. Jefferson Davis that the two cities could no longer be held, and the evacuation was carried out that night. After Lee's plan to join with Gen. Joseph E. Johnston was thwarted, he surrendered to General Grant on April 9 at Appomattox Court House.

SURRENDER AT APPOMATTOX COURT HOUSE

After an engagement with Federal cavalry, the Confederate Army of Northern

Federal soldiers at Appomattox Court House, Appomattox, Va. Photograph by Timothy H. O'Sullivan, April 1865. Library of Congress, Washington, D.C. (LC-B8171-7169 DLC)

Virginia was surrounded at Appomattox, Virginia, 25 miles (40 km) east of Lynchburg, and surrendered to Union forces on April 9, 1865, thus effectively ending the Civil War. The site of the surrender was the former county seat, known as Appomattox Court House, where Gen. Robert E. Lee met Gen. Ulysses S. Grant. This location was virtually deserted after removal of the county seat to the new town of Appomattox in 1892, but was made a national historical monument in 1940; its buildings, including the McLean House, in which the formal surrender took place, were restored to their 1865 condition. In 1954 the entire 968-acre area was designated a historical park.

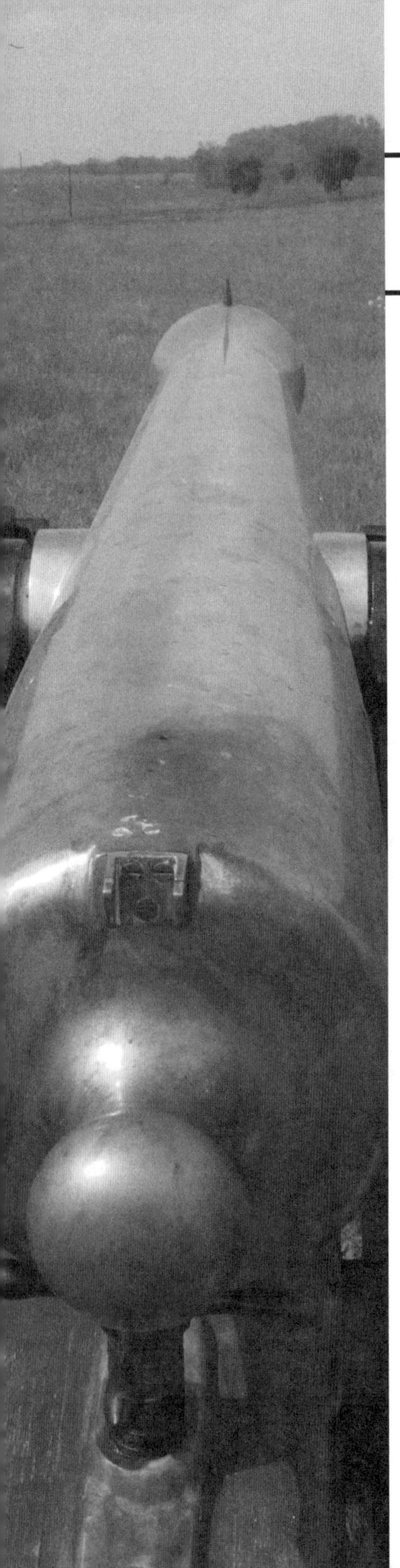

CHAPTER 7

MILITARY LEADERS

It is generally agreed that Northern military leadership was less talented and less battle-tested than that of the South, not least because so many military professionals refused to fight for the North, instead putting themselves at the service of the Confederacy. That said, the North's diverse group of military leaders clearly triumphed, be it because of their growing skills, innovations, and perseverance; more and better supplies; a larger fighting force; or the overarching leadership from Pres. Lincoln—this, though the Commander-in-Chief himself had no military experience.

THE UNION

SAMUEL CHAPMAN ARMSTRONG

(b. Jan. 30, 1839, Maui, Hawaii—d. May 11, 1893, Hampton, Va.)

Samuel Chapman Armstrong commanded black Union troops during the Civil War and and later founded Hampton Institute, a vocational educational school for blacks.

The son of American missionaries to Hawaii, Armstrong attended Oahu College for two years before going to the United States in 1860. He enrolled at Williams College; but, on the outbreak of the Civil War, he left school to accept a commission as captain in the 125th New York Regiment.

He recruited and trained his own troops and led them in several battles, including Gettysburg.

First promoted to major and then to colonel, Armstrong was put in command of the 9th Regiment, a corps consisting entirely of black troops. Determined to show the full capabilities of black soldiers, he trained his men rigorously. By the end of the war, he held the rank of brigadier general, and the troops under his command had distinguished themselves on many occasions.

After the war, Armstrong became an agent of the Freedmen's Bureau and, in 1866, took charge of a huge camp of former slaves in Hampton, Va. Recognizing the need for those blacks to receive an education, in 1867 Armstrong convinced the American Missionary Association and a private benefactor to purchase land in Hampton and establish a vocational training institution there. Hampton Normal and Industrial Institute opened in 1868. For the next 25 years, Armstrong laboured to sustain and administer the school, which became a leading centre for both vocational training and academic education for Southern blacks.

Nathaniel P. Banks

(b. Jan. 30, 1816, Waltham, Mass.—d. Sept. 1, 1894, Waltham)

A politician of long standing, Nathaniel P. Banks was the governor of Massachusetts when he was commissioned a general in the Union army.

Banks received only a common school education and at an early age began work as a bobbin boy in a cotton factory. He subsequently edited a weekly paper at Waltham, studied law, and, after being admitted to the bar, became active in politics. He served in the Massachusetts legislature (1849–53) and as president of the state constitutional convention in 1853. In that year he entered the U.S. Congress, holding the support of Democrats and Free-Soilers for a time, and later of the Know-Nothing Party. He joined the newly formed Republican Party in 1855 and in 1856, after a bitter and protracted contest, was elected speaker of the House of Representatives on the 133rd ballot. He served in Congress until elected governor of Massachusetts in 1858.

Although while governor he had been a strong advocate of peace, Banks was one of the earliest to offer his services to President Lincoln, who in 1861 appointed him a major general of volunteers. Banks served in the campaigns of early 1862 in the Shenandoah Valley and later in the year was in command of the Department of the Gulf in New Orleans. Forces under his command laid siege to Port Hudson, La., which finally fell in July 1863. In 1863 and 1864 Banks organized a number of expeditions in Texas, but he proved unsuccessful as a tactician, and his Red River expedition (March–May 1864) ended in disaster.

After the war Banks reentered politics, serving several more terms in

Congress and as U.S. marshal for Massachusetts (1879–88).

DON CARLOS BUELL
(b. March 23, 1818, near Marietta, Ohio—d. Nov. 19, 1898, Rockport, Ky.)

Union General Don Carlos Buell graduated from the U.S. Military Academy at West Point, N.Y., in 1841 and was a company officer of infantry in the Seminole War of 1841–42 and the Mexican War. From 1848 to 1861 he acted chiefly as assistant adjutant general. On the outbreak of the Civil War he was appointed lieutenant colonel, then brigadier general of volunteers and major general of volunteers in March 1862. He aided in organizing the Army of the Potomac and was sent, in November 1861, to Kentucky to succeed Gen. William T. Sherman in command. There he organized and trained the Army of the Ohio, which to the end of its career retained a standard surpassed only by that of the Army of the Potomac. In the spring of 1862 Buell pursued the retiring Confederates under Gen. Sidney Johnston, served under Gen. Henry W. Halleck in the Union advance on Corinth, and in the autumn commanded in the campaign in Kentucky against the Confederate general Braxton Bragg. A period of maneuvering ended in the indecisive Battle of Perryville. The alleged tardiness of his pursuit and his objection to a plan of campaign ordered by the Washington authorities brought about his removal from command. The complaints made against him were investigated in 1862–63, but the result was not published.

Subsequently, he was offered military employment, which he declined. He resigned his volunteer commission in May and his regular commission in June 1864. After the war he settled in Kentucky, where he engaged in mining.

AMBROSE EVERETT BURNSIDE
(b. May 23, 1824, Liberty, Ind.—d. Sept. 13, 1881, Bristol, R.I.)

Union General Ambrose Everett Burnside is perhaps best remembered as the originator in the United States of the fashion of side whiskers (later known as sideburns).

Burnside, a graduate of the U.S. Military Academy at West Point, N.Y. (1847), resigned his commission in 1853 and for the next five years manufactured firearms at Bristol, R.I. Soon after the Civil War broke out, Burnside took command of a Rhode Island militia regiment. He was later commissioned a brigadier general in the Union Army and fought in the North Carolina coast campaign. Promoted to major general (1862), he was transferred to the Virginia theatre of war. In command of Gen. George McClellan's left wing at the Battle of Antietam, Md. (September), he was criticized for his ineffectiveness.

When McClellan was removed from the command of the Army of the Potomac (Nov. 7, 1862), Burnside (over his own protests) was chosen to replace him. After a crushing defeat at the Battle of

Fredericksburg (December), Burnside was replaced by Gen. Joseph Hooker (Jan. 26, 1863). Transferred to Ohio, Burnside helped to crush Gen. John Morgan's Ohio raid in July. He then marched into Tennessee, taking Knoxville and holding it against a siege by Confederate troops under Gen. James Longstreet. Returning to the Eastern theatre in 1864, Burnside led his old corps under Gen. Ulysses S. Grant in the Wilderness campaign. In Virginia the fiasco of the "Burnside mine" at Petersburg—a mine was exploded under part of the Confederate line, but the assaulting troops were repulsed with heavy losses because of mismanagement—brought about Burnside's resignation. After the war he served as governor of Rhode Island (1866–69) and as U.S. senator from 1875 until his death.

Benjamin F. Butler

(b. Nov. 5, 1818, Deerfield, N.H.—d. Jan. 11, 1893, Washington, D.C.)

A politician turned soldier, Benjamin F. Butler served as a general in the Union army, then returned to government as a Radical Republican member of the House of Representatives during the Reconstruction era. He is remembered as a champion of the rights of workers and black people.

A prominent attorney at Lowell, Mass., Butler served two terms in the state legislature (1853, 1859), where he distinguished himself by vigorously supporting the cause of labour and of naturalized citizens. Though he was affiliated with the Southern wing of the Democratic Party in the 1860 elections, he strongly supported the Union after the Civil War broke out. He was appointed a Union officer for political reasons, and his military career was mercurial and often controversial. As a brigadier general of the Massachusetts militia, he commanded the troops that occupied Baltimore, Md., and in May 1861 was promoted to the rank of major general in command of Fort Monroe, Virginia. There he refused to return fugitive slaves to the Confederacy, using the logic that they constituted "contraband of war"—an interpretation later upheld by his government. In June 1861 he lost the engagement at Big Bethel, Va., but succeeded in capturing the forts guarding the inlet at Hatteras, N.C., two months later.

Early in 1862 Butler was given command of the land forces that accompanied the victorious Union expedition against New Orleans. The city fell late in April, and from May to December Butler ruled it with an iron hand: he executed a citizen who had torn down the U.S. flag, undertook sanitary measures to prevent an outbreak of yellow fever, and confiscated the property of Confederate sympathizers. Partly because of difficulties arising from his relations with foreign consuls concerning confiscated property, he was recalled at the end of the year.

As commander of the Army of the James in Virginia in 1864, Butler became bottled up in Bermuda Hundred, Va., and was unsuccessful in operations before

Richmond and Petersburg, Va. After the failure of an expedition against Fort Fisher, North Carolina, he was relieved of his command (January 1865).

After the war, Butler became a Radical Republican in the U.S. House of Representatives (1867– 75, 1877–79), supporting firm Reconstruction measures toward the South and playing a leading role in the impeachment trial of Pres. Andrew Johnson. Although a staunch supporter of Pres. Ulysses S. Grant after 1868, he broke with the party in 1878 because of his sympathy with the inflationary Greenback movement. After two unsuccessful tries, he was elected Democratic governor of Massachusetts in 1882 and two years later became the presidential candidate of the Greenback-Labor Party and the Anti-Monopoly Party. He advocated the eight-hour day and national control of interstate commerce but failed to win a single electoral vote.

At various times in his career Butler was accused of corruption, but no charges against him were ever proved.

JACOB DOLSON COX

(b. Oct. 27, 1828, Montreal, Que., Can.—d. Aug. 8, 1900, Magnolia, Mass., U.S.)

A political leader who became one of the great "civilian" Union generals, Jacob Dolson Cox went on to make his mark as one of the country's foremost military historians.

After dipping into the fields of theology and education, Cox was admitted to the Ohio bar in 1853 and served in the state senate (1859–61). Appointed by the governor as one of three generals of militia (1860), Cox studied tactics, strategy, and military history. He subsequently raised troops for the Union and was commissioned brigadier general, U.S. volunteers. Cox took part in the West Virginia campaign (1861) and was in supreme command of the Kanawha region from spring to August 1862. His troops were then ordered to Virginia to join Gen. Ambrose E. Burnside's IX Corps, which he commanded during the Battle of Antietam (September). In April–December 1863 Cox headed the Department of Ohio, also participating in the Atlanta campaign (1864).

After the war, Cox was active in Republican politics, legal practice, and university administration. He was elected governor of Ohio in 1866 and served as secretary of the interior in Pres. Ulysses S. Grant's Cabinet (1869–70), in which post he effectively opposed the patronage system. His last public office was a term in the U.S. House of Representatives, to which he was elected in 1876. Cox's extensive writings on the Civil War include *Military Reminiscences of the Civil War*, 2 vol. (1900).

WILLIAM BARKER CUSHING

(b. Nov. 4, 1842, Delafield, Wis.—d. Dec. 17, 1874, Washington, D.C.)

Naval officer William Barker Cushing won acclaim for his daring exploits for the Union during the Civil War .

Appointed to the U.S. Naval Academy at Annapolis, Md., in 1857, Cushing was obliged to resign four years later because of his irreverent attitude and practical jokes. The onset of the Civil War gave him a chance to redeem himself, however, and in four years' time he had risen to the rank of lieutenant commander. Exhibiting courage and exceptional resourcefulness, he also experienced amazing good fortune and escaped a number of hazardous incidents without harm; the more superstitious sailors regarded him as invulnerable.

Cushing performed numerous feats throughout the war, the most spectacular being the destruction of the Confederate ironclad *Albemarle* in the Roanoke River, N.C., in October 1864. This vessel, which had done much damage to Union naval forces, was at anchor when Cushing, in a steam launch, eluded the Confederate lookout and exploded against the ship a spar torpedo with such success that it sank. Cushing's own launch was destroyed and the crew compelled to take to the water; only he and one other man escaped capture or death. For this achievement he was thanked by Congress and promoted.

After the war, he continued to serve in the navy and was promoted to commander at the early age of 30.

David Farragut

(b. July 5, 1801, near Knoxville, Tenn.—d. Aug. 14, 1870, Portsmouth, N.H.)

An admiral who achieved fame for his outstanding Union naval victories during the Civil War, David Farragut was befriended as a youth in New Orleans by Captain (later Commodore) David Porter (of the U.S. Navy), who adopted him. Farragut served under Porter aboard the frigate *Essex* in the War of 1812; this vessel captured so many British whaling vessels that Farragut, then age 12, was put in charge of one of the prize ships. By the age of 20 he was already an accomplished ship's officer. In 1823 he served under Porter in a squadron that suppressed pirates in the Caribbean. He was given his first independent command in 1824.

In December 1861, after many years of routine service, Farragut was assigned to command the Union blockading squadron in the western Gulf of Mexico with orders to enter the Mississippi River and capture New Orleans, a port through which the South was receiving much of its war supplies from abroad. Although the War Department had recommended that he first reduce the two forts that lay some distance downstream of the city by mortar fire, he successfully carried out his own, bolder plan of running past them with guns blazing in the dark (April 24, 1862). His naval force then destroyed most of the Confederate river squadron that was stationed just upstream of the forts. Troops from Union transports could then land almost under Farragut's protecting batteries, resulting in the surrender of both forts and city.

The following year, when Gen. Ulysses S. Grant was advancing toward Vicksburg, Miss., Farragut greatly aided him by passing the heavy defensive works at Port Hudson below the Red River and stopping Confederate traffic below that tributary. Vicksburg fell in July 1863, and the entire Mississippi River was soon in Federal control.

Farragut next turned his attention to Mobile Bay, Ala., which was defended by several forts, the largest of which was Fort Morgan. A line of mines ("torpedoes") on one side of the bay's channel obliged any attacking ships to pass close to Fort Morgan on the other side of the channel, and the Confederate ironclad *Tennessee* was also stationed in the bay. Farragut's force entered the bay in two columns (Aug. 5, 1864), with armoured monitors leading and a fleet of wooden frigates following. When the lead monitor *Tecumseh* was demolished by a mine, the leading wooden ship *Brooklyn* stopped in alarm, and the whole line of ships drifted in confusion under the guns of Fort Morgan. As disaster seemed imminent, Farragut shouted his famous words, "Damn the torpedoes, full speed ahead!" to the hesitating *Brooklyn*. He swung his own ship, the *Hartford*, clear and headed across the mines, which failed to explode. The rest of the fleet followed and anchored above the forts. Then the *Tennessee* emerged from the shelter of the fort and, after a hard fight during which it was repeatedly rammed, surrendered. The forts were now isolated and surrendered one by one, with Fort Morgan the last to do so. This battle was the capstone of Farragut's career, but poor health precluded further active service. Having become a rear admiral in 1862 and a vice admiral in 1864, he was made a full admiral in 1866. He went the next year to Europe and paid ceremonial visits to the seaports of the great powers.

Andrew Foote

(b. Sept. 12, 1806, New Haven, Conn.—d. June 26, 1863, New York, N.Y.)

A career naval officer, Andrew Hull Foote already had years of experience under his belt when he distinguished himself through his service with the Union navy during the Civil War.

The son of a U.S. senator and governor of Connecticut, Foote was appointed a midshipman in the U.S. Navy in 1822. He rose through the ranks, eventually commanding the Perry off the African coast. While in that command he was particularly zealous in apprehending slavers; his book, *Africa and the American Flag* (1854), is considered to have influenced public opinion away from traffic in slaves. In 1856–58 Foote commanded the Portsmouth. Sailing the Asian seas in that capacity, Foote became embroiled in hostilities between England and China and, after being fired upon, led a party of seamen in the destruction of four Cantonese barrier forts.

In August 1861, at the outset of the Civil War, Foote was put in charge of naval defense on the upper Mississippi River. He oversaw the outfitting of a flotilla that included three wooden paddleboats converted into gunboats and seven newly commissioned ironclad gunboats, as well as a number of smaller and partially armoured gunboats. The following February, he and his command sailed on the Tennessee River to Fort Henry, which he captured easily on February 6, and then (February 12–16) down the Cumberland River to Fort Donelson. There the flotilla was heavily damaged, and Foote sustained injuries. He went on to help capture Island Number Ten (about 55 miles [88 km] below Cairo, Ill.), in the Mississippi, but his injuries and additional ailments soon forced him to relinquish all but nominal command. He was promoted to rear admiral on July 16. In June of the following year he was once again appointed to the command of a squadron of ships, this time near Charleston, but he died before he could take up the position.

William Buel Franklin

(b. Feb. 27, 1823, York, Pa.—d. March 8, 1903, Hartford, Conn.)

Union General William Buel Franklin was particularly active in the early years of fighting around Washington, D.C.

Franklin graduated from the U.S. Military Academy at West Point, N.Y., in 1843 and served in the Mexican War (1846–48). When the Civil War broke out, he was appointed a brigadier general of volunteers and fought at the First Battle of Bull Run (July 1861). He was then advanced to division commander in the Army of the Potomac and served in the Peninsular Campaign in 1862.

Franklin was a major general at the Battle of Antietam, Md. (September 1862); he was later partially blamed for the disastrous defeat at the Battle of Fredericksburg (December 1862) by both his commanding officer, Gen. A.E. Burnside, and a congressional committee on the conduct of the war. However, the committee did not have access to a copy of Burnside's orders to his subordinates, which were acknowledged to be confusing. Franklin was inactive for some months before serving inauspiciously in the Southwest. He resigned from the army in 1866 and was engaged in business at Hartford after the war.

Ulysses S. Grant

(b. April 27, 1822, Point Pleasant, Ohio—d. July 23, 1885, Mount McGregor, N.Y.)

The Union's most successful general and the commander of the Union armies during the late years (1864–65) of the Civil War, Ulysses S. Grant also served as the 18th president of the United States (1869–77).

Early Life

The son of an Ohio tanner, Grant attended the U.S. Military Academy at West Point, N.Y. He served in the Mexican War (1846–48) under Zachary Taylor. After two years' service on the Pacific coast (1852–54), during which he attempted to supplement his army pay

Ulysses S. Grant. Library of Congress, Washington, D.C.

with ultimately unsuccessful business ventures, he resigned his commission. His decision might have been influenced by his fondness for alcohol, which he reportedly drank often during this period. He worked unsuccessfully at farming in Missouri and at his family's leather business in Illinois.

The Civil War

At the outbreak of the Civil War in April 1861, Grant helped recruit, equip, and drill troops in Galena, then accompanied them to the state capital, Springfield, where Governor Richard Yates made him an aide and assigned him to the state adjutant general's office. Yates appointed him colonel of an unruly regiment (later named the 21st Illinois Volunteers) in June 1861. Before he had even engaged the enemy, Grant was appointed brigadier general through the influence of Elihu B. Washburne, a U.S. congressman from Galena. On learning this news and recalling his son's previous failures, his father said, "Be careful, Ulyss, you are a general now—it's a good job, don't lose it!" To the contrary, Grant soon gained command of the District of Southeast Missouri, headquartered at Cairo, Illinois.

In January 1862, dissatisfied with the use of his force for defensive and diversionary purposes, Grant received permission from Gen. Henry Wager Halleck to begin an offensive campaign. On February 16 he won the first major Union victory of the war, when Fort Donelson, on the Cumberland River in Tennessee, surrendered with about 15,000 troops. When the garrison's commander, Gen. Simon B. Buckner, requested his Union counterpart's terms for surrender, Grant replied, "No terms except unconditional surrender can be accepted."

Promoted to major general, Grant repelled an unexpected Confederate attack on April 6–7 at Shiloh Church, near Pittsburg Landing, Tennessee, but the public outcry over heavy Union losses in the battle damaged Grant's reputation, and Halleck took personal command of the army. However, when Halleck was called to Washington as general in chief in July, Grant regained command. Before the end of the year, he began his advance toward Vicksburg, Mississippi, the last major Confederate stronghold on the Mississippi River. Displaying his characteristic aggressiveness, resilience, independence, and determination, Grant brought about the besieged city's surrender on July 4, 1863. When Port Hudson, Louisiana, the last post on the Mississippi, fell a few days later, the Confederacy was cut in half.

Command Over Union Armies

Grant was appointed lieutenant general in March 1864 and was entrusted with command of all the U.S. armies. His basic plan for the 1864 campaign was to immobilize the army of Gen. Robert E. Lee near the Confederate capital at Richmond, Va., while Gen. William Tecumseh Sherman led the western Union army southward through Georgia. It worked. By mid-June, Lee was pinned down at Petersburg, near Richmond, while Sherman's army cut and rampaged through Georgia and cavalry forces under Gen. Philip Sheridan destroyed railroads and supplies in Virginia. On April 2, 1865, Lee was forced to abandon his Petersburg defensive line, and the surrender of Lee's army followed on April 9 at Appomattox Court House. This surrender, in effect, marked the end of the Civil War. The South's defeat saddened Grant. As he wrote in his *Personal Memoirs*, he felt "sad and depressed . . . at the downfall of a foe who had fought so long and valiantly, and had suffered so much for a cause, though that cause was, I believe, one of the worst for which a people ever fought." That Grant's army vastly outnumbered Lee's at the close of the conflict should not obscure Grant's achievements: the Union had numerical superiority in Virginia throughout the war, yet Grant was the first general to make these numbers count. Earlier, he had rebounded from initial defeat to triumph at Shiloh. His success as a commander was due in large measure to administrative ability, receptiveness to innovation, versatility, and the ability to learn from mistakes.

In late 1865 Grant, by then immensely popular, toured the South at Pres. Andrew Johnson's request, was greeted with surprising friendliness, and submitted a report recommending a lenient Reconstruction policy. In 1866 he was appointed to the newly established rank of general of the armies of the United States. In 1867 Johnson removed Secretary of War Edwin M. Stanton and thereby tested the constitutionality of the Tenure of Office Act, which dictated that removals from office be at the assent of Congress, and in August appointed Grant interim secretary of war. When Congress insisted upon Stanton's reinstatement, Grant resigned (January 1868), thus infuriating Johnson, who believed that Grant had agreed to remain in office to provoke a court decision.

Johnson's angry charges brought an open break between the two men and strengthened Grant's ties to the Republican Party, which led to his nomination for president in 1868. The last line of his letter of acceptance, "Let us have peace," became the Republican campaign slogan. Grant's Democratic opponent was Horatio Seymour, former governor of New York. The race was a close one, and Grant's narrow margin of victory in the popular vote (300,000 ballots) may have been attributable to newly enfranchised black voters. The vote of the electoral college was more one-sided, with Grant garnering 214 votes, compared with 80 for Seymour.

Grant's Presidency

Grant entered the White House on March 4, 1869, politically inexperienced and, at age 46, the youngest man theretofore elected president. His appointments to office were uneven in quality but sometimes refreshing. Notably, Grant named Ely S. Parker, a Seneca Indian who had served with him as a staff officer, commissioner of Indian affairs, and Grant's wife persuaded him to appoint Hamilton Fish secretary of state. Strong-willed and forthright, Julia Grant also later claimed credit for helping to persuade her husband to veto the Finance Bill, but she did not often involve herself in presidential decisions. She daringly—for that time—supported women's rights and considered Susan B. Anthony to be a friend. As a result, it is said, Anthony supported Grant when he ran for reelection in 1872, rather than the first woman candidate for the presidency, Victoria Claflin Woodhull of the Equal Rights Party, a

Print of a Republican campaign banner for the 1868 presidential election invoking the working-class origins of Ulysses S. Grant and his running mate, Henry Wilson. Library of Congress, Washington, D.C. (neg. no. lc-usz62-3983)

splinter group that had bolted from the National Woman Suffrage Association convention.

Julia was not beautiful—she had a cast in her left eye and squinted—but Grant was attracted to her liveliness, and his devotion to her was unbounded. Photography was just becoming part of the political scene when Julia rose to prominence as first lady, and, self-conscious about her looks, she contemplated having surgery to correct her eyes. Grant vetoed the idea, saying he loved her as she was. Consequently, almost all pictures of her were taken in profile.

The Grants had four children. Their daughter, Nellie, became a national darling, and when she was married in the White House in 1874, the public was entranced by the details of the wedding. The executive mansion was also the home for both the president's father and his father-in-law, whose squabbling with each other was general knowledge and aroused considerable public amusement. Because the Gilded Age was at hand, Americans did not seem to mind that the Grants enjoyed ostentatious living. They redecorated the White House lavishly and entertained accordingly, with state dinners sometimes consisting of 29 courses complemented by nine French wines.

On March 18, 1869, Grant signed his first law, pledging to redeem in gold the greenback currency issued during the Civil War, thus placing himself with the financial conservatives of the day. He appointed the first Civil Service Commission, but after initially backing its recommendations he abandoned his support for the group when faced with congressional intransigence. Grant was more persistent but equally unsuccessful when the Senate narrowly rejected a treaty of annexation with the Dominican Republic (which Grant had been persuaded would be of strategic importance to the building of a canal connecting the Atlantic and Pacific oceans). His negotiation of the Treaty of Washington provided for the settlement by international tribunal of American claims against Great Britain arising from the wartime activities of the British-built Confederate raider *Alabama*, whose sale had violated Britain's declared neutrality.

Grant won reelection easily in 1872, defeating Horace Greeley, the editor of the *New York Tribune* and the candidate for the coalition formed by Democrats and Liberal Republicans. Grant won by nearly 800,000 votes in the popular election, capturing 286 of 366 electoral votes. During the campaign, newspapers discovered that prominent Republican politicians were involved in the Crédit Mobilier of America, a shady corporation designed to siphon profits of the Union Pacific Railroad. More scandal followed in 1875, when Secretary of the Treasury Benjamin Helm Bristow exposed the operation of the "Whiskey Ring," which had the aid of high-placed officials in defrauding the government of tax revenues. When the evidence touched the president's private secretary, Orville E.

Babcock, Grant regretted his earlier statement, "Let no guilty man escape." Grant blundered in accepting the hurried resignation of Secretary of War William W. Belknap, who was impeached on charges of accepting bribes; because he was no longer a government official, Belknap escaped conviction. Discouraged and sickened, Grant closed his second term by assuring Congress, "Failures have been errors of judgment, not of intent."

Scandals have become the best-remembered feature of the Grant administration, obscuring its more positive aspects. Grant supported both amnesty for Confederate leaders and civil rights for former slaves. He worked for ratification of the Fifteenth Amendment and went to Capitol Hill to win passage of the Ku Klux Klan Act of 1871, although he was largely ineffective in enforcing the civil rights laws and other tenets of Reconstruction. His 1874 veto of a bill to increase the amount of legal tender diminished the currency crisis during the next quarter century, and he received praise two years later for his graceful handling of the controversial election of 1876, when both Republican Rutherford B. Hayes and Democrat Samuel Jones Tilden claimed election to the presidency.

Henry W. Halleck

(b. Jan. 16, 1815, Westernville, N.Y.—d. Jan. 9, 1872, Louisville, Ky.)

Despite his administrative skill as general in chief (1862–64), Henry W. Halleck failed to achieve an overall battle strategy for Union forces.

A graduate of the U.S. Military Academy at West Point, N.Y. (1839), Halleck was commissioned in the engineers and sent in 1844 to visit the principal military establishments of Europe. After his return to the United States, he delivered a course of lectures on the science of war, published in 1846 as Elements of Military Art and Science, which was widely used as a textbook by volunteer officers during the Civil War. When the Mexican War broke out (1846), he served with the U.S. expedition to the Pacific Coast and became California's secretary of state under the military government; in 1849 he helped frame the state constitution. Five years later he resigned his commission and took up the practice of law.

When war erupted between the states (1861), Halleck returned to the army as a major general and was charged with the supreme command of the Western theatre. There he was instrumental in bringing order out of chaos in the hurried formations of large volunteer armies, but the military successes of the spring of 1862 were due mainly to the military skill of such subordinate generals as Ulysses S. Grant and John Pope. In July, however, with some misgivings President Lincoln called Halleck to Washington as his military adviser and general in chief of the armies. Held responsible for subsequent reverses of Union generals in Virginia and frequently at odds with his subordinates and with the secretary of war, Edwin M. Stanton, he was replaced by Grant in March 1864. He then served as chief of staff until the end of the war.

Winfield Scott Hancock

(b. Feb. 14, 1824, Montgomery County, Pa.—d. Feb. 9, 1886, Governor's Island, N.Y.)

Union General Winfield Scott Hancock is remembered for his military service during both the Civil War and Reconstruction. His Reconstruction policies in Louisiana and Texas so endeared him to the Democratic Party that he became its presidential candidate in 1880.

A graduate of the U.S. Military Academy at West Point, N.Y. (1844), he served with distinction in the Mexican War (1846–48). Hancock was appointed a brigadier general of volunteers on the outbreak of the Civil War and served in the Peninsular Campaign of 1862. In May 1863 he was made head of the II Corps, Army of the Potomac, which he led for most of the remaining two years of the war. He served with distinction at the Battle of Gettysburg (July 1863) and participated in the drive on Richmond, Va., the following spring. As a major general after the war, he commanded (1866–68) various army departments, including the military division composed of Louisiana and Texas. Although great discretionary power had been conferred upon him, Hancock insisted on the maintenance of the civil authorities in their "natural and rightful dominion." This stand enraged some Republicans, who were counting on military power to protect black and white Republicans in the South, but his policy won him the support of the Democrats, who nominated him for the presidency in 1880. After narrowly losing the election to the Republican candidate, James A. Garfield, he returned to military life.

Joseph Hooker

(b. Nov. 13, 1814, Hadley, Mass.—d. Oct. 31, 1879, Garden City, N.Y.)

Union General Joseph Hooker successfully reorganized the Army of the Potomac in early 1863 but thereafter earned a seesaw reputation for defeat and victory in battle.

A graduate of the U.S. Military Academy at West Point, N.Y., and veteran of the Mexican War (1846–48), Hooker left his California home at the outbreak of the Civil War to serve as brigadier general of volunteers. In 1862 he participated in all the major Eastern campaigns and was dubbed "Fighting Joe" because of his vigorous leadership in the field. When Gen. A.E. Burnside resigned command of the Army of the Potomac after the Union disaster at Fredericksburg (November–December), Hooker was appointed to succeed him.

Immediately, the new commander effected several much-needed organizational reforms and prepared to challenge the South at the Battle of Chancellorsville (May 1–4, 1863). His grave defects as a commanding officer became apparent

Union Gen. Joseph Hooker and his horse. Fighting "Joe" Hooker, a veteran of the Mexican War, succeeded Gen. Ambrose Burnside as the commander of the Army of the Potomac. Photograph by Mathew Brady. National Archives, Brady Collection, Civil War Photographs

when Confederate Gen. Robert E. Lee, with fewer than half the number of troops, outmaneuvered him and caused a Union retreat. This defeat resulted in the loss of 17,000 Union soldiers. When Lee advanced into Pennsylvania in June, Hooker followed him closely until, rebuffed by Washington in his request for additional troops to meet the enemy at Gettysburg in July, he sensed his superiors' distrust and resigned his command on the eve of battle.

Three months later Hooker was sent by rail in command of two corps of the

Army of the Potomac to help relieve Gen. W.S. Rosecrans, besieged at Chattanooga, Tenn. On Nov. 24, 1863, he won the "Battle Above the Clouds" on Lookout Mountain, clearing the way for the crowning Union victory on Missionary Ridge. Denied advancement during the Atlanta Campaign in 1864, he thereafter ceased to play any active part in the war.

Oliver O. Howard

(b. Nov. 8, 1830, Leeds, Maine—d. Oct. 26, 1909, Burlington, Vt.)

A Union general who was involved in some of the Civil War's most important campaigns, Oliver O. Howard also headed the Freedmen's Bureau (1865–72) during the period of Reconstruction.

A graduate of the U.S. Military Academy at West Point, N.Y. (1854), Howard resigned his regular army commission at the beginning of the war to become colonel of a Maine volunteer regiment. He was given the rank of major general (1862) after fighting in Virginia at the First Battle of Bull Run, the Peninsular Campaign, the Battle of Fair Oaks (Seven Pines)—in which he lost his right arm—and at Antietam. He also took part in the Battle of Chancellorsville (May) and in the Tennessee and Atlanta campaigns (1863–64). Promoted to command the Army of the Tennessee (July 1864), he marched with Gen. William T. Sherman through Georgia to the sea (November–December) and fought in the Carolinas campaign (early 1865).

Unusually interested in the welfare of the nearly four million slaves who had been freed during the war, Howard was appointed by Pres. Andrew Johnson as commissioner of the Bureau of Refugees, Freedmen, and Abandoned Lands (the Freedmen's Bureau). Because he was not a skilled administrator, many abuses appeared in the bureau, much of the staff being poorly trained. Nevertheless, his agency fed millions of the indigent, built hospitals, provided direct medical aid, and negotiated thousands of labour contracts for the former slaves. Most important, it established a multitude of schools and training institutes for blacks; Howard University, Washington, D.C. (founded 1867), was named in recognition of his work in the bureau and as one of the university's founders. He served as the university's third president (1869–74), after which he resigned to return to military service.

Howard fought against Indians in the West and served as superintendent at West Point (1880–82). He wrote several books on military history in addition to his autobiography, published in 1907.

David Hunter

(b. July 21, 1802, Washington, D.C.—d. Feb. 2, 1886, Washington, D.C.)

Union officer David Hunter issued an emancipation proclamation on May 9, 1862, that was annulled by President Lincoln on May 19.

Hunter graduated from the U.S. Military Academy at West Point, N.Y., in 1822 and served in the Mexican War (1846–48). In 1862, while in command of Federal troops along the South Atlantic coast, he proclaimed the freedom of slaves in Georgia, Florida, and South Carolina; Lincoln, determined to maintain his executive prerogatives, revoked the order. In South Carolina General Hunter organized the Union Army's first African American regiment and was soon described by the Confederacy as a "felon to be executed if captured." He took command in West Virginia (May 21, 1864) but was defeated by Gen. Jubal Early at Lynchburg, Va., on June 18 and resigned his command on August 8. After Lincoln's assassination, Hunter served as chairman of the commission that tried the conspirators.

John A. Logan

(b. Feb. 9, 1826, Jackson County, Ill.—d. Dec. 26, 1886, Washington, D.C.)

A congressman who rose to the rank of general in the Union army, John A. Logan was the originator of Memorial Day.

Logan graduated in law from the University of Louisville (Kentucky) in 1851. He served as a Democratic congressman (1859–61) from Illinois, resigning his seat to join the Union Army as colonel of the 31st Illinois Infantry, which he had organized. He served under Gen. Ulysses S. Grant until the capture of Vicksburg (July 1863), rising to the rank of major general of volunteers. In 1864 Logan succeeded Gen. James McPherson as commander of the Army of the Tennessee but was later relieved of his command, apparently because Gen. William T. Sherman felt Logan did not pay enough attention to logistics.

After the war, Logan, by then a Republican, represented Illinois in the U.S. House of Representatives (1867–71) and the Senate (1871–77, 1879–86). In 1865 he helped found the Grand Army of the Republic (GAR), an organization of Union Army veterans, and was its head for three successive terms. In 1868, as commander in chief of the GAR, he inaugurated the observance of Memorial, or Decoration, Day when he asked GAR members to decorate soldiers' graves with flowers on May 30.

George B. McClellan

(b. Dec. 3, 1826, Philadelphia, Pa.—d. Oct. 29, 1885, Orange, N.J.)

Although he skillfully reorganized Union forces in the first year of the Civil War, Gen. George B. McClellan (1861–65) drew wide criticism for repeatedly failing to press his advantage over Confederate troops and ultimately lost the confidence of President Lincoln. That he voiced opposition to the emancipation of slaves and professed little respect for Lincoln also put him at odds with the Republican Party. Such stances, coupled with his battlefield performances, have made him a fiercely debated figure to this day.

Graduating second in his class at the U.S. Military Academy at West Point, N.Y. (1846), McClellan served in the Mexican War (1846–48) and taught military engineering at West Point (1848–51). He was then assigned to conduct a series of surveys for railroad and military installations, concluding with a mission to the Crimea (1855–56) to report on European methods of warfare.

McClellan resigned his commission in 1857 to become chief of engineering for the Illinois Central Railroad and, in 1860, president of the Ohio and Mississippi Railroad. Although a states' rights Democrat, he was nevertheless a staunch Unionist, and, a month after the outbreak of the Civil War (April 1861), he was commissioned in the regular army and placed in command of the Department of the Ohio with responsibility for holding western Virginia. By July 13 the Confederate forces there were defeated, and McClellan had established a reputation as the "Young Napoleon of the West."

After the disastrous Union defeat at the First Battle of Bull Run the same month, McClellan was placed in command of what was to become the Army of the Potomac. He was charged with the defense of the capital and destruction of the enemy's forces in northern and eastern Virginia. In November he succeeded Gen. Winfield Scott as general in chief of the army. His organizing abilities and logistical understanding brought order out of the chaos of defeat, and he was brilliantly successful in whipping the army into a fighting unit with high morale, efficient staff, and effective supporting services. Yet he refused to take the offensive against the enemy that fall, claiming that the army was not prepared to move. Pres. Abraham Lincoln was disturbed by McClellan's inactivity and consequently issued his famous General War Order No. 1 (Jan. 27, 1862), calling for the forward movement of all armies. "Little Mac" was able to convince the president that a postponement of two months was desirable and also that the offensive against Richmond should take the route of the peninsula between the York and James rivers in Virginia.

In the Peninsular Campaign (April 4–July 1, 1862), McClellan was never really defeated and actually achieved several victories. But he was overly cautious and seemed reluctant to pursue the enemy. Coming to within a few miles of Richmond, he consistently overestimated the number of troops opposing him, and, when Confederate forces under Gen. Robert E. Lee began an all-out attempt to destroy McClellan's army in the Seven Days' Battles (June 25–July 1), McClellan retreated. Lincoln's discouragement over McClellan's failure to take Richmond or to defeat the enemy decisively led to the withdrawal of the Army of the Potomac from the peninsula.

Returning to Washington as news of the Union defeat at the Second Battle of Bull Run (August 29–30) was received, McClellan was asked to take command of the army for the defense of the capital. Again exercising his organizing capability, he was able to rejuvenate Union forces. When Lee moved north into Maryland, McClellan's army stopped the invasion at the Battle of Antietam (September 17). But he again failed to move rapidly to destroy Lee's army, and, as a result, the exasperated president removed him from command in November.

In 1864 McClellan was nominated for the presidency by the Democratic Party, though he repudiated its platform, denouncing the war as a failure. On election day he resigned his army commission and later sailed for Europe. Returning in 1868, he served as chief engineer of the New York Department of Docks (1870–72) and in 1872 became president of the Atlantic and Great Western Railroad. He served one term as governor of New Jersey (elected 1877) and spent his remaining years traveling and writing his memoirs.

James B. McPherson

(b. Nov. 14, 1828, Sandusky county, Ohio—d. July 22, 1864, near Atlanta, Ga.)

When Union General James B. McPherson was killed during the Atlanta Campaign, Gen. Ulysses S. Grant is reported to have said, "The country has lost one of its best soldiers, and I have lost my best friend."

After graduation from the U.S. Military Academy at West Point, N.Y., at the head of the class of 1849, McPherson was commissioned in the Corps of Engineers and held minor army assignments until the outbreak of the Civil War (1861). Following several months with Gen. H. W. Halleck in Missouri, he was assigned to General Grant's staff as chief engineer in the Tennessee campaign and, after distinguished service at the battles of Shiloh, Tenn., and Corinth, Miss., was promoted to major general of volunteers. He participated in the second advance on Vicksburg, Miss. (1863), and, after the city fell, was promoted to brigadier general in the regular army. In March 1864 he took command of the Army of the Tennessee, which moved against Atlanta under Gen. William T. Sherman's supreme command. Shortly after reporting to Sherman, the youthful officer was killed by a Confederate skirmisher.

George Gordon Meade

(b. Dec. 31, 1815, Cádiz, Spain—d. Nov. 6, 1872, Philadelphia, Pa.)

Union General George Gordon Meade played a critical role in the Civil War by defeating the Confederate Army at the Battle of Gettysburg. As commander of the 3rd Military District in the south, Meade was also noted for his firm justice, which helped to make the Reconstruction period following the war less painful.

The son of a U.S. naval agent in Spain, Meade graduated from the U.S. Military

Academy at West Point, N.Y., in 1835. He was commissioned in the artillery but resigned after a year's service to work for a time as a surveyor. He reentered the army in 1842 and in August 1861 was commissioned brigadier general of volunteers in command of the 2nd Brigade of the Pennsylvania Reserves. After the disastrous Union defeat at Fredericksburg, Va., he was assigned the V Corps, which participated in the Chancellorsville, Va., campaign (April–May 1863).

On June 28, 1863, President Lincoln appointed Meade to replace Gen. Joseph Hooker in command of the Army of the Potomac. Meade repulsed Gen. Robert E. Lee at Gettysburg (July 1–3) with great tactical skill; however, he has been criticized by some for allowing Lee's army to escape after this decisive victory. Although Meade retained command of the Army of the Potomac until the end of the war, his independence of action was sharply curtailed after March 1864, when Gen. Ulysses S. Grant was placed in command of all Union forces. Meade was respected by his associates though he engaged in frequent quarrels. He was promoted to major general in the regular army (August 1864), and after the war he commanded several military departments.

John Pope

(b. March 16, 1822, Louisville, Ky.—d. Sept. 23, 1892, Sandusky, Ohio)

Union General John Pope was relieved of command following the Confederate triumph at the Second Battle of Bull Run.

A graduate of the U.S. Military Academy at West Point in 1842, Pope served as a topographical engineer with the army throughout most of the 1840s and '50s. He did, however, see combat during the Mexican War, serving with distinction in the campaigns of Gen. Zachary Taylor.

Following the outbreak of the Civil War, Pope was appointed brigadier general of volunteers in 1861 and was promoted to major general in 1862. After securing the Mississippi River for the Union almost as far south as Memphis, Pope attracted the admiration of Pres. Abraham Lincoln. He was made a brigadier general of the regular army and transferred to Washington, D.C., where he was given command of the Army of Virginia.

In August 1862 a Confederate force under Gen. Thomas J. "Stonewall" Jackson moved toward Pope's army. Jackson's force was reinforced by troops under generals James Longstreet and Robert E. Lee, and Pope—misgauging the number and location of the enemy—issued muddled and confusing orders. The result was the decisive defeat at the Second Battle of Bull Run, August 29–30, and the loss of about 15,000 Union troops. Pope attempted to blame his subordinate officers—especially Gen. Fitz-John Porter—for the debacle, but in September Pope was relieved of his command and sent to Minnesota to quell a Sioux uprising.

After the Civil War, Pope served in various posts, notably as commander of the Department of the Missouri (1870–83), in which he was primarily engaged in protecting settlers in the Northwest and Southwest from Indian attacks. On Oct. 26, 1882, he was promoted to major general of the regular army, a rank he held until he retired in 1886.

David Dixon Porter

(b. June 8, 1813, Chester, Pa.—d. Feb. 13, 1891, Washington, D.C.)

The son of Commodore David Porter, David Dixon Porter served in the Mexican War (1846–48) before holding important Union naval commands during the Civil War. Promoted to commander early in the war, he participated in Union expeditions against New Orleans, La., and Vicksburg, Miss. (April to June 1862), under his foster brother, Commander David Farragut.

In the spring of 1863 Porter succeeded in running his fleet past the Confederate fortress at Vicksburg, halfway between Memphis, Tenn., and New Orleans on the Mississippi River. He next overcame the Confederate forts at Grand Gulf, Miss., south of Vicksburg, enabling a rendezvous of his fleet there with the troops of the invading Union army under Gen. Ulysses S. Grant at Bruinsburg, Miss. Grant's troops then took Vicksburg, and the joint army-navy effort effectively cut the Confederacy in two. Porter received the thanks of Congress for "opening the Mississippi" and was promoted to rear admiral. He next cooperated in the Red River Campaign (March to May 1864), in which his gunboats, held above Alexandria, La., by shallow water and rapids, narrowly escaped isolation. In October he assumed command of the North Atlantic blockading squadron and was eventually responsible for the fall of Fort Fisher, N.C. (January 1865).

From 1865 to 1869 Porter was superintendent of the U.S. Naval Academy at Annapolis, Md. He was promoted to admiral in 1870. He wrote several naval books and two novels.

Fitz-John Porter

(b. Aug. 31, 1822, Portsmouth, N.H.—d. May 21, 1901, Morristown, N.J.)

Union General Fitz-John Porter was court-martialed and cashiered—but later vindicated—for disobeying orders at the Second Battle of Bull Run.

Porter was educated at Phillips Exeter Academy and at the U.S. Military Academy at West Point, N.Y., graduating from the latter in 1845. He fought in the Mexican War (1846–48) and from 1849 to 1855 was an instructor at West Point. After the outbreak of the Civil War, Porter was made a brigadier general of volunteers (May 1861). He distinguished himself during Gen. George B. McClellan's 1862 Peninsular Campaign, but on August 29 of that year he failed to comply with Gen. John Pope's orders to attack the right flank of Thomas J. "Stonewall" Jackson's forces at the Second Battle of Bull Run. Pope claimed that the subsequent Confederate victory resulted from Porter's disobedience and misconduct.

In November 1862 Porter was relieved of his command and court-martialed. The trial continued on into January 1863, Porter claiming that Pope's orders had been vague, contradictory, and impossible to execute. But on January 21, Porter was found guilty and immediately cashiered.

After the end of the war, Porter entered the mercantile business in New York. He later served as commissioner of public works, police commissioner, and fire commissioner of New York City. The most notable aspect of Porter's postwar career, however, was his dogged pursuit of vindication for his alleged misdeeds at Bull Run. No sooner was his court-martial concluded than he started efforts to clear his name. Finally, in 1879, he won a review of his case, a review that supported his claim of innocence. But it was not until 1886 that he was reappointed an army officer and placed, at his own request, on the retired list.

William S. Rosecrans

(b. Sept. 6, 1819, Kingston Township, Ohio—d. March 11, 1898, Redondo Junction, Calif.)

Although he proved himself to be an excellent strategist early in the Civil War, Gen. William S. Rosecrans was relieved of his command after his defeat in the Battle of Chickamauga (September 1863).

Graduated from the U.S. Military Academy at West Point, N.Y., in 1842, Rosecrans served 12 years as an army officer and then resigned to become an architect and civil engineer in Ohio and Virginia. Returning to active service upon the outbreak of the war, he served under Gen. George B. McClellan and Gen. John Pope, each of whom he succeeded when he moved east to larger commands. During 1862 Rosecrans led Union forces to victory in the battles of Iuka and Corinth, Miss., after which he moved on to Nashville, Tenn., to take command of the Army of the Cumberland. He fought well at the intense but indecisive Battle of Stones River, or Murfreesboro (Dec. 31, 1862–Jan. 2, 1863).

About this time, Rosecrans' earlier aggressive quality seemed to give way to an excess of caution and a disposition to worry and to argue with his superiors, who he felt were hampering the effectiveness of his command. Finally, on June 23, 1863, after six months of delay in the face of official pressure to take the offensive, he began an advance that forced Confederate Gen. Braxton Bragg into Chattanooga, Tenn., then manoeuvred him out of the city without a battle. There his customary hesitancy vanished, and he followed Bragg, who turned upon him and precipitated the bloody Battle of Chickamauga (September 19–20). An ill-advised move opened a gap in Rosecrans' lines and allowed Southern forces to pour through and put to rout part of his army, which was driven back into Chattanooga. Only the strong stand of Gen. George H. Thomas on the North's left averted complete defeat. Gen. Ulysses S. Grant was now charged with the relief and defense of the besieged city; Grant promptly removed Rosecrans, ending any important role for him in the war.

Rosecrans resigned his army commission in 1867, serving as minister to Mexico during the next two years. Later he represented California in the U.S. House of Representatives (1881–85) and served as register of the U.S. Treasury (1885–93).

Winfield Scott

(b. June 13, 1786, Petersburg, Va.—d. May 29, 1866, West Point, N.Y.)

The foremost American military figure between the Revolution and the Civil War, an officer who held the rank of general in three wars and was the unsuccessful Whig candidate for president in 1852, Winfield Scott commanded the Union army at the beginning of the Civil War.

Scott was commissioned a captain of artillery in 1808 and fought on the Niagara frontier in the War of 1812. He was captured by the British in that campaign, but was exchanged in 1813 and went on to fight in the battles of Chippewa (July 5, 1814) and Lundy's Lane (July 25), where his success made him a national hero. By war's end he had attained the rank of major general. Scott remained in military service, studying tactics in Europe and taking a deep interest in maintaining a well-trained and disciplined U.S. Army. In 1838 he supervised the removal of the Cherokee Indians from Georgia and other Southern states to reservations west of the Mississippi River. Scott became commanding general of the U.S. Army in 1841, serving in that capacity until 1861.

With the outbreak of the Mexican War (1846–48), Scott recommended Gen. Zachary Taylor for command of the U.S. forces. When Taylor appeared to be making little progress, however, Scott set out himself with a supplementary force on a seaborne invasion of Mexico that captured Veracruz (March 1847). Six months later, after a series of victories, including those at Cerro Gordo, Contreras, Churubusco, Molino del Rey, and Chapultepec, Scott entered Mexico City on September 14, thus ending the war. For this service he was honoured by appointment to the brevet rank of lieutenant general. Despite—or perhaps because of—the fact that he was clearly the most capable American military leader of his time, Scott was bedeviled by political opposition throughout his career. And though he was highly popular with his men, he earned the nickname "Old Fuss and Feathers" because of his emphasis on military formalities and proprieties.

A prominent Whig, Scott won his party's presidential nomination in 1852 but lost the election to Democrat Franklin Pierce, mainly because the Whigs were divided over the issue of slavery. In 1855 he was promoted to lieutenant general, becoming the first man since George Washington to hold that rank. Scott was still commander in chief of the U.S. Army when the Civil War broke out in April 1861, but his proposed strategy of splitting the Confederacy—the plan eventually adopted—was ridiculed. Age forced his retirement the following November.

Philip H. Sheridan

(b. March 6, 1831, Albany, N.Y.?—d. Aug. 5, 1888, Nonquitt, Mass.)

A highly regarded Union cavalry officer, Gen. Philip H. Sheridan played a pivotal role during the last year of the Civil War in the defeat of the Confederate Army.

A graduate of the U.S. Military Academy at West Point, N.Y. (1853), Sheridan served mostly at frontier posts until the spring of 1862, when he was appointed colonel of the 2nd Michigan Cavalry. In July he skillfully split his outnumbered command to rout a large Confederate force at Booneville, Miss. Made a brigadier general, he led the 11th Division, Army of the Ohio, at Perryville, Ky., in October, as it held its position against repeated attacks. At the Battle of Stones River, or Murfreesboro, Tenn. (December 1862–January 1863), he was made a major general of volunteers for his unyielding defense of the Federal right centre.

Sheridan was unable to prevent defeat at the Battle of Chickamauga, Ga. (September 1863), but his assault on Missionary Ridge below Chattanooga, Tenn., in November, brought his fighting in the West to a brilliant close. This victory so impressed Gen. Ulysses S. Grant that Sheridan was called east in the spring of 1864 to head the cavalry of the Army of the Potomac. Following action in the Battle of the Wilderness (May 1864), he led a raid toward Richmond, Va., that destroyed considerable Confederate supplies and rolling stock and resulted in the death of the South's great cavalry leader, Gen. J.E.B. ("Jeb") Stuart.

On August 4 Sheridan was given command of the Army of the Shenandoah and charged with forcing the Confederates from that valley and its rich farms, which had sustained the defense of the Southern capital for more than three years. In the Third Battle of Winchester, Va. (September), he drove General Jubal A. Early out of Winchester and gained two more victories during the next few weeks. Sheridan systematically destroyed the capacity of the Shenandoah Valley to support military operations by the South. For this feat he was made a major general and received the thanks of Congress.

Having completed his mission in the valley, Sheridan rejoined his cavalry before Petersburg in March 1865. With the 5th Corps Infantry added to his command, he circled south and west of the city to cut the Confederate general Robert E. Lee's rail communications. At the end of the month, he twice broke into the Confederate right and rear, forcing Lee to retire westward from his Richmond-Petersburg lines. Sheridan continued his pressure against Lee's southern flank and at the end helped close off his escape near Appomattox.

After the war Sheridan reported to the Gulf of Mexico, where his presence along the Texas border hastened the fall of Maximilian, the French puppet emperor in Mexico, in 1867. He was later named military commander of Louisiana and Texas (1867), but his harsh administration of Reconstruction measures led to his removal soon thereafter by Pres. Andrew Johnson. He spent the remaining years until 1883 in Western command. He planned and conducted a successful Indian campaign (1868–69), after which he was promoted to lieutenant general. He became general-in-chief of the army in 1883 and five years later was commissioned as general of the army of the United States. He spent his last months writing his memoirs.

William Tecumseh Sherman

(b. Feb. 8, 1820, Lancaster, Ohio—d. Feb. 14, 1891, New York, N.Y.)

Considered a major architect of modern warfare, General William Tecumseh Sherman led Union forces in crushing campaigns through the South, marching through Georgia and the Carolinas (1864–65).

Early Life and Career

Sherman graduated from the U.S. Military Academy at West Point, N.Y., but the Mexican War, in which so many future generals of the Civil War received their experience, passed Sherman by; he served instead in Florida and California, then resigned his commission in 1853 to pursue a banking career. The Panic of 1857 interrupted his promising career in business, however, and after several more disappointments, his old friends, the Southerners Braxton Bragg and P. G. T. Beauregard, found him employment (January 1860) as superintendent of a newly established military academy in Louisiana. When Louisiana seceded from the Union in January 1861, Sherman resigned his post and returned to St. Louis. His devotion to the Union was strong, but he was greatly distressed at what he considered an unnecessary conflict between the states. He used the influence of his younger brother, Sen. John Sherman, to obtain an appointment in the U.S. Army as a colonel in May 1861.

Civil War Years

Sherman was soon assigned to command a brigade in Gen. Irvin McDowell's army, and he fought in the disastrous first Battle of Bull Run (July 21, 1861). Though afterward promoted to brigadier general, he was convinced by his experience at Bull Run that he was unfit for such responsibility, and he begged Pres. Abraham Lincoln not to trust him in an independent command. Lincoln nevertheless sent Sherman to Kentucky as second-in-command under Gen. Robert Anderson. In October 1861 Sherman succeeded to the command in Kentucky, but he was nervous and unsure of himself, and his hallucinations concerning opposing Confederate forces led him to request so many reinforcements from his superiors that some newspapers

Gen. William T. Sherman (leaning on the breech of the cannon) and staff at Union Fort No. 7, Atlanta, Ga., 1864. Photograph by George N. Barnard. Library of Congress, Washington, D.C. (LC-B8171-3626 DLC)

described him as insane. He lost his Kentucky command, but with the support of Gen. Henry Halleck, he then served as a divisional commander under Gen. Ulysses S. Grant. Sherman distinguished himself at the Battle of Shiloh (April 6–7, 1862) and won promotion to the rank of major general.

Grant had a calming influence on Sherman. Together they fought brilliantly to capture Vicksburg, Miss. (1862–63), shattering the Confederate defenses and opening the Mississippi River to Northern commerce once more. Though Sherman began his part in the campaign with a defeat at Chickasaw Bluffs, his capture of

Gen. William Tecumseh Sherman and staff (from left to right): Generals Oliver O. Howard, John A. Logan, William B. Hazen, Sherman, Jefferson C. Davis, Henry W. Slocum, and Joseph Mower. Photograph by Mathew B. Brady. National Archives, Brady Collection, Civil War Photographs

Fort Hindman, Ark., served to restore his reputation. In Grant's final Vicksburg campaign Sherman commanded the 15th Corps.

Sherman's star, along with Grant's, was now in the ascendant, and their careers were thenceforth closely linked as they worked together to bring about a Union victory in the war. When Grant was placed in supreme command in the west, Sherman succeeded to the command of the Army of the Tennessee and in that capacity took part with Grant in the Chattanooga campaign in November 1863. In March 1864, when Grant became general-in-chief of the Union armies,

Union soldiers wrecking railroad lines (making "Sherman's neckties"—created by heating and then twisting the rails, rendering them useless), Atlanta, Ga. Library of Congress, Washington, D.C. (B8184-10488)

Sherman was made commander of the military division of the Mississippi, with three armies under his overall command. Assembling about 100,000 troops near Chattanooga, Tenn., in May 1864, he began his invasion of Georgia. The opposing Confederate forces led by Gen. Joseph E. Johnston retreated slowly ahead of him, and on Sept. 2, 1864, Sherman's forces were able to occupy Atlanta, a vital industrial centre and the hub of the Southern railway network. The Union war effort was not proceeding well in the east, and Sherman's capture of Atlanta was a much-needed victory that restored Northern morale and helped ensure Lincoln's reelection that November.

Union superiority in manpower was now having its effect, and Sherman was able to detach part of his army and lead the remaining 62,000 troops on the celebrated "March to the Sea" from Atlanta to Savannah on the Atlantic coast. Separated from its supply bases and completely isolated from other Union forces, Sherman's army cut a wide swath as it moved south through Georgia, living off the countryside, destroying railroads and supplies, reducing the war-making potential of the Confederacy, and bringing the war home to the Southern people.

Sherman reached Savannah in time for Christmas and "presented" the city to Lincoln with 150 captured cannons and 25,000 bales of cotton. By February 1865 he was heading north through the Carolinas toward Virginia, where Grant and the Confederate commander Gen. Robert E. Lee were having a final showdown. The opposing Confederate forces led by Johnston could offer Sherman only token resistance by now. Lee surrendered to Grant in Virginia on April 9, and Johnston surrendered the remnants of his forces to Sherman on April 26 near Durham, North Carolina.

Sherman remained a soldier to the end, though his view of warfare was succinctly put in his oft-quoted assertion that "war is hell." When Grant became a full general in 1866, Sherman moved up to the rank of lieutenant general, and when Grant became president in 1869, he made Sherman commanding general of the army, a post he held until 1884. Unlike Grant, Sherman declined all opportunities to run for political office, saying he would not run if nominated and would not serve if elected. He died in New York City in 1891.

Sherman was one of the ablest Union generals in the Civil War. He saw that conflict in its broadest strategic terms, and his March to the Sea is generally regarded as the first example of the use of total war in the modern era.

George Henry Thomas

(b. July 31, 1816, Southampton county, Va.—d. March 28, 1870, San Francisco, Calif.)

Union General George Henry Thomas became known as "the Rock of Chickamauga" after his unyielding defense in combat near that stream in northwestern Georgia in September 1863.

A graduate of the U.S. Military Academy at West Point, N.Y., in 1840, Thomas served in the Mexican War (1846–48) and as an instructor at West Point. Despite his Southern birth he remained loyal to the Union when the Civil War broke out. In command of an independent force in eastern Kentucky, he attacked the Confederates on Jan. 19, 1862, at Mill Springs and gained the first important Union victory in the west. He served under Gen. Don Carlos Buell and was offered but refused the chief command. Under Gen. William S.

Rosecrans, he was engaged at Stones River (Murfreesboro), Tenn., and was in charge of the most important part of the maneuvering from Decherd to Chattanooga, Tenn. On Sept. 19–20, 1863, after two days of conflict along Chickamauga Creek in Georgia 12 miles (19 km) south of Chattanooga, General Thomas adroitly organized Union defenses and withstood violent attack on the left wing until reserve units allowed an orderly withdrawal of Union troops. For this action he was promoted to brigadier general and succeeded Rosecrans in command of the Army of the Cumberland shortly before the great victory at Chattanooga (November), in which he and his army played a conspicuous role.

In the autumn of 1864, Union General William Tecumseh Sherman called on Thomas to deal with the threat to Union communications by the Confederate forces of Gen. John B. Hood. Thomas had achieved his objective by Christmas, checking the enemy army at Franklin, Tenn. (November 30), and finally at Nashville, Tenn. (December 15–16). At that historic battle, Thomas inflicted on Hood the worst defeat sustained in the open field on either side during the war. Thomas was made a major general and received the thanks of Congress.

After the war Thomas commanded the military departments in Kentucky and Tennessee until 1869, when he was placed in charge of the Division of the Pacific with headquarters at San Francisco.

JOHN L. WORDEN

(b. March 12, 1818, Westchester county, N.Y.—d. Oct. 18, 1897, Washington, D.C.)

U.S. Naval officer John L. Worden commanded the Union warship *Monitor* against the Confederate *Virginia* (formerly *Merrimack*) in the first battle between ironclads (March 9, 1862) in the Civil War .

Appointed a midshipman in 1834, Worden received his early naval training with the Brazilian squadron (1835–38). He served on the Pacific Coast during the Mexican War (1846–48) and afterward in both the Mediterranean and the home fleets.

On Jan. 16, 1862, Worden was appointed to command John Ericsson's experimental ship, the *Monitor*. In March he took the cumbersome "cheese box on a raft" down the Atlantic Coast in perilous, stormy weather and engaged the larger ironclad *Virginia* at the mouth of the James River. The three-hour battle ended when both withdrew from the conflict. Worden, stationed in the pilothouse, had been wounded in the face, however, and nearly blinded by a shell.

For the rest of the war, he commanded monitors stationed with the South Atlantic blockading squadron. Afterward he was promoted to rear admiral (1872) and commanded the European squadron (1875–77). He was retired by Congress in 1886 at full pay for life.

THE CONFEDERACY

Richard Heron Anderson

(b. Oct. 7, 1821, Statesburg, S.C.— d. June 26, 1879, Beaufort, S.C.)

Confederate General Richard Heron Anderson graduated from the U.S. Military Academy at West Point, N.Y., in 1842 and won the brevet of first lieutenant in the Mexican War, becoming first lieutenant in 1848 and captain in 1855; he took part in the following year in the Kansas troubles.

At the outbreak of the Civil War in 1861, he resigned from the U.S. Army and entered the Confederate service as a brigadier general, being promoted major general on July 14, 1862. Except for a few months spent with the army under Braxton Bragg in 1862, Anderson's service was wholly in the Army of Northern Virginia under Gen. Robert E. Lee.

In the Wilderness campaign, in May 1864, he succeeded to the command of the 1st Corps when Longstreet was wounded. After saving Spotsylvania by a brilliant night march on May 7–8, at the outset of the punishing Battle of Spotsylvania Courthouse, Anderson was given the rank of temporary lieutenant general. He later participated in the defense of Petersburg and Richmond. After the war Anderson became a railroad official in South Carolina and then state phosphate inspector.

P. G. T. Beauregard

(b. May 28, 1818, near New Orleans, La.—d. Feb. 20, 1893, New Orleans)

Confederate General P. G. T. (Pierre Gustave Toutant) Beauregard graduated from the U.S. Military Academy at West Point, N.Y. (1838), and served in the Mexican War (1846–48).

After the secession of Louisiana from the Union (January 1861), Beauregard resigned from the U.S. Army and was commissioned a brigadier general in the Confederate Army; he eventually became one of the eight full generals of the Confederacy and participated in almost every important theatre of the war. He commanded the forces that bombarded Fort Sumter, S.C., was on the field at the First Battle of Bull Run (1861), and assumed command at Shiloh after the death of General Albert Sidney Johnston (1862). He later conducted the defense of Charleston and toward the end of the war defended the southern approaches to Richmond. Though he proved to be a capable combat commander and often displayed sound strategic sense, Beauregard revealed serious deficiencies as a general officer. His penchant for questioning orders bordered on insubordination.

After the war he returned to Louisiana, where he became a railroad director, adjutant general of the state, and manager of the Louisiana lottery. His last years were marked by bitter quarrels with Joseph E. Johnston, Jefferson Davis, and

William Preston Johnston over their published accounts of the war and Beauregard's role in it. Beauregard was the author of *Principles and Maxims of the Art of War* (1863) and *Report on the Defense of Charleston* (1864).

Braxton Bragg

(b. March 22, 1817, Warrenton, N.C.—d. Sept. 27, 1876, Galveston, Texas)

Confederate General Braxton Bragg experienced early success in the Civil War's Western theatre but often failed to push his advantage and eventually was relieved of command.

After graduating in 1837 from the U.S. Military Academy at West Point, N.Y., Bragg served in the Seminole Wars and the Mexican War (1846–48). As a major general in the Confederate Army, he commanded a corps at Shiloh (April 1862) and, upon the death of Gen. Albert Sidney Johnston in that battle, was promoted to full general's rank. In the autumn of that year, having succeeded Gen. P. G. T. Beauregard in the command of the Army of Tennessee, Bragg led a bold advance from eastern Tennessee across Kentucky to Louisville. Tactically, the ensuing Battle of Perryville (October) was a draw; unwilling to fight to a decision, Bragg withdrew into Tennessee. Though he was bitterly censured, the personal favour of Confederate Pres. Jefferson Davis kept him at the head of the Army of Tennessee, and in December–January 1862–63 he fought the indecisive Battle of Stones River (Murfreesboro) against Gen. William Starke Rosecrans. The following September he inflicted a crushing defeat on Rosecrans at Chickamauga and for a time besieged the Union forces at Chattanooga. But large Federal reinforcements were concentrated upon the threatened spot under Gen. Ulysses S. Grant, and the great Battle of Chattanooga (November) ended in the rout of Bragg's army. Bragg was then relieved of his command, but President Davis made him his military adviser. After the war he was a civil engineer in Alabama and Texas.

Franklin Buchanan

(b. Sept. 17, 1800, Baltimore, Md.—d. May 11, 1874, Talbot County, Md.)

After serving as the first superintendent of the U.S. Naval Academy at Annapolis, Md. (1845–47), Franklin Buchanan became senior naval officer for the Confederacy.

A midshipman in 1815, Buchanan served until 1845, when he submitted a plan for organizing a national naval academy at Annapolis. When the academy was founded in the same year, he was appointed to head it. In 1847–48 he saw active service in the Mexican War, and in 1852–54 he accompanied Commodore Matthew C. Perry's expedition to Japan.

In April 1861, on the eve of the Civil War, Buchanan resigned his commission, believing that Maryland would secede from the Union. He tried to recall his resignation but was dismissed the following month and entered the Confederate Navy. He commanded the ironclad ram *Virginia* (*Merrimack*) when it sank the Union frigates *Cumberland* and *Congress* in Hampton Roads (March 1862). Promoted to the rank of admiral in August, he served as senior officer thereafter. In Mobile Bay (August 1864) he fought Union ships with the ram *Tennessee* after other vessels of his own squadron were disabled or captured.

Simon Bolivar Buckner

(b. April 1, 1823, near Mundfordville, Ky.—d. Jan. 8, 1914, near Mundfordville)

A native of the border state of Kentucky, Simon Bolivar Buckner served as a Confederate general during the Civil War and eventually as the governor of Kentucky (1887–91).

A graduate of the U.S. Military Academy at West Point, N.Y., Buckner served in the Mexican War (1846–48) and thereafter at various army posts until 1855, when he resigned his commission to become manager of family property in Chicago. At the outbreak of the Civil War, he worked to build up the state guard of Kentucky and to ensure the neutrality of the state, but eventually he espoused the Confederate cause and was commissioned a brigadier general.

Ordered to reinforce Fort Donelson, Tenn, he found the military situation hopeless and surrendered unconditionally to Gen. Ulysses S. Grant (Feb. 16, 1862). After a war-prisoner exchange he served the Confederacy in many capacities and was a lieutenant general when the war ended.

In 1868 Buckner returned to Kentucky, became editor of the *Louisville Courier* for a short time, and eventually recovered his valuable real estate in Chicago. After some years in private business he entered politics as a Democrat and served as governor of Kentucky from 1887 to 1891. In 1896 Buckner ran unsuccessfully for the vice presidency on the same ticket with John M. Palmer, as a

Simon Bolivar Buckner. © Photos.com/ Jupiterimages

gold Democrat, in opposition to the Free Silver majority.

Jubal A. Early

(b. Nov. 3, 1816, Franklin County, Va.—d. March 2, 1894, Lynchburg, Va.)

Confederate General Jubal A. Early, who earned command of Confederate forces in the Shenandoah Valley, menaced Washington, D.C., late in the war but was ultimately responsible for a series of defeats during the Shenandoah Valley campaigns of late 1864 and early 1865 that contributed to the final collapse of the South. A graduate of the U.S. Military Academy at West Point, N.Y., Early served in the Second Seminole War in Florida (1835–42) and the Mexican War (1846–48). In the period leading up to the Civil War, he strongly opposed secession, but when Virginia decided to withdraw from the Union in 1861, he felt obliged to conform to the action of his state.

As an officer in the Confederate Army of Northern Virginia, he rendered conspicuous service at the First Battle of Bull Run (July 1861), near Manassas, Va., and served throughout the Virginia campaigns of 1862–63 and at Gettysburg (July 1863). The climax of his career came in the summer of 1864 when Gen. Robert E. Lee placed him in command of all Southern forces in the strategic Shenandoah Valley. His first action was to drive the Union forces under Gen. David Hunter out of the state and to move down the valley unopposed. He then crossed the Potomac River, reaching Hagerstown and Frederick in Maryland, and defeated a small Union force at the Battle of Monocacy (July 9, 1864). Two days later he led 8,000 troops past Silver Spring and brought them into sight of Washington before withdrawing.

Northern pride was wounded by Early's threat, and Gen. Ulysses S. Grant dispatched Gen. Philip Sheridan to clear the valley once and for all. Bowing to numerically superior forces, Early suffered three decisive defeats at Sheridan's hands between September 19 and October 19—at Winchester, Fishers Hill, and Toms Brook—after which the valley was laid waste. Early then carried out a well-planned attack at Cedar Creek but was forced to retreat up the valley to Waynesboro, where he experienced the final defeat (March 2, 1865) that ended Confederate resistance in that area and opened the way to Union capture of Richmond.

After the Confederate surrender (April 1865) Early went to Mexico and then Canada, where he published *A Memoir of the Last Years of the War of Independence in the Confederate States of America* (1866). In 1869 he returned to Virginia, where he practiced law and wrote historical essays.

Nathan Bedford Forrest

(b. July 13, 1821, near Chapel Hill, Tenn.,—d. Oct. 29, 1877, Memphis, Tenn.)

Confederate General Nathan Bedford Forrest was often described as a "born military genius"; his rule of action, "Get there first with the most men," became one of the most often quoted statements of the war. A major blemish on his record, however, was the Massacre of Ft. Pillow (April 12, 1864)—the slaughter by his soldiers of more than 300 blacks after the surrender of Ft. Pillow, Tenn.

A self-taught man, Forrest bought and sold horses, cattle, and slaves before acquiring considerable wealth as a cotton planter in Mississippi. At the outbreak of the war, he raised a cavalry unit and, as a lieutenant colonel, took part in the defense of Ft. Donelson, Tenn. (February 1862). Refusing to capitulate with the rest of the Confederate forces, he made his way out before the fort was surrendered. After fighting with distinction at the Battle of Shiloh, Tenn. (April), he was promoted to brigadier general and took a brilliant part in the autumn campaign. The following winter he was continually active in raiding hostile lines of communication.

In keeping with Confederate policy at that time, Forrest—by then a major general—ordered his troops to "take no more Negro prisoners" when they assaulted and captured Ft. Pillow. A Congressional investigation committee verified the slaughter of more than 300 black men, women, and children within the fort.

In June 1864 Forrest decisively defeated a superior Union force at Brice's Cross Roads, Miss., and throughout the year he conducted successful raids in Mississippi, Tennessee, and Alabama. He was once more with the main Confederate Army of the West in the last disastrous campaign of Nashville (December) and fought a stubborn rearguard action to cover the retreat of the broken army. He was forced back at Selma, Ala., in April 1865 and surrendered his entire command in May.

After the war he was active in the railroad business, and was a leading organizer and the first Grand Wizard of the original Ku Klux Klan, a secret society advocating white supremacy.

A. P. Hill

(b. Nov. 9, 1825, Culpeper, Va.—d. April 2, 1865, Petersburg, Va.)

Confederate General A.P. Hill led a force called the "Light Division" that was considered one of the best in the South. He and his men were particularly active in the fighting around Washington, D.C.

After graduating from the U.S. Military Academy at West Point, N.Y., in 1847, Hill saw routine service before the outbreak of war. He joined the Confederate Army as a colonel, serving primarily in northern Virginia. His regiment was held in reserve at the First Battle of Bull Run (July 1861), and, as brigadier general, he fought at Williamsburg (May 1862) in the Peninsular Campaign. As major general he led his "Light Division" in the Seven Days' Battles (June) at Mechanicsville, Gaines's Mill, and Frayser's Farm. Hill's troops helped repel the Federal attacks at the Second Battle of Bull Run (August) and assisted in capturing Harpers Ferry (September 14). Three days later he arrived at Antietam in time to check decisively the Federal assault against Gen. Robert E. Lee's right wing. Hill participated in the Battle of Fredericksburg (December) and was wounded at Chancellorsville (May 1863).

Promoted to lieutenant general in command of the III Corps, he had a prominent role in the Battle of Gettysburg (July). He was engaged in the Battle of the Wilderness (May 1864) and at Petersburg (April 1865), where he was killed.

John B. Hood

(b. June 1, 1831, Owingsville, Ky.—d. Aug. 30, 1879, New Orleans, La.)

Confederate General John B. Hood had a reputation as a resolute fighter, but his vigorous defense of Atlanta failed to stem the advance of Gen. William T. Sherman's superior Federal forces through Georgia in late 1864.

A graduate of the U.S. Military Academy at West Point, N.Y., who served in the U.S. Cavalry until the outbreak of hostilities, Hood rapidly rose to the rank of colonel in the Confederate Army. He was seriously wounded at the Battle of Gettysburg (July 1863), where he commanded an assault on the Federal left at Round Top, and lost a leg at the Battle of Chickamauga (September).

In the spring of 1864, Hood was appointed a lieutenant general under Gen. Joseph E. Johnston to help defend Atlanta against Sherman's forces. Johnston's continual withdrawals impelled Confederate president Jefferson Davis to transfer the command in July to Hood, whom he considered more aggressive. In a vain effort to save Atlanta, Hood promptly attacked but was forced back into the city, which he held for five weeks. He then led his men on a long march north and west, intending to strike Sherman's rear. This plan was thwarted, however, when he was confronted by the Army of the Cumberland, under Gen. George H. Thomas, which had moved back to check him. Two battles ensued in Tennessee—Franklin (November) and Nashville (December)—both decisive defeats for Hood, whose retreating army was pursued by Thomas and virtually destroyed. His command ended at his own request the following month. He spent his retirement years in New Orleans in business and in writing his memoirs.

Thomas Jonathan Jackson

(b. Jan. 21, 1824, Clarksburg, Va. [now in W.Va.]—d. May 10, 1863, Guinea Station [now Guinea], Va.)

Renowned as one of the most skilled tacticians of the Civil War, Confederate General Thomas Jonathan Jackson gained his well-known sobriquet "Stonewall" as a result of his heroic stand at the First Battle of Bull Run in 1861.

Early Life and Career

Despite little formal education, Jackson secured an appointment to the U.S. Military Academy at West Point, N.Y.; he then served with distinction in the Mexican War. Finding service in the peacetime army tedious, he resigned his commission and became professor of artillery tactics and natural philosophy at the Virginia Military Institute (VMI) in 1851. Upon the outbreak of the Civil War he offered his services to his state of Virginia and was ordered to bring his VMI cadets from Lexington to Richmond. Soon after, he received a commission as colonel in the state forces of Virginia and was charged with organizing volunteers into an effective Confederate army brigade, a feat that rapidly gained him fame and promotion. His untimely death only two years later cut Jackson down at the height of an increasingly successful career, leaving unanswered the question of his capacity for independent command, which his rapid rise suggests he might have achieved.

Jackson's first assignment in the Confederate cause was the small command at Harpers Ferry, Va. (now West Virginia), where the Shenandoah River flows into the Potomac. His mission was to fortify the area and hold it if possible. When Gen. Joseph E. Johnston took over the Confederate forces in the valley, with Jackson commanding one of the brigades, Jackson withdrew to a more defensible position at Winchester.

Battle of Manassas

In July 1861 the invasion of Virginia by Federal army troops began, and Jackson's brigade moved with others of Johnston's army to unite with Gen. P. G. T. Beauregard on the field of Bull Run in time to meet the advance of Gen. Irvin McDowell's Federal army. It was here that he stationed his brigade in a strong line, withholding the enemy against overwhelming odds and earning the nickname "Stonewall." The spring of 1862 found Jackson again in the Shenandoah Valley, where his diversionary tactics prevented reinforcements being sent to Federal army general George B. McClellan, who was waging the Peninsular Campaign against Richmond, the Confederate capital. Jackson's strategy possibly accounted for Lee's victory later in the Seven Days' Battles. Lee, then chief military adviser to Confederate president Jefferson Davis, suggested to Jackson that he use his troops to attack Federal troops in the valley and thus threaten Washington. By rapid movement, Jackson closed separately with several Federal units and defeated them. In April he struck in the mountains of western Virginia; then on May 24–25 he turned on Gen. Nathaniel P. Banks and drove him out of Winchester and back to the Potomac River.

He then quickly turned his attention to the southern end of the valley, defeating the Federals at Cross Keys, Va., on June 8, and at Port Republic on the next day. Lee then brought Jackson's troops by road and railroad to Richmond to envelop the right wing of McClellan's army. But Jackson arrived a day late, and his reputation lost some of its lustre, possibly because of his lack of experience in large-scale action; nevertheless, McClellan was beaten back and was ordered to evacuate the peninsula.

Lee at once joined Jackson against the Federal forces regrouping under Gen. John Pope. He sent Jackson, by a wide encircling movement, to attack the rear of Pope's forces and bring on the Second Battle of Bull Run, in which Pope was soundly beaten. Lee next crossed the Potomac for the "liberation" of Maryland. To protect Richmond, Lee detached Jackson to capture Harpers Ferry, which he did in time (September 13–15) to rejoin Lee at Antietam. After his return to Virginia, Lee divided his army into two corps, Gen. James Longstreet commanding the first and Jackson, now a lieutenant general, the second. At Fredericksburg, Va., in December, Jackson was in command of the Confederate right when Federal general Ambrose E. Burnside's rash attack was easily repulsed and he was crushingly defeated.

In April, Gen. Joseph Hooker, Burnside's successor, attempted to turn the Confederate position on the Rappahannock River, south of Washington. There the seemingly invincible team of Lee and Jackson made its boldest move. Leaving a small detachment to meet Federal troops on the Rappahannock, Lee moved his main body, including Jackson's corps, to meet Hooker's threatened envelopment in the woods of Chancellorsville. He then divided his army again, keeping only 10,000 men to demonstrate against Hooker's front, and he sent Jackson to move secretly around Hooker's right with his entire corps.

Stonewall Jackson Monument, Manassas National Battlefield Park, Virginia. Milt and Joan Mann/ CameraMann International

Death

The maneuver was completely successful. On the evening of May 2, Jackson rolled up the flank of the unsuspecting Federal forces. Then, in the moment of victory, tragedy struck. Jackson, who had ridden forward to organize the pursuit, was accidentally shot down by his own men when he returned at dusk and was seriously, but not mortally, wounded. Although his left arm was amputated successfully, pneumonia set in and he died a week later. Lee could not replace him; for while Jackson had lost his left arm, Lee had, indeed, lost his right arm.

Albert Sidney Johnston

(b. Feb. 2, 1803, Washington, Ky.—d. April 6, 1862, Shiloh, Tenn.)

Albert Sidney Johnston was one of the highest-ranking Confederate generals, and his death in the second year of the war was considered an irreparable loss by the South.

An 1826 graduate of the U.S. Military Academy at West Point, N.Y., Johnston fought in the Black Hawk War (1832) and the Mexican War (1846–48) and was in the bloodless expedition against the Mormons in Utah (1857). When his adopted state of Texas seceded from the Union in 1861, he resigned his commission as commander of the U.S. Pacific Department and was appointed second-ranking general in the Confederate Army by Pres. Jefferson Davis, whom he had known at West Point. Assuming command of the Western Department in September, Johnston succeeded in raising and organizing an army to guard a long and vulnerable line from the Mississippi River to the Allegheny Mountains. His forces were no match, however, for the superior numbers of the North, which forced the Confederates to retreat from Forts Henry and Donelson, in Tennessee, and from Bowling Green, Ky., and led to the fall of Nashville, Tenn., in February 1862. Nevertheless, bitter criticism of Johnston did not affect Davis' confidence in him.

Concentrating his army at Corinth, Miss., Johnston determined to attack Gen. Ulysses S. Grant at Pittsburg Landing. His surprise assault upon the Union forces at the Battle of Shiloh (April 6 and 7) was almost successful, but he was mortally wounded in the first afternoon's fighting.

Joseph E. Johnston

(b. Feb. 3, 1807, near Farmville, Va.—d. March 21, 1891, Washington, D.C.)

Confederate General Joseph E. Johnston never suffered a direct defeat during the Civil War; however, his military effectiveness was hindered by a long-standing feud with the president of the Confederacy, Jefferson Davis.

A graduate of the U.S. Military Academy at West Point, N.Y. (1829), Johnston resigned his commission at the outbreak of the Civil War to offer his services to his native state of Virginia. Given the rank of brigadier general in the Confederate Army of the Shenandoah

(May 1861), he was credited in July with the first important Southern victory at the First Battle of Bull Run (Manassas). He was promoted to general, but his dissatisfaction with his seniority was the start of his lengthy differences with Davis, president of the Confederacy. When the Peninsular Campaign began in April 1862, Johnston withdrew to defend the capital at Richmond. Although objecting to the strategy prescribed by Davis, he fought well against the Union forces. Severely wounded at the Battle of Fair Oaks (Seven Pines) in May, he was replaced by Gen. Robert E. Lee.

A year later Johnston assumed control of Confederate forces in Mississippi threatened by the Federal advance on Vicksburg. He warned Gen. John C. Pemberton to evacuate the city, but President Davis counterordered Pemberton to hold it at all costs. Lacking sufficient troops, Johnston could not relieve Pemberton, and Vicksburg fell on July 4, 1863. Bitterly criticized, he nonetheless took command of the Army of the Tennessee in December as the combined armies of the North advanced toward Atlanta, Ga. Subsequent events demonstrated the soundness of Johnston's strategy of planned withdrawal to avoid a defeat by superior forces and the disintegration of the Confederate Army; nevertheless, Davis, dissatisfied with his failure to defeat the invaders, replaced him in July.

Restored to duty in February 1865, Johnston took command of his old army, now in North Carolina, and succeeded in delaying the advance of Gen. William T. Sherman at Bentonville, in March. But lack of men and supplies forced Johnston to order continued withdrawal, and he surrendered to Sherman at Durham Station, N.C., on April 26.

After the war, Johnston engaged in business ventures, wrote his memoirs, served in the U.S. House of Representatives (1879–81), and was named U.S. commissioner of railroads in 1885.

E. Kirby-Smith

(b. May 16, 1824, St. Augustine, Fla.—d. March 28, 1893, Sewanee, Tenn.)

Confederate General E. Kirby-Smith controlled the area west of the Mississippi River for the Confederacy for almost two years after it had been severed from the rest of the South.

Born Edmund Kirby Smith, he later signed his name E. Kirby Smith; the hyphenated form of the name was adopted by his family after his death. Graduated from the U.S. Military Academy at West Point, N.Y., in 1845, Kirby-Smith fought in the Mexican War (1846–48) and in Indian warfare on the frontier before he reached the rank of major in 1860. When Florida seceded from the Union (January 1861), he entered the Confederate Army and was made a brigadier general in June. Commanding a brigade at the First Battle of Bull Run (First Manassas; July 1861), he was seriously wounded. In 1862 he led the advance in the Kentucky campaign, defeated the Union forces at Richmond,

Ky., and fought at Perryville, Ky., and Stones River (Murfreesboro) in Tennessee. He was promoted to lieutenant general in October and the following February was given command of the Trans-Mississippi Department.

Cut off from the East by the fall of Vicksburg (July 1863), Kirby-Smith exercised both civil and military powers and made his section self-supporting. In April 1864 he met and defeated the Federal Red River expedition. On June 2, 1865, he formally surrendered the last armed Confederate force at Galveston, Texas.

After the war Kirby-Smith headed a military academy until 1870, when he became president of the University of Nashville. He resigned in 1875 to teach mathematics at the University of the South.

Robert E. Lee

(b. Jan. 19, 1807, Stratford, Westmoreland county, Va.—d. Oct. 12, 1870, Lexington, Va.)

Confederate General Robert E. Lee was the commander of the Army of Northern Virginia, the most successful of the Southern armies, and in February 1865 he was given command of all the Southern armies. His surrender at Appomattox Courthouse April 9, 1865, is commonly viewed as signifying the end of the Civil War.

Heritage and Youth

Robert Edward Lee was the fourth child of Colonel Henry Lee and Ann Hill Carter. On both sides, his family had produced many of the dominant figures in the ruling class of Virginia. Lee's father, Henry ("Light-Horse Harry") Lee, had been a cavalry leader during the Revolution, a post-Revolution governor of Virginia, and the author of the famous congressional memorial eulogy to his friend, George Washington.

Early Military Career

After graduating from the U.S. Military Academy at West Point, N.Y., Robert E. Lee was commissioned into the elite engineering corps. Later transferring to the cavalry because of slow advancement in the engineers, he did the best he could at routine assignments and on relatively uninspiring engineering projects. Not until the Mexican War (1846–48), when he was a captain on the staff of Gen. Winfield Scott, did he have the opportunity to demonstrate the brilliance and heroism that prompted General Scott to write that Lee was "the very best soldier I ever saw in the field."

In October 1859, while on leave at Arlington to straighten out the entangled affairs of his late father-in-law, he was ordered to suppress the slave insurrection attempted by John Brown at Harpers Ferry, Va. Although Lee put down the insurgency in less than an hour, the very fact that it was led by a white man made him aware of the gathering crisis between the North and the South.

Lee was back at his command in Texas when on Feb. 1, 1861, Texas became the seventh Southern state to secede, and, with the rest of the U.S. Army forces, he was ordered out of the state. Without a command, he returned to Arlington to wait to see what Virginia would do. On April 18 he was called to Washington and offered command of a new army being formed to force the seceded states back into the Union. Lee, while he opposed secession, also opposed war, and "could take no part in an invasion of the Southern states." Meanwhile, President Lincoln called on Virginia to furnish troops for the invasion. A Virginia convention, which had previously voted 2 to 1 against secession, now voted 2 to 1 against furnishing troops for an invasion and to secede, and Lee resigned from the army in which he had served for 36 years to offer his services to the "defense of [his] native state."

Role in Civil War

As commander in chief of Virginia's forces, Lee saw it as his first task to concentrate troops, armaments, and equipment at major points where the invasion might be expected. During this period, Confederate troops joined the Virginia forces and subdued the Federal Army at the first Battle of Bull Run. The attempt at a quick suppression of the Southern states was over and, as Lee was one of the first to realize, a long, all-out war began. Between July 1861 and June 1862, Confederate president Jefferson Davis appointed Lee to several unrewarding positions, the last of which was the trying post of military adviser to the president. Here, however, Lee, working independently of Davis, was able to introduce a coherent strategy into the Confederacy's defense.

During May 1862, General Johnston was leading a heterogeneous collection of Confederate troops back toward Richmond from the east, before the methodical advance of Gen. George B. McClellan's superbly organized, heavily equipped Army of the Potomac. Lee collaborated with Thomas J. "Stonewall" Jackson to concentrate scattered garrisons in Virginia into a striking force in the Shenandoah Valley, where he surprised the Federal forces into retreating and posed a threat to Washington. Jackson's threat from the valley caused Lincoln to withhold from McClellan the large corps of Gen. Irvin McDowell, with whom McClellan planned a pincer movement on Richmond from the east and north. On May 31, Johnston delivered an attack on McClellan's forces seven miles east of Richmond in the indecisive Battle of Fair Oaks (Seven Pines). The battle became a turning point for Lee: Johnston was seriously wounded, and Lee was at last given field command.

In three weeks he organized Confederate troops into what became the famed Army of Northern Virginia; he tightened command and discipline, improved morale, and convinced the soldiers that headquarters was in full command. McClellan, waiting vainly for McDowell to join the wing of his army on the north side of the Chickahominy River, was moving heavy siege artillery from the east for the subjugation of Richmond when Lee struck. Combining with Jackson, who moved in from the valley, Lee defeated Porter's right wing and was on McClellan's supply line to his base on the York River.

In a series of hard fights, the Seven Days' Battles (around Richmond), McClellan withdrew his army to the wharves of Berkeley Plantation, where he was aided by the U.S. Navy. Because it was the first major victory for the Confederacy since Bull Run, and because it halted a succession of military reversals, Lee emerged overnight as the people's hero, and his soldiers developed an almost mystical belief in him.

Lee never believed that the Confederate troops had the strength to win in the field; for the next two years his objectives were to keep the enemy as far away as possible from the armament-producing centre of Richmond as well as from the northern part of the state, where farmers were harvesting their crops, and, finally, to inflict defeats of such decisiveness as to weaken the enemy's will to continue the war. To nullify the Federals' superiority in manpower, armaments, and supply, Lee always sought to seize the initiative by destroying the enemy's prearranged plans.

Until the spring of 1864, he was successful in keeping the enemy away from Richmond and from the northern part of the state, twice expelling the enemy out of Virginia altogether. He inflicted several severe defeats on the enemy, most strikingly at the Second Battle of Bull Run (Second Manassas), Aug. 29–30, 1862. To shift the fighting out of Virginia, Lee crossed into Maryland, where he hoped for support from Southern sympathizers. But his plans fell into Northern hands, and his forces were nearly destroyed at Antietam (Sharpsburg) on Sept. 17, 1862. He was, however, able to withdraw the remnants across the Potomac, to reorganize his army, and to resume his series of victories at Fredericksburg in December of that year. At Chancellorsville (May 1–4, 1863) he achieved another notable victory, although outnumbered two to one, by splitting up his army and encircling the enemy in one of the most audacious moves in military history.

But he was producing no more than a stalemate on the Virginia front, while Federal forces won important victories in other parts of the Confederacy, and time was against him. While the Federals always replaced their losses, Lee's army was dwindling in size, suffering an irreplaceable drain in its command—particularly through the loss of Thomas J. "Stonewall" Jackson, who had been mortally wounded at Chancellorsville—and increasingly acute shortages of food and clothing, which undermined the physical condition of the soldiers.

Largely to resupply his troops and to draw the invading armies out of Virginia, Lee once more crossed the Potomac. The first invasion had ended with the Battle of Antietam, and the second ended in Lee's repulse at Gettysburg (July 1–3,

1863). There, operating for the first time without Jackson, Lee was failed by three of his top generals in using the discretionary orders that had worked so effectively with Jackson, his "right arm."

Then, in May 1864, Ulysses S. Grant, the newly appointed commanding general of all Union forces, drove at Lee with enormous superiority in numbers, armaments, and cavalry. The horses of the troopers of Confederate Gen. Jeb Stuart were in poor condition, and Stuart was killed early in the campaign. Grant could neither defeat nor outmaneuver Lee, however, and the superb army Grant inherited sustained losses of 50,000 men in the May and early June battles of the Wilderness, Spotsylvania Court House, the North Anna, and Cold Harbor.

Grant, however, his losses replaced by fresh recruits, had advanced within seven miles of Richmond, while Lee, his soldiers too weakened physically and his officers too inexperienced to attempt countering manoeuvres, had lost the initiative. Lee himself was, moreover, physically declining and frequently incapacitated by illness. When Grant, abandoning his advance on Richmond, moved south of the James River to Petersburg—Richmond's rail connection with the South—Lee could only place his starving tatterdemalions in defensive lines in front of Petersburg and Richmond.

Beginning at Spotsylvania Court House, Lee had nullified Grant's numbers by using his engineering experience to erect fortifications that were in advance of any fieldworks previously seen in warfare. At Petersburg, Lee extended the field fortifications into permanent lines that presaged trench warfare. While Lee's lines enabled him to withstand Grant's siege of the two cities from late June 1864 to April 1, 1865, once his mobile army was reduced to siege conditions, Lee said the end would be "a mere question of time."

The time came on Sunday, April 2, when his defensive lines were stretched so thin that the far right broke under massive assaults, and Lee was forced to evacuate Petersburg and at last uncover Richmond. When the survivors of his army pulled out of the trenches, an agonizing week of a forlorn retreat began for him; his men fell out from hunger, animals dropped in the traces, and units dissolved under demoralized officers. At Appomattox Court House on April 9, 1865, his way west was blocked and there was nothing left except to bear with dignity the ordeal of surrender, which was made less painful for him by Grant's considerate behaviour.

Postwar Years and Position in History

Lee spent several months recuperating from the physical and mental strain of retreat and surrender, but he never regained his health; however, both to earn subsistence for his family and to set an example for his unemployed fellow officers, he accepted the post of president of Washington College (later Washington and Lee University) in Lexington, Va.

He died in 1870 at his home at Washington College.

Although history knows him mostly as "the Rebel General," Lee was a disbeliever in slavery and secession and was devoutly attached to the republic that his father and kinsmen had helped bring into being. He was, moreover, very advanced in his rejection of war as a resolution of political conflicts—a fact that has been almost entirely ignored by posterity. As a U.S. Army colonel in Texas during the secession crises of late 1860, he wrote, "[If] strife and civil war are to take the place of brotherly love and kindness, I shall mourn for my country and for the welfare and progress of mankind."

The Lee Chapel and Museum, on the campus of Washington and Lee University, Lexington, Va. The chapel contains the crypt of Robert E. Lee and his family. Library of Congress, Washington, D.C.; Carol M. Highsmith Archive (digital file no. LC-DIG-pplot-13600-01102)

As the idol of a defeated people, Lee served as an example of fortitude and magnanimity during the ruin and dislocations, the anguish and bitterness of the war's long aftermath. In those years, he became an enduring symbol to the Southern people of what was best in their heritage.

James Longstreet

(b. Jan. 8, 1821, Edgefield District, S.C.—d. Jan. 2, 1904, Gainesville, Ga.)

James Longstreet was one of the Confederacy's best-known generals. A graduate of the U.S. Military Academy at West Point, N.Y. (1842), he resigned from the U.S. Army when his native state seceded from the Union (December 1860); he was made a brigadier general in the Confederate Army. He fought in the first and second battles of Bull Run, called First and Second Manassas by the Confederates (July 1861; August–September 1862); was a division commander in the Peninsular Campaign (March–July 1862); and at Antietam (September 1862) and Fredericksburg (November–December 1862) commanded what was soon called the I Corps in the Army of Northern Virginia. Promoted to lieutenant general (1862), Longstreet participated in the Battle of Gettysburg as Gen. Robert E. Lee's second in command. His delay in attacking and his slowness in organizing "Pickett's Charge," his critics argue, were responsible for the Confederate defeat at Gettysburg; others, however, place the blame on Lee, citing his inability to cope with unwilling officers. In September 1863 Longstreet directed the attack at Chickamauga that broke the Federal lines. He was severely wounded in the Wilderness Campaign. In November 1864, although with a paralyzed right arm, he resumed command of his corps. He surrendered with Lee at Appomattox.

After the war Longstreet became unpopular in the South—partly because of his admiration for Pres. Ulysses S. Grant and partly because he joined the Republican Party. He served as U.S. minister to Turkey (1880–81) and commissioner of Pacific railways (1898–1904). His reminiscences, *From Manassas to Appomattox*, appeared in 1896.

JOHN HUNT MORGAN

(b. June 1, 1825, Huntsville, Ala.—d. Sept. 4, 1864, Greenville, Tenn.)

John Hunt Morgan led and gave his name to "Morgan's Raiders," a Confederate guerrilla force best known for its July 1863 attacks in Indiana and Ohio—the farthest north Confederate troops penetrated during the Civil War.

In 1830 Morgan's parents moved from Alabama to a farm near Lexington, Ky. He received a public-school education in Lexington. In 1846 he enlisted in the army and saw action at Buena Vista during the Mexican War.

In the 1850s Morgan concentrated on his prosperous hemp-manufacturing business. In September 1861 he joined the Confederate army as a scout, but by early 1862 he held the rank of captain and had a cavalry squadron under his command. He then launched lightning-like raids on Union supply lines in Kentucky and Tennessee, avoiding open combat whenever possible. Swift movement, interruption of enemy telegraphic communications, destruction of Union transportation facilities, and the dismounting of horse soldiers for combat characterized Morgan's cavalry methods. By April 1862 he had been promoted to colonel, and before the end of the year he was a brigadier general in command of a cavalry division.

Morgan began a new series of raids in spring 1863 and was authorized to raid Kentucky with 2,000 men in June and July. But Morgan went beyond his authorization and on July 8 crossed the Ohio River into Indiana. Hotly pursued by Union troops and local forces, Morgan and his men were unable to inflict much damage and suffered heavy casualties. The raid succeeded only in taking Union pressure off Gen. Braxton Bragg's army and prolonging Confederate control of eastern Tennessee.

On July 19 most of Morgan's men surrendered, but Morgan rode on until surrounded and captured near New Lisbon, Ohio, on July 26. Four months later, he escaped from the Ohio State Penitentiary, and by spring 1864 he was back in command of a Confederate army (the Department of Southwest Virginia). He began raiding Kentucky once again and then decided to attack Union forces at Knoxville, Tenn. But on Sept. 4, 1864, he was surprised by a Federal force at Greenville and killed while trying to join his men.

John Singleton Mosby

(b. Dec. 6, 1833, Edgemont, Va.—d. May 30, 1916, Washington, D.C.)

Confederate ranger John Singleton Mosby led a guerrilla band that frequently attacked and disrupted Union supply lines in Virginia and Maryland.

Reared near Charlottesville, Va., Mosby entered the University of Virginia in 1849 and graduated in 1852. While there, he shot at and wounded a few students, but his resulting jail sentence was later annulled by the state legislature. In 1855 Mosby was admitted to the bar, and he practiced law in Bristol, Va., until the start of the Civil War in 1861. Enlisting in the Confederate cavalry, he saw action at Bull Run and spent most of 1862 as a scout with Gen. J.E.B. Stuart's forces. It was not until Jan. 2, 1863, that Mosby, with just nine men, launched the ranger attacks for which he is best remembered.

Mosby's band struck isolated Union posts in northern Virginia and Maryland in an effort to cut communications and disrupt supply lines. The rangers furnished their own guns (mostly revolvers), food, horses, and uniforms. They did not keep a common camp, boarding instead where they chose. At the end of a mission or when danger threatened, they scattered, only to link up once again at a predetermined time and location. They divided captured goods among themselves, leading Union officials to regard them as criminals rather than soldiers.

The lack of regimentation, combined with Mosby's success as a commander, drew additional rangers to his band. The best known of their exploits took place on March 9, 1863, when they slipped through federal lines at Fairfax Court House and captured a Union general along with 100 of his men. This mission and subsequent triumphs earned Mosby promotions to captain, major, and, eventually (December 1864), colonel.

By April 1865, Mosby had eight companies of well-equipped, well-trained rangers under his command. But his last raid took place on April 10, the day following Robert E. Lee's surrender at Appomattox. On April 21, he disbanded his men, and two months later he personally surrendered.

Mosby returned to private law practice in Warrenton, Va. At first a hero to Southerners, he lost their admiration when he entered politics as a Republican and backed Ulysses S. Grant for president. From 1878 to 1885 he served as U.S.

consul at Hong Kong, and from 1904 to 1910 he was an assistant attorney in the Justice Department. He wrote two books about his war experiences: *Mosby's War Reminiscences,* and *Stuart's Cavalry Campaigns* (1887) and *Stuart's Cavalry in the Gettysburg Campaign* (1908).

JOHN C. PEMBERTON

(b. Aug. 10, 1814, Philadelphia, Pa.—d. July 13, 1881, Penllyn, Pa.)

Confederate General John C. Pemberton is remembered for his tenacious but ultimately unsuccessful defense of Vicksburg.

Pemberton grew up and was educated in Philadelphia, entered the U.S. Military Academy at West Point, N.Y., in 1833, and graduated four years later. He fought in the Mexican War and was cited for bravery while participating in many of the crucial battles of 1846 and 1847.

Upon the outbreak of the Civil War, Pemberton resigned his commission on April 24, 1861, and went to Richmond to offer his services to the Confederacy. Made a lieutenant colonel on April 28, 1861, Pemberton began organizing the cavalry and artillery in Virginia. On May 8 he was promoted to colonel and on June 17 to brigadier general; on Feb. 13, 1862, he became a major general in command of South Carolina, Georgia, and Florida. In October 1862 Pemberton was made lieutenant general and given command over Mississippi, Tennessee, and eastern Louisiana.

Ordered by Pres. Jefferson Davis to hold Vicksburg at all costs, Pemberton conducted a stubborn defense despite his lack of adequate food, ammunition, and manpower. Gen. Ulysses S. Grant laid siege on both land and water, and by early July 1863 the Confederate defenders were suffering from starvation and exhaustion. On July 4 Pemberton accepted Grant's terms for surrender. Shortly thereafter he resigned his commission as lieutenant general and served out the balance of the war as an ordnance inspector with the rank of colonel.

After Appomattox, Pemberton retired to a farm near Warrenton, Va. In 1876 he moved to Philadelphia.

GEORGE E. PICKETT

(b. Jan. 25, 1825, Richmond, Va.—d. July 30, 1875, Norfolk, Va.)

Confederate General George E. Pickett will forever be associated with the Battle of Gettysburg, where he led the disastrous assault on the centre of the Union lines known as Pickett's Charge.

After graduating last in his class from the U.S. Military Academy at West Point, N.Y. (1846), Pickett served with distinction in the Mexican War (1846–47). He resigned his commission in June 1861 and entered the Confederate Army, in which he was made brigadier general in February 1862. Pickett rose to major general in October and was given command of a Virginia division. At the Battle of Fredericksburg he commanded the centre of Gen. Robert E. Lee's line but saw little action.

At Gettysburg (July 3, 1863) three brigades of Pickett's division (4,300 men) constituted somewhat less than half the force in the climactic attack known as Pickett's Charge. The attack was actually under the command of Gen. James Longstreet. Its bloodily disastrous repulse is often considered the turning point of the war. Although Pickett was much criticized and charged by some with cowardice, Lee retained him in divisional command throughout the Virginia Campaign of 1864. Eight days before the surrender at Appomattox (April 9, 1865), Pickett's division was almost destroyed at Five Forks while he was attending a shad bake. After the war he worked in an insurance business in Norfolk, Va.

WILLIAM C. QUANTRILL

(b. July 31, 1837, Canal Dover, Ohio—d. June 6, 1865, Louisville, Ky.)

The captain of a guerrilla band irregularly attached to the Confederate army, William C. Quantrill was notorious for overseeing the sacking of the free-state stronghold of Lawrence, Kan. (Aug. 21, 1863), in which at least 150 people were burned or shot to death.

After growing up in Ohio, Quantrill taught school in Ohio and then Illinois and, in 1857, moved to Kansas, where he first tried farming, without much enthusiasm. By the end of 1860, while living near Lawrence, he fell into thievery and murder, was charged with horse stealing, and began life on the run. After the outbreak of the Civil War he first served with the Confederate Army in Missouri but then, independently, put together a gang of guerrillas, who raided and robbed towns and farms with Union sympathies. The Union forces declared Quantrill's Raiders to be outlaws; the Confederates made them an official troop in August 1862, giving Quantrill the rank of captain.

On Aug. 21, 1863, his troop of about 450 men raided Lawrence, pillaging, burning, and killing. Two months later, donning Federal uniforms, the raiders surprised a detachment of Union soldiers at Baxter Springs, Kan., and slaughtered about 90 of them. As the Civil War drew to a close, dissension caused Quantrill's followers to break up into smaller bands to continue their criminal pursuits. Quantrill was mortally wounded on a raid into Kentucky in May 1865.

RAPHAEL SEMMES

(b. Sept. 27, 1809, Charles County, Md.—d. Aug. 30, 1877, Mobile, Ala.)

As the commander of the Confederate man-of-war *Alabama*, Raphael Semmes led daring raids on Union merchant shipping during the middle two years of the Civil War.

Appointed a midshipman in the U.S. Navy in 1826, Semmes studied law while awaiting orders and was admitted to the bar in 1834. In the Mexican War (1846–48), he superintended the landing of troops at Veracruz (March 1847) and marched inland to Mexico City with Gen. Winfield Scott.

When Alabama, his home state, seceded from the Union (January 1861), Semmes resigned his commission as commander, and with the outbreak of war in April he received a similar appointment in the Confederate Navy. After capturing 17 Union merchant ships while in command of the packet *Sumter*, he was assigned to command the *Alabama*, newly built in England. Between 1862 and 1864 he made a series of brilliant and successful cruises, capturing, sinking, or burning 82 Union ships valued at more than $6,000,000. Finally he met the Union ship *Kearsarge* in the English Channel and, after a 90-minute battle, was forced to surrender. After being rescued from the water by an English yacht, he rested in Switzerland and returned to the Confederacy via Mexico.

As a rear admiral, Semmes subsequently helped command the Confederate Navy in the James River. After the war he returned to Mobile to practice law. He also wrote several books on the Mexican and Civil wars.

Jeb Stuart

(b. Feb. 6, 1833, Patrick county, Va., U.S.—d. May 12, 1864, Yellow Tavern, near Richmond, Va.)

Confederate cavalry officer Jeb Stuart provided reports of enemy troop movements that were of particular value to Robert E. Lee and the Southern command during the Civil War.

An 1854 graduate of the U.S. Military Academy at West Point, N.Y., James Ewell Brown ("Jeb") Stuart resigned his commission to share in the defense of his state when Virginia seceded from the Union (April 1861). At the First Battle of Bull Run (First Manassas) that July, he distinguished himself by his personal bravery. Later in the year he was promoted to brigadier general and placed in command of the cavalry brigade of the Army of Northern Virginia. Just before the Seven Days' Battle—fought in June 1862 in defense of Richmond—Stuart was sent out by Confederate Gen. Robert E. Lee to locate the right flank of the Federal army under Gen. George B. McClellan. He not only successfully achieved his mission but also rode completely around McClellan's army to deliver his report to Lee. In the next campaign he had the good fortune, in his raid against Federal communications, to bring back a staff document from which Lee was able to discover the strength and position of Federal forces.

Stuart, promoted to a major general and commander of the cavalry corps, was present at the Second Battle of Bull Run (Second Manassas, August 1862) and again circled the Federal army, returning with 1,200 enemy horses. During the Maryland campaign that followed, he brilliantly defended one of the passes of South Mountain (Crampton's Gap), thus enabling Lee to concentrate his army in time to meet McClellan's attack. By the winter of 1862 Stuart's extraordinary skill as an intelligence officer was fully recognized, and Lee called him the "eyes of the army."

At the Battle of Fredericksburg (December 1862) Stuart's horse artillery rendered valuable service by checking the Federal attack on Gen. Thomas J. "Stonewall" Jackson's corps. The following May at the Battle of Chancellorsville, Stuart was appointed by Lee to take command of the 2nd Army Corps after Jackson had been wounded.

The next campaign at Gettysburg, Pa. (July 1863), was preceded by the cavalry Battle of Brandy Station (June 9), at which for the first time Stuart and his men were met by worthy opposition from the Federal cavalry. The Confederates' northward march to the Potomac River was screened by Stuart's cavalry corps, which held the various approaches on the right flank of the army. Stuart's conduct at Gettysburg was long a subject of controversy. Though ordered by Lee to deploy his cavalry as a screen while also gathering intelligence for the advancing Confederate army, Stuart instead struck off on a raid, was delayed, and arrived at Gettysburg too late to provide Lee with vital information on the positions and movements of the Union forces. When Stuart did rejoin Lee's army at Gettysburg on July 2, the battle had already begun, and his exhausted forces were of little help.

Throughout the winter of 1863–64 Stuart continued to supply the Confederate command with accurate knowledge of Northern troop movements. But soon after the opening of the 1864 campaign his corps was drawn away from Lee's army by Gen. Philip Sheridan's Federal cavalry forces. In attempting to keep the enemy from reaching Richmond, during the engagement generally known as Spotsylvania Courthouse, Stuart's army met defeat (May 11), and he himself was mortally wounded at close range the next day.

Joseph Wheeler

(b. Sept. 10, 1836, near Augusta, Ga.—d. Jan. 25, 1906, Brooklyn, N.Y.)

Joseph Wheeler entered the U.S. cavalry after graduating from the U.S. Military Academy at West Point, N.Y., in 1859 but resigned to join the Confederate cavalry.

He commanded a brigade at the Battle of Shiloh (April 6–7, 1862), but soon afterward he returned to the cavalry arm, in which he won a reputation second only to Gen. Jeb Stuart's. After the action of Perryville he was promoted to brigadier general and, in 1863, to major general. Throughout the campaigns of Chickamauga, Chattanooga, and Atlanta, he commanded the cavalry of the Confederate Army in the west and was given the task of harassing Gen. William Tecumseh Sherman's army during its march to the sea. In the closing operations of the war, with the rank of lieutenant general, he commanded the cavalry of Gen. Joseph Johnston's weak army in North Carolina and was included in its surrender.

In 1898, during the Spanish-American War, Wheeler commanded the cavalry in the actions of Guasimas and San Juan. He wrote *The Santiago Campaign* (1898).

CHAPTER 8

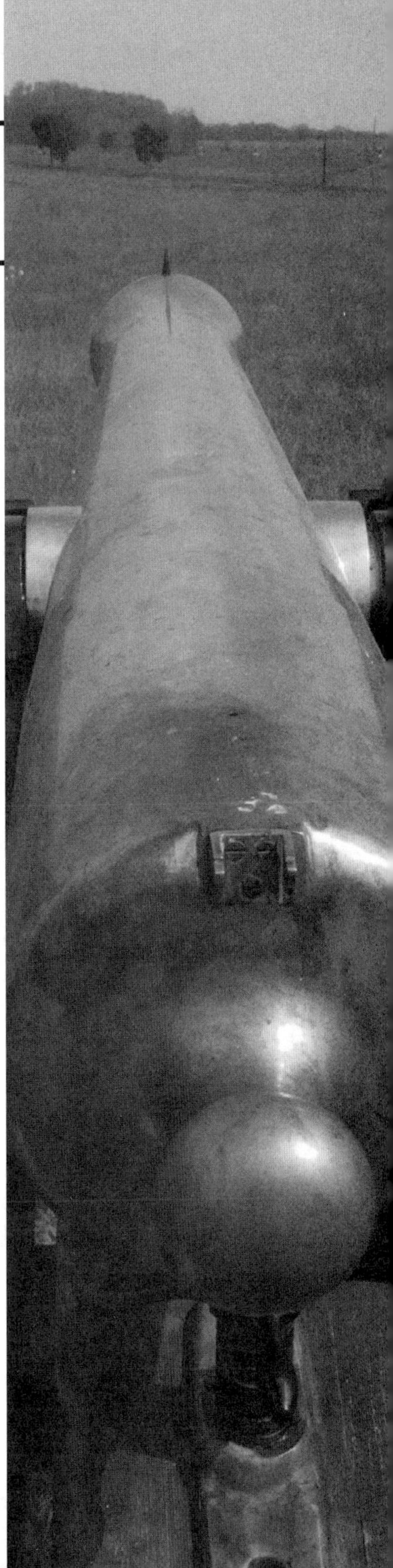

Non-Military Leaders

The contributions of the following civilians—encompassing those engaged in the highest levels of politics, medicine, engineering, journalism, and more—helped shape the form, tone, and trajectory of the war.

THE UNION

Charles Francis Adams
(b. Aug. 18, 1807, Boston, Mass.—d. Nov. 21, 1886, Boston)

Diplomat Charles Francis Adams played an important role in keeping Britain neutral during the Civil War and in promoting the arbitration of the important *Alabama* claims.

The son of Pres. John Quincy Adams and the grandson of Pres. John Adams, Charles was introduced early on to a cosmopolitan way of life when his father was appointed minister to Russia in 1809. In the 1840s Charles Adams served for six years as a member of the Massachusetts legislature and as the editor of a party journal, the *Boston Whig*. He felt, however, that the Whigs should take a more forthright position against the extension of slavery into the territories. When, in 1848, the so-called Conscience Whigs broke with the party to form the antislavery Free-Soil Party, Adams received the vice-presidential nomination of the new coalition.

The emergence of the Republican Party in 1856 offered Adams the permanent political affiliation he was seeking, and he was elected to the U.S. Congress from his father's old district in 1858. When the Republicans won at the polls two years later, Adams was named ambassador to Great Britain by his close friend William H. Seward, the new secretary of state.

When Adams arrived in London one month after the war broke out, he found that Great Britain had already recognized Confederate belligerency. So much sympathy was shown in England for the South that Adams' path for the next seven years was strewn with difficulties, but his logic, reserve, and directness appealed to the British, and gradually he won their support. His main mission was to prevent the British from abandoning neutrality, and, with the issuance of the Emancipation Proclamation (Jan. 1, 1863), the immediate danger of diplomatic recognition of the South was over.

Adams then laboured to prevent the building or the outfitting at British shipyards of privateers for Confederate use. He had not been able to prevent the sailing of the highly effective commerce destroyer *Alabama* in May 1862, but his vigorous protestations of the obligations of neutrals succeeded in preventing further launchings. Furthermore, he persistently argued the British government's responsibility for the estimated $6 million worth of damage done by the *Alabama* to Federal merchant vessels. From 1871 to 1872 Adams served as U.S. arbiter on the international commission that met at Geneva to settle the *Alabama* claims. During this long and taxing period in Anglo-American relations, Adams' judicious and balanced conduct greatly enhanced the reputation of his country abroad.

Clara Barton

(b. Dec. 25, 1821, Oxford, Mass.—d. April 12, 1912, Glen Echo, Md.)

Long before she founded the American Red Cross in 1881, Clara Barton earned a reputation for compassionate caring during the Civil War.

At the outbreak of the war, Barton, who had initially worked as a schoolteacher, showed characteristic initiative in organizing facilities to recover soldiers' lost baggage and in securing medicine and supplies for men wounded in the first battle of Bull Run. She gained permission to pass through the battle lines to distribute supplies, search for the missing, and nurse the wounded. Barton carried on this work through the remainder of the Civil War, traveling with the army as far south as Charleston in 1863. In June 1864 she was formally appointed superintendent of nurses for the Army of the James. In 1865, at the request of Pres. Abraham Lincoln, she set up a bureau of records to aid in the search for missing men.

Edward Bates

(b. Sept. 4, 1793, Goochland county, Va., U.S.—d. March 25, 1869, St. Louis, Mo.)

Whig politician Edward Bates joined the Republican Party before the Civil War and served as Abraham Lincoln's attorney general.

Educated largely at home, Bates moved from Virginia to Missouri in 1814 and shortly thereafter began the study of law. By 1816 he was practicing law in St. Louis. Over the next decade he served in a number of territorial and state offices. Elected in 1826 to a term in the U.S. House of Representatives, Bates was defeated in a bid for a Senate seat by followers of Democrat Thomas Hart Benton. As a Whig in a strongly pro–Andrew Jackson state, Bates also lost his reelection attempt in 1828 for another term in the House.

Although his career in national politics was largely dormant for more than three decades, Bates served in the Missouri legislature, drew national attention as president of the River and Harbor Improvement Convention of 1847, and in 1850 declined appointment as secretary of war during the administration of Whig Millard Fillmore. After serving as president of the Whig convention of 1856, he broke with the party and joined the newly created Republican Party.

Bates had long been a free-soil advocate. He freed his own slaves, opposed the Kansas–Nebraska Bill, and spoke out against the admission of Kansas under the Lecompton Constitution. As a Southern-born border-state politician, Bates attracted support for the 1860 Republican presidential nomination. His followers believed he could maintain party principles opposing the extension of slavery without alienating the South and provoking secession.

When Bates's presidential bid failed, the triumphant Lincoln offered his erstwhile rival a choice of Cabinet positions. Bates chose the attorney generalship,

Edward Bates. Library of Congress, Washington, D.C.

and for a time exercised some influence in the administration. But he opposed the admission of West Virginia as a state, the subjugation of constitutional rights to military control, and the increasing power of the Radical Republicans. On Nov. 24, 1864, weary of a position in which he wielded little authority, Bates resigned as attorney general. He returned to Missouri and fought the Radical Republicans in his home state by writing newspaper articles and letters to prominent citizens.

John Bell

(b. Feb. 15, 1797, near Nashville, Tenn.—d. Sept. 10, 1869, Dover, Tenn.)

John Bell was the presidential nominee of the Constitutional Union party in the 1860 election.

Bell entered the U.S. House of Representatives in 1827 and served there as a Democrat until 1841. He broke with Pres. Andrew Jackson in 1834 and supported Hugh Lawson White for president in 1836. After White's defeat, Bell became a Whig and, in March 1841, as a reward for party services, was made secretary of war in Pres. William Henry Harrison's Cabinet. A few months later, after the death of President Harrison, he resigned in opposition to Pres. John Tyler's break with the Whigs.

After six years' retirement from political life, Bell was elected as a U.S. senator for Tennessee in 1847, serving in the Senate until 1859. Although a large slaveholder, Bell opposed efforts to expand slavery to the U.S. territories. He vigorously opposed Pres. James Knox Polk's Mexican War policy and voted against the Compromise of 1850, the Kansas-Nebraska Bill (1854), and the attempt to admit Kansas as a slave state. Bell's temperate support of slavery, combined with his vigorous defense of the Union, brought him the presidential nomination on the Constitutional Union ticket in 1860, but he carried only Virginia, Kentucky, and Tennessee.

Bell initially opposed secession. However, following Pres. Abraham Lincoln's call for troops, he openly advocated resistance and henceforth classed himself a rebel. Bell spent the war years in retirement in Georgia, returning to Tennessee in 1865.

Mary Ann Bickerdyke

(b. July 19, 1817, Knox county, Ohio—d. Nov. 8, 1901, Bunker Hill, Kan.)

Mary Ann Bickerdyke was the organizer and chief of nursing, hospital, and welfare services for the Western armies under the command of Gen. Ulysses S. Grant during the Civil War.

Mary Ann Ball grew up in the houses of various relatives. She attended Oberlin College and later studied nursing. In 1847 she married a widower, Robert Bickerdyke, who died in 1859. Thereafter Mary Ann Bickerdyke supported herself in Galesburg, Illinois, by the practice of "botanic" medicine.

Soon after the outbreak of the Civil War, she volunteered to accompany and distribute a collection of supplies taken up for the relief of wounded soldiers at a makeshift army hospital in Cairo, Ill. On her arrival there she found conditions to be extremely unsanitary, and she set to work immediately at cleaning, cooking, and nursing. She became matron when a general hospital was organized in Cairo in November 1861.

Following the fall of Fort Donelson in February 1862, Bickerdyke made a number of forays onto the battlefield to search for wounded. Such exploits began to attract general attention. Her alliance with the U.S. Sanitary Commission began about this time.

Bickerdyke soon attached herself to the staff of Gen. Ulysses S. Grant, by whom she was given a pass for free transportation anywhere in his command. She followed Grant's army down the Mississippi River, setting up hospitals as they were needed, and later accompanied the forces of Gen. William Tecumseh Sherman on their march through Georgia to the sea. Through her efforts, provisions were made for frequent medical examinations and transporting men who could no longer walk. Under Bickerdyke's supervision, about 300 field hospitals were built with the help of U.S. Sanitary Commission agents.

Having scavenged supplies and equipment and established mobile laundries and kitchens, Bickerdyke had generally endeared herself to the wounded and sick, among whom she became known as "Mother" Bickerdyke. To incompetent officers and physicians she was brutal, succeeding in having several dismissed. She retained her position largely through the influence of Grant, Sherman, and others who recognized the value of her services. After the war Bickerdyke continued to work tirelessly with and on behalf of veterans and the disadvantaged.

John Bigelow

(b. Nov. 25, 1817, Bristol, N.Y.—d. Dec. 19, 1911, New York, N.Y.)

As U.S. consul in Paris during the Civil War, John Bigelow prevented the delivery of warships constructed in France for the Confederacy.

Long the managing editor and, with the poet William Cullen Bryant, part owner of the *New York Evening Post* (1849–61), Bigelow also was a principal adviser of the Republican Party's first presidential candidate, John Charles Frémont. Appointed consul in Paris (1861), Bigelow adroitly gained support for the Union cause, emphasizing ideological considerations to the French liberal press and the trading potential of the Northern industrial states to French businessmen. In *France and the Confederate Navy, 1862–1868* (1888), he recounted the episode of the French-built warships, which, if manned by Confederate crews, might have broken the Union blockade of the South. As U.S. minister to France (April 1865–September 1866), he dealt tactfully with the problem of the French-backed Mexican empire of Maximilian. Bigelow also was the discoverer and first editor of Benjamin Franklin's long-lost *Autobiography*.

Mathew B. Brady

(b. c. 1823, near Lake George, N.Y.—d. Jan. 15, 1896, New York, N.Y.)

Well-known 19th-century photographer Mathew B. Brady was celebrated for his portraits of politicians and his photographs of the Civil War.

Brady learned to make daguerreotypes from Samuel F.B. Morse. In 1844 he opened the first of two studios in New York City and began photographing famous people, including Daniel Webster, Edgar Allan Poe, and Henry Clay. In 1847 Brady opened a studio in Washington, D.C., and there created, copied, and collected portraits of U.S. presidents. He achieved international fame with *A Gallery of Illustrious Americans* (1850).

At the outbreak of the Civil War in 1861, Brady decided to make a complete record of that conflict. He hired a staff of about 20 photographers, the best known of whom were Alexander Gardner and Timothy H. O'Sullivan, and dispatched them throughout the war zones. Brady's main activities in the endeavour involved organizing and supervising the operation of his employees and studios; he himself probably photographed only occasionally on such battlefields as Bull Run, Antietam, and Gettysburg. Since Brady refused to give individual credit to photographers, a number of them, including Gardner and O'Sullivan, left his employ.

The Civil War project ruined Brady financially. He had invested $100,000 in it and had bought supplies on credit, confident that the government would buy his photographs after the war ended. The government, however, showed no interest. The financial panic of 1873 forced him to sell his New York studio and declare bankruptcy. He was unable to pay the storage bill for his negatives, which the War Department finally bought at public auction for $2,840. Through the efforts of his friends in government, Brady was finally granted $25,000 by Congress in 1875, but he never regained financial solvency and died alone and virtually forgotten in a hospital charity ward.

Simon Cameron

(b. March 8, 1799, Maytown, Pa.—d. June 26, 1889, Donegal Springs, Pa.)

After being Pennsylvania's favourite-son candidate for the presidential nomination at the Republican National Convention in 1860, Simon Cameron threw his support to Abraham Lincoln, thereby gaining a seat in Lincoln's Cabinet as the secretary of war. He administered the War Department with such favouritism, however, that Lincoln replaced him with Edwin M. Stanton (Jan. 11, 1862), and Cameron was censured for his conduct by the House of Representatives. Lincoln then appointed him minister to Russia, from which post he resigned (Nov. 8, 1862).

In 1867 Cameron returned to the Senate (where he had represented Pennsylvania in 1845–49 and again in 1857–61), serving as chairman of the Foreign Relations Committee from 1872. He wielded such power in Republican circles that he was able to obtain the appointment of his son as secretary of war by Pres. Ulysses S. Grant.

Anna Ella Carroll

(b. Aug. 29, 1815, near Pokomoke City, Somerset County, Md.—d. Feb. 19, 1894, Washington, D.C.)

Political pamphleteer and constitutional theorist Anna Ella Carroll claimed she played a role in determining Union strategy during the Civil War.

From a prominent family, Carroll emerged in the 1850s as a spokesperson for the virulently anti-Catholic and anti-foreign Know-Nothing Party. She published a series of lectures on the "Catholic menace" in 1854 and *The Great American Battle*, a Know-Nothing apology, in 1856. In the latter year she campaigned widely for Millard Fillmore, the Know-Nothing candidate for president. At the outbreak of the Civil War, she settled in Washington, D.C., and began writing letters, articles, and pamphlets in support of the Union.

In *The War Powers of the General Government* (1861) and *The Relation of the National Government to the Revolted Citizens Defined* (1862), both published at her own expense, Carroll outlined a constitutional theory under which the secession of Southern states and the formation of the Confederacy were legal nullities. She held that the general rebellion was merely the sum of individual acts of rebellion, and the states would automatically resume their former relation to the central government when the rebellion had been put down; therefore, the executive power superseded the legislative in prosecuting both war and reconstruction. This theory was precisely that under which Pres. Abraham Lincoln exercised wartime authority and which he pressed against the competing claims of Congress.

In mid-1862, in the belief that she had a firm agreement to be paid for her services—a former assistant secretary of war had made her some vague assurances—Carroll carried a demand for $50,000 all the way to Lincoln and was rebuffed. She continued to press her claim in various ways, but in 1870 it was eclipsed by a far more spectacular one, namely, that she had originated the military strategy that had broken the Confederacy.

In 1861 she had visited St. Louis, Missouri, and there met Charles Scott, a riverboat pilot and amateur strategist who outlined to her his plan for a Union invasion of the South along the Tennessee River. Later that year she submitted a lengthy memorandum to the War Department on the plan, crediting Scott. Gen. Ulysses S. Grant's successful drive up the Tennessee to Forts Henry and Donelson in February 1862 seemed to prove that the Scott plan had been adopted, and as late as 1865 Carroll acknowledged Scott's authorship publicly. In 1870, however, she claimed it herself and petitioned Congress for payment. By various questionable means she secured affidavits from a number of prominent people, and apparently altered many of the documents to strengthen their positions. Her petitions and memorials to Congress continued to appear until her death. While the claim was never officially accepted, she became something of a cause célèbre among feminists.

Henry Winter Davis

(b. Aug. 16, 1817, Annapolis, Md.—d. Dec. 30, 1865, Baltimore, Md.)

A Maryland unionist during the secession crisis, Henry Winter Davis was a harsh critic of Abraham Lincoln and the coauthor of the congressional plan for Reconstruction during the Civil War.

A lawyer intent upon a political career, Davis joined the Whig Party and campaigned for Winfield Scott in 1852. As the Whig Party faded during the 1850s, Davis' conservatism and apparent lack of interest in the sectional crisis led him to the Know-Nothing Party. In 1854 he ran successfully on the Know-Nothing ticket for a seat in the U.S. House of Representatives.

During the second half of the 1850s, Davis tried to avoid taking sides between North and South. But in 1860 he aligned himself with the House Republicans, even though he backed the Union Party in that year's presidential contest. The Union Party triumphed in Maryland, and it was largely due to Davis that Maryland did not secede. When the Union Party crumbled in the face of secession, Davis found himself without a party. On June 13, 1861, he lost his reelection race to a pro-Southerner.

As a private citizen, Davis toured the North, becoming a national figure while speaking for the Union. Increasingly, however, he took issue with Lincoln's wartime policies, especially the suspension of habeas corpus. A Republican at odds with his party's leader, he was nonetheless elected once again to the House of Representatives in 1863. He continued to criticize Lincoln and members of the cabinet, and before long he had become a highly influential member of the House.

In response to Lincoln's plan for reconstruction, Davis formulated the congressional policy that became embodied in the Wade-Davis Bill. This bill stymied the conciliatory policy Lincoln planned toward the South by placing reconstruction in the hands of Congress. The bill required a majority of voters (not Lincoln's 10 percent) to establish a legal government in a seceded state. It disfranchised a large number of former Confederates (not just the Confederate leadership) and compelled immediate emancipation, rather than, according to the presidential plan, leaving individual states to handle emancipation on their own.

The Wade-Davis Bill passed the House and Senate, but Lincoln pocket-vetoed it, enraging Davis, who lost his House seat in 1864.

Stephen A. Douglas
(b. April 23, 1813, Brandon, Vt.—d. June 3, 1861, Chicago, Ill.)

The leader of the Democratic Party and an orator who espoused the cause of popular sovereignty in relation to the issue of slavery in the territories before the Civil War, Stephen A. Douglas was re-elected senator from Illinois in 1858 after a series of eloquent debates with the Republican candidate, Abraham Lincoln, who defeated him in the presidential race two years later.

Douglas left New England at the age of 20 to settle in Jacksonville, Ill., where he quickly rose to a position of leadership in the Illinois Democratic Party. In 1843 he was elected to the U.S. House of Representatives. One of its youngest members, Douglas gained early prominence as a dedicated worker and gifted speaker. Heavyset and only five feet four inches tall, he was dubbed the "Little Giant" by his contemporaries.

Douglas embraced a lifelong enthusiasm for national expansion, giving consistent support to the annexation of Texas (1845), the Mexican War (1846–48), taking a vigorous stance toward Great Britain in the Oregon boundary dispute (1846), and advocating both government land grants to promote transcontinental railroad construction and a free homestead policy for settlers.

Douglas was elected in 1846 to the U.S. Senate. There he became deeply involved in the nation's search for a solution to the slavery problem. As chairman of the Committee on Territories, he was particularly prominent in the bitter debates between North and South on the extension of slavery westward. Trying to remove the onus from Congress, he developed the theory of popular sovereignty (originally called squatter sovereignty), under which the people in a territory would themselves decide whether to permit slavery within their region's boundaries. Douglas himself was not a slaveholder, though his wife was. He was influential in the passage of the Compromise of 1850, which tried to maintain a congressional balance between free and slave states. The organization of the Utah and New Mexico territories under popular sovereignty was a victory for his doctrine.

The climax of Douglas' theory was reached in the Kansas-Nebraska Act (1854), which substituted local options toward slavery in the Kansas and Nebraska territories for that of congressional mandate, thus repealing the Missouri Compromise of 1820. The act's passage was a triumph for Douglas, although he was bitterly condemned and vilified by antislavery forces. A strong contender for the Democratic presidential nomination in both 1852 and 1856, he was too outspoken to be chosen by a party that was still trying to bridge the sectional gap.

The Supreme Court struck indirectly at popular sovereignty in the Dred Scott decision (1857), which held that neither Congress nor territorial legislatures could prohibit slavery in a territory. The following year Douglas engaged in a number of widely publicized debates with Lincoln in a close contest for the Senate seat in Illinois. Although Lincoln won the popular vote, Douglas was elected 54 to 46 by the legislature. In the debates, Douglas enunciated his famous "Freeport Doctrine," which stated that the territories could still determine the existence of slavery through unfriendly legislation and the use of police power, in spite of the Supreme Court decision. As a result, Southern opposition to Douglas intensified, and he was denied reappointment to the committee chairmanship he had previously held in the Senate.

When the "regular" (Northern) Democrats nominated him for president in 1860, the Southern wing broke away and supported a separate ticket headed by John C. Breckinridge of Kentucky. Although Douglas received only 12 electoral votes, he was second to Lincoln in the number of popular votes polled. Douglas then urged the South to acquiesce in the results of the election. At the outbreak of the Civil War, he denounced secession as criminal and was one of the strongest advocates of maintaining the integrity of the Union at all costs. At President Lincoln's request, he undertook a mission to the Border States and to the Northwest to rouse Unionist sentiments among their citizenry. Douglas's early and unexpected death was partly the result of these last exertions on behalf of the Union.

James B. Eads

(b. May 23, 1820, Lawrenceburg, Ind., U.S.—d. March 8, 1887, Nassau, Bah.)

James B. Eads, a wealthy self-educated engineer best known for his triple-arch steel bridge over the Mississippi River at St. Louis, Mo., also invented a "submarine" that he used to make a fortune in salvage. As the Civil War threatened, Eads foresaw the struggle that would take place for control of the Mississippi system, and he advanced a radical idea. He proposed that ironclad steam-powered warships of shallow draft be built to operate on the rivers.

The U.S. government was slow to take up his offer to build such a flotilla. When it did, Eads built the ships in record time, working 4,000 men on day and night shifts seven days a week. The novel craft he set afloat spearheaded Grant's offensive against Forts Henry and Donelson, the first important Union victories of the war. They continued to play a conspicuous role under Andrew Foote and David Farragut at Memphis, Island No. 10, Vicksburg, and Mobile Bay. The vessels were the first ironclads to fight in North America and the first in the world to engage enemy warships. (The *Monitor* and *Merrimack*, both ironclads that battled in the Civil War, were the first such vessels to close against each other in combat.)

Immediately after the war, Eads was chosen to direct a construction project of extraordinary difficulty, the bridging of the Mississippi at St. Louis. Eads was the first U.S. engineer to be honoured with the Albert Medal of the Royal Society of Arts in London.

Edward Everett

(b. April 11, 1794, Dorchester, Mass.—d. Jan. 15, 1865, Boston, Mass.)

Statesman and orator Edward Everett is mainly remembered for delivering the speech immediately preceding Pres. Abraham Lincoln's Gettysburg Address (Nov. 19, 1863) at the ceremony dedicating the Gettysburg National Cemetery (Pa.) during the Civil War.

By 1820 Everett had established a formidable reputation as a lecturer and orator, based on careful preparation, an extraordinary memory, and brilliance of style and delivery. He served in the U.S. House of Representatives (1825–35), as governor of Massachusetts (1835–39), and as U.S. minister to England (1841–45). With his election as president of Harvard in 1846, he withdrew from politics for several years, returning in 1852 as secretary of state during the last four months of Pres. Millard Fillmore's administration. In 1853 he entered the U.S. Senate, but his generally conciliatory stand on the issue of slavery aroused the ire of his abolitionist constituents, and he resigned the following year.

In 1860 Everett was the unsuccessful vice presidential candidate of the Constitutional Union Party, which sought to bridge sectional differences by stressing common devotion to the Union and the Constitution. His desire for compromise ended at the outbreak of the Civil War, throughout which he traveled and spoke in support of the Union cause.

Barbara Hauer Frietschie

(b. Dec. 3, 1766, Lancaster, Pa.—d. Dec. 18, 1862, Frederick, Md.)

Union patriot Barbara Frietschie became the focus of highly embellished legend and the subject of literary treatment when she purportedly defied Confederate invaders of Maryland in September 1862.

When the Army of Northern Virginia marched through Frederick, Md., on September 10, the troops passed Frietschie's house, and she may have waved a small Union flag from the porch or a second-floor window. There may also have been some small incident as a result. Whatever the actual case, the story soon grew up in Frederick that Frietschie, who was known to be intensely patriotic, had somehow confronted the Confederate army. The story's connection with fact was broken by Frietschie's death in 1862.

The tale was heard by the novelist Emma D.E.N. Southworth, who passed it on to John Greenleaf Whittier. In October 1863 Whittier published in the *Atlantic Monthly* his verse version, "Barbara Frietchie," in which the story of Frietschie's encounter with Gen. Thomas J. "Stonewall" Jackson was much elaborated. Whittier's version quickly became canonical, and the enduring popularity of the poem kept Frietschie's name alive.

Despite its meagre factual basis—the one thing known certainly of the events of that day is that Jackson did not pass Frietschie's house—the endurance of the tale led to the erection of a memorial in 1913 and the building in 1926 of a replica of her house, the original having been razed a few years after her death.

Alexander Gardner

(b. Oct. 17, 1821, Paisley, Renfrew, Scot.—d. 1882, Washington, D.C.)

Scots immigrant Andrew Gardner, who was working as a portrait photographer for Mathew B. Brady when the Civil War erupted in 1861, assisted Brady in his effort to make a complete photographic record of the conflict. Brady, however, refused to give Gardner public credit for his work. Gardner therefore left Brady in 1863, opened a portrait gallery in Washington, and continued to photograph the hostilities on his own.

Gardner's photographs "President Lincoln on the Battlefield of Antietam" (1862) and "Home of a Rebel Sharpshooter, Gettysburg" (1863) and his portraits of Abraham Lincoln are among the best-known photographs of the war period. Gardner's *Photographic Sketch Book of the Civil War*, a two-volume collection of 100

Dead Confederate soldier at the foot of Little Round Top, Gettysburg, Pa., July 1863. Photograph by Alexander Gardner. Library of Congress, Washington, D.C.

original prints, was published in 1866. When Brady petitioned Congress to buy his photographs of the war, Gardner presented a rival petition, claiming that it was he, not Brady, who had originated the idea of providing the nation with a photographic history of the conflict. Congress eventually bought both collections.

Hannibal Hamlin

(b. Aug. 27, 1809, Paris Hill, Maine—d. July 4, 1891, Bangor, Maine)

The 15th vice president of the United States (1861–65), Hannibal Hamlin served in the first Republican administration of Pres. Abraham Lincoln.

An antislavery Jacksonian Democrat, Hamlin served in the Maine state legislature (1836–40). He was elected to the United States House of Representatives in 1842 and to the Senate in 1848. In his first term as a senator, he took an antislavery position on sectional issues, and left the Democratic Party in 1856 because of its endorsement of the Kansas-Nebraska Act (1854), which proponents of abolitionism had attacked as a capitulation to the interests of the slave states. He was elected Maine's first Republican governor (1856) but resigned in February 1857 to return to the Senate.

The Republican National Convention of 1860 nominated Hamlin for vice president—a post he said he would have declined had he attended the convention in Chicago—in the belief that as an Easterner and former Democrat he would provide both regional and partisan balance to Lincoln. Although Lincoln rarely consulted him in office, Hamlin was an early supporter of emancipation and the arming of freedmen, steps that Lincoln later adopted. After failing to secure renomination in 1864—an outcome in which Lincoln played a decisive role—he became collector of the port of Boston, but he resigned in 1866 when he found himself out of step with the policies of Pres. Andrew Johnson. Elected to the Senate again (1869–81), Hamlin supported radical Reconstruction.

B. F. Isherwood

(b. Oct. 6, 1822, New York City—d. June 19, 1915, New York City)

Naval engineer Benjamin Franklin Isherwood was greatly responsible for the development of the Union navy's steam-powered fleet during the Civil War.

Having learned mechanics and engineering while working on railroads, at various U.S. Treasury lighthouses, and at the Novelty Iron Works (New York City), Isherwood joined the Engineer Corps of the U.S. Navy in 1844, serving thereafter on several ships and land-based posts. After the Civil War began, he became engineer in chief of the Union navy and, in 1862, the first chief of its Bureau of Steam Engineering. At the beginning of the war the navy had but 28 steam-powered ships and boats; by the end of the war it had about 600. Isherwood oversaw the design and construction of most of these ships and, in large part, personally designed the machinery and hulls of ships of the Wampanoag class, which, when built, were the world's fastest at 17 $^{3}/_{4}$ knots.

Andrew Johnson

(b. Dec. 29, 1808, Raleigh, N.C., U.S.—d. July 31, 1875, near Carter Station, Tenn.)

The 17th president of the United States (1865–69), Andrew Johnson took office upon the assassination of Pres. Abraham Lincoln during the closing months of the Civil War. His lenient Reconstruction policies toward the South embittered the Radical Republicans in Congress and led to his political downfall and to his impeachment, though he was acquitted.

Early Life and Career

Born into poverty, Johnson never attended school, and he taught himself to read and write. After a short apprenticeship as a tailor, he moved with his family to Greeneville, Tenn., where he opened his own tailor shop. From a book containing some of the world's great orations he began to learn history. Another subject he studied was the Constitution of the United States, which he was soon able to recite from memory in large part.

Before he was 21, Johnson organized a workingman's party. Elected to the state legislature (1835–43), he found a natural home in the states' rights Democratic Party of Andrew Jackson and emerged as the spokesman for mountaineers and small farmers against the interests of the landed classes. In that role, he was sent to Washington for 10 years as a U.S. representative (1843–53), after which he served as governor of Tennessee (1853–57). Elected a U.S. senator in 1856, he generally adhered to the dominant Democratic views favouring lower tariffs and opposing antislavery agitation.

Johnson had achieved a measure of prosperity and owned a few slaves himself. In 1860, however, he broke dramatically with the party when, after Lincoln's election, he vehemently opposed Southern secession. When Tennessee seceded in June 1861, he alone among the Southern senators remained at his post and refused to join the Confederacy. Sharing the race and class prejudice of many poor white people in his state, he explained his decision: "Damn the negroes, I am fighting those traitorous aristocrats, their masters." Although denounced throughout the South, he remained loyal to the Union. In recognition of this unwavering support, Lincoln appointed him (May 1862) military governor of Tennessee, by then under federal control.

The Presidency

To broaden the base of the Republican Party to include loyal "war" Democrats, Johnson was selected to run for vice president on Lincoln's reelection ticket of 1864. His first appearance on the national stage was a fiasco. On Inauguration Day he imbibed more whiskey than he should have to counter the effects of a recent illness, and he swayed on his feet and stumbled over his words. He embarrassed his colleagues in the administration and dismayed onlookers. Northern newspapers were appalled. His detractors later seized on this incident to accuse him of habitual drunkenness. Less than five weeks later he was president.

Thrust so unexpectedly into the White House (April 14, 1865), Johnson was faced with the enormously vexing problem of reconstructing the Union and settling the future of the former Confederate states. Congressional Radical Republicans, who favoured severe measures toward the defeated yet largely impenitent South, were disappointed with the new president's program, with its lenient policies begun by Lincoln and its readmission of seceded states into the Union with few provisions for reform or civil rights for freedmen—who, although emancipated, were destitute, uneducated, and subject to exploitation and mistreatment. This element in Congress was outraged at the return of power to traditional white aristocratic hands and protested the emergence of restrictive black codes aimed at controlling and suppressing the former slaves. The Republican majority refused to seat the Southern congressmen and set up a Joint Committee of Fifteen on Reconstruction. Johnson viewed their actions as a usurpation of his power, and he believed that continued punitive measures in the South, along with a guarantee of suffrage to blacks, was not supported by majority opinion nationwide. He was reluctant to insist on suffrage for blacks in the South when it had not been granted in the North. He believed that placing power over whites in the hands of former slaves would create an intolerable situation.

Johnson's vetoing of two important pieces of legislation aimed at protecting blacks, an extension of the Freedman's Bureau Bill and the Civil Rights Act of 1866, was disastrous. His vetoes united Moderate and Radical Republicans in outrage and further polarized a situation already filled with acrimony. Congress at first failed to override the Freedman's Bureau veto (a second attempt carried the measure) but succeeded with the Civil Rights Act; it was the first instance of a presidential veto's being overridden. In addition, Congress passed the Fourteenth Amendment to the Constitution, conferring citizenship on all people born or naturalized in the United States and guaranteeing them equal protection under the law. Against Johnson's objections, the amendment was ratified.

In the congressional elections of 1866, Johnson undertook an 18-day speaking tour throughout the Midwest, which he called "a swing around the circle," in order to explain and defend his policies and defeat congressional candidates opposing them. His effort proved a failure. His speeches were often rabble-rousing and ill-tempered as he tried to deal with hecklers sympathetic to the Radicals. In Indianapolis, Indiana, a confrontation with a crowd led to violence in which one man was killed. A result was sweeping electoral victories everywhere for the Radicals. With strong majorities in the House and Senate, they would now have sufficient votes to override any presidential veto of their bills. The president was unable to block legislation that tipped the balance of power to Congress over the Chief Executive.

In March 1867 the new Congress passed, over Johnson's veto, the first of the Reconstruction acts, providing for suffrage for male freedmen and military administration of the Southern states. With Reconstruction virtually taken out of his hands, the president, by exercising his veto and by narrowly interpreting the law, managed to delay the program so seriously that he contributed materially to its failure. He maintained that the Reconstruction acts were unconstitutional because they were passed without Southern representation in Congress. Seen as being aloof, gruff, and undiplomatic, Johnson constantly antagonized the Radicals. They became his sworn enemies.

Impeachment

Johnson played into the hands of his enemies by an imbroglio over the Tenure of Office Act, passed the same day as the Reconstruction acts. It forbade the chief executive from removing without the Senate's concurrence certain federal officers whose appointments had originally been made by and with the advice and consent of the Senate. The question of the power of the president in this matter had long been a controversial one. Johnson plunged ahead and dismissed from office Secretary of War Edwin M. Stanton—the Radicals' ally within his cabinet— to provide a court test of the act's constitutionality. In response, the House of Representatives voted articles of impeachment against the president—the first such occurrence in U.S. history.

While the focus was on Johnson's removal of Stanton in defiance of the Tenure of Office Act, the president was also accused of bringing "into disgrace, ridicule, hatred, contempt, and reproach the Congress of the United States." The evidence cited was chiefly culled from the speeches he had made during his "swing around the circle." What was at stake in the trial was not only the fate of a president but the very nature of the federal government. If Congress were able to remove the president, then, many Americans believed, the United States would be a dictatorship run by the leaders of Congress.

In a theatrical proceeding before the Senate, presided over by Chief Justice Salmon P. Chase, the charges proved weak, despite the passion with which they were argued, and the key votes (May 16 and 26, 1868) fell one short of the necessary two-thirds for conviction, seven Republicans voting

Andrew Johnson's impeachment trial in the Senate, 1868. Library of Congress, Washington, D.C. (neg. no. lc-usz61-269)

with Johnson's supporters. These men had been placed under the keenest pressure to vote to convict. One of them, Edmund Ross of Kansas, declared that, as he cast his ballot, "I almost literally looked into my open grave." When a messenger brought Johnson the news that the Senate had failed to convict him, he wept, declaring that he would devote the remainder of his life to restoring his reputation.

Despite his exoneration, Johnson's usefulness as a national leader was over. During his remaining days in office, he extended his grants of amnesty to all of the former rebels. The vexing problem of black suffrage was addressed by Congress's passage of the Fifteenth Amendment (ratified during the ensuing administration of Ulysses S. Grant), which forbade denial of suffrage on the basis of "race, color, or previous condition of servitude." At the 1868 Democratic National Convention, Johnson received a modest number of votes, but he did not actively seek renomination.

Abraham Lincoln

(b. Feb. 12, 1809, near Hodgenville, Ky.—d. April 15, 1865, Washington, D.C.)

The 16th president of the United States (1861–65), Abraham Lincoln preserved the Union during the Civil War and brought about the emancipation of the slaves.

Among American heroes, Lincoln continues to have a unique appeal for his fellow countrymen and also for people of other lands. This charm derives from his remarkable life story—the rise from humble origins, the dramatic death—and his distinctively human and humane personality, as well as from his historical role as saviour of the Union and emancipator of the slaves. His relevance endures and grows especially because of his eloquence as a spokesman for democracy. In his view, the Union was worth saving not only for its own sake but because it embodied an ideal—the ideal of self-government.

Early Life

Born in a Kentucky log cabin, Lincoln moved to Indiana in 1816 and to Illinois in 1830. After working as a storekeeper, a rail-splitter, a postmaster, and a surveyor, he enlisted as a volunteer in the Black Hawk War (1832) and was elected captain of his company. He taught himself law and, having passed the bar examination, began practicing in Springfield, Ill., in 1836. By the time he began to be prominent in national politics, about 20 years after launching his legal career, Lincoln had made himself one of the most distinguished and successful lawyers in Illinois. He was noted not only for his shrewdness and practical common sense, which enabled him always to see to the heart of any legal case, but also for his invariable fairness and utter honesty (earning the nickname "Honest Abe").

Early Politics

When Lincoln first entered politics, Andrew Jackson was president. Lincoln shared the sympathies that the Jacksonians professed for the common man, but he disagreed with the Jacksonian view that the government should be divorced from economic enterprise. "The legitimate object of government," he was later to say, "is to do for a community of people whatever they need to have done, but cannot do at all, or cannot do so well, for themselves, in their separate and individual capacities." Among the prominent politicians of his time, he most admired Henry Clay and Daniel Webster, who advocated using the powers of the federal government to encourage business and develop the country's resources by means of a national bank, a protective tariff, and a program of internal improvements for facilitating transportation. In Lincoln's view, Illinois, and the West as a whole, desperately needed such aid for economic development. From the outset, he associated himself with the party of Clay and Webster, the Whigs.

Abraham Lincoln, 1863. Library of Congress, Washington, D.C.

As a Whig member of the Illinois State Legislature, to which he was elected four times from 1834 to 1840, Lincoln devoted himself to a grandiose project for constructing with state funds a network of railroads, highways, and canals. Whigs and Democrats joined in passing an omnibus bill for these undertakings, but the panic of 1837 and the ensuing business depression brought about the abandonment of most of them. While in the legislature he demonstrated that, though opposed to slavery, he was no abolitionist. In 1837, in response to the mob murder of Elijah Lovejoy, an antislavery newspaperman of Alton, the legislature introduced resolutions condemning abolitionist societies and defending slavery in the Southern states as "sacred" by virtue of the federal Constitution. Lincoln refused to vote for the resolutions. Together with a fellow member, he drew up a protest that declared, on the one hand, that slavery was "founded on both injustice and bad policy" and, on the other, that "the promulgation of abolition doctrines tends rather to increase than to abate its evils."

During his single term in Congress (1847–49), Lincoln, as the lone Whig from Illinois, gave little attention to legislative matters. He proposed a bill for the gradual and compensated emancipation of slaves in the District of Columbia, but, because it was to take effect only with the approval of the "free white citizens" of the district, it displeased abolitionists as well as slaveholders and never was seriously considered.

Lincoln devoted much of his time to presidential politics—to unmaking one president, a Democrat, and making another, a Whig. He found an issue and a candidate in the Mexican War. With his "spot resolutions," he challenged the statement of Pres. James K. Polk that Mexico had started the war by shedding American blood on American soil. Along with other members of his party, Lincoln voted to condemn Polk and the war while also voting for supplies to carry it on. At the same time, he laboured for the nomination and election of the war hero Zachary Taylor.

After Taylor's success at the polls, Lincoln expected to be named commissioner of the general land office as a reward for his campaign services. He was bitterly disappointed when he failed to get the job. His criticisms of the war, meanwhile, had not been popular among the voters in his own congressional district. At the age of 40, frustrated in politics, he seemed to be at the end of his public career.

THE ROAD TO THE PRESIDENCY

For about five years Lincoln took little part in politics, and then a new sectional crisis gave him a chance to reemerge and rise to statesmanship. In 1854 his political rival Stephen A. Douglas maneuvered through Congress a bill for reopening the entire Louisiana Purchase to slavery and allowing the settlers of Kansas and Nebraska (with "popular sovereignty") to decide for themselves whether to permit slaveholding in those territories. The Kansas-Nebraska Act provoked violent opposition in Illinois and the other states of the old Northwest. It gave rise to the Republican Party while speeding the Whig Party on its way to disintegration. Along with many thousands of other homeless Whigs, Lincoln soon became a Republican (1856). Before long, some prominent Republicans in the East talked of attracting Douglas to the Republican fold, and with him his Democratic following in the West. Lincoln would have none of it. He was determined that he, not Douglas, should be the Republican leader of his state and section.

Lincoln challenged the incumbent Douglas for the Senate seat in 1858, and the series of debates they engaged in throughout Illinois was political oratory of the highest order. Both men were shrewd debaters and accomplished stump speakers, though they could hardly have been more different in style and appearance—the short and pudgy

Douglas, whose stentorian voice and graceful gestures swayed audiences, versus the tall, homely, almost emaciated-looking Lincoln, who moved awkwardly and whose voice was piercing and shrill. Lincoln's prose and speeches, however, were eloquent, pithy, powerful, and free of the verbosity so common in communication of his day. The debates were published in 1860, together with a biography of Lincoln, in a best-selling book that Lincoln himself compiled and marketed as part of his campaign.

In their basic views, Lincoln and Douglas were not as far apart as they seemed in the heat of political argument. Neither was abolitionist or pro-slavery. But Lincoln, unlike Douglas, insisted that Congress must exclude slavery from the territories. He disagreed with Douglas's belief that the territories were by nature unsuited to the slave economy and that no congressional legislation was needed to prevent the spread of slavery into them. In one of his most famous speeches, he said: "A house divided against itself cannot stand. I believe the government cannot endure permanently half slave and half free." He predicted that the country eventually would become "all one thing, or all the other." Again and again he insisted that the civil liberties of every U.S. citizen, white as well as black, were at stake. The territories must be kept free, he further said, because "new free states" were "places for poor people to go and better their condition."

He agreed with Thomas Jefferson and other founding fathers, however, that slavery should be merely contained, not directly attacked. In fact, when it was politically expedient to do so, he reassured his audiences that he did not endorse citizenship for blacks or believe in the equality of the races. "I am not, nor ever have been, in favour of bringing about in any way the social and political equality of the white and black races," he told a crowd in Charleston, Illinois. "I am not nor ever have been in favour of making voters or jurors of Negroes, nor of qualifying them to hold office, nor to intermarry with white people." There is, he added, "a physical difference between the white and black races which I believe will forever forbid the two races living together on terms of social and political equality." Lincoln drove home the inconsistency between Douglas's "popular sovereignty" principle and the Dred Scott decision (1857), in which the U.S. Supreme Court held that Congress could not constitutionally exclude slavery from the territories.

In the end, Lincoln lost the election to Douglas. Although the outcome did not surprise him, it depressed him deeply. Lincoln had, nevertheless, gained national recognition and soon began to be mentioned as a presidential prospect for 1860.

On May 18, 1860, after Lincoln and his friends had made skillful preparations, he was nominated on the third

Election poster of the Abraham Lincoln and Hannibal Hamlin, campaign of 1860, lithograph. Library of Congress, Washington, D.C.

ballot at the Republican National Convention in Chicago. He then put aside his law practice and, though making no stump speeches, gave full time to the direction of his campaign. His "main object," he had written, was to "hedge against divisions in the Republican ranks," and he counseled party workers to "say nothing on points where it is probable we shall disagree."

With the Republicans united, the Democrats divided, and a total of four candidates in the field, Lincoln carried the election on November 6. Although he received no votes from the Deep South and no more than 40 out of 100 in the country as a whole, the popular votes were so distributed that he won a clear and decisive majority in the electoral college.

U.S. President Abraham Lincoln (seated centre) and his cabinet, with Lieutenant General Winfield Scott, in the council chamber at the White House, lithograph, 1866. Library of Congress, Washington, D.C.

President Lincoln

After Lincoln's election and before his inauguration, the state of South Carolina proclaimed its withdrawal from the Union. To forestall similar action by other Southern states, various compromises were proposed in Congress. The most important, the Crittenden Compromise, included constitutional amendments guaranteeing slavery forever in the states where it already existed and dividing the territories between slavery and freedom. Although Lincoln had no objection to the first of these amendments, he was unalterably opposed to the second and indeed to any scheme infringing in the slightest on the free-soil plank of his party's platform. "I am inflexible," he privately wrote. He feared that a territorial division, by sanctioning the principle of slavery extension, would only encourage planter imperialists to seek new slave territory south of the American border and thus would "put us again on the high-road to a slave empire." From his home in Springfield he advised Republicans in Congress to vote against a division of the territories, and the proposal was killed in committee. Six additional states then seceded and, with South Carolina, combined to form the Confederate States of America.

Thus, before Lincoln had even moved into the White House, a disunion crisis was upon the country. Attention, by the North and South, focused in particular upon Fort Sumter, in Charleston Harbor, South Carolina. This fort, still under construction, was garrisoned by U.S. troops under Major Robert Anderson. The Confederacy claimed it and, from other harbour fortifications, threatened it. Foreseeing trouble, Lincoln, while still in Springfield, confidentially requested Winfield Scott, general in chief of the U.S. Army, to be prepared "to either hold, or retake, the forts, as the case may require, at, and after, the inauguration."

In his inaugural address (March 4, 1861), besides upholding the Union's indestructibility and appealing for sectional harmony, Lincoln restated his Sumter policy as follows:

> *The power confided to me, will be used to hold, occupy, and possess the property, and places belonging to the government, and to collect the duties and imposts; but beyond what may be necessary for these objects, there will be no invasion—no using of force against, or among the people anywhere.*

Then, near the end, addressing the absent Southerners, he said, "You can have no conflict, without being yourselves the aggressors."

OUTBREAK OF WAR

No sooner was he in office than Lincoln received word that the Sumter garrison, unless supplied or withdrawn, would shortly be starved out. Still, for about a month, Lincoln delayed acting. He was beset by contradictory advice. On the one hand, General Scott, Secretary of State William H. Seward, and others urged him to abandon the fort. Additionally, Seward, through a go-between, gave a group of Confederate commissioners to understand that the fort would in fact be abandoned. On the other hand, many Republicans insisted that any show of weakness would bring disaster to their party and to the Union. Finally Lincoln ordered the preparation of two relief expeditions, one for Fort Sumter and the other for Fort Pickens, in Florida. (He afterward said he would have been willing to withdraw from Sumter if he could have been sure of holding Pickens.) Before the Sumter expedition, he sent a messenger to tell the South Carolina governor:

> *I am directed by the President of the United States to notify you to expect an attempt will be made to supply Fort-Sumpter* [sic] *with provisions only; and that, if such attempt be not resisted, no effort to throw in men, arms, or ammunition, will be made, without further notice, or in case of an attack upon the Fort.*

Without waiting for the arrival of Lincoln's expedition, the Confederate authorities presented to Major Anderson a demand for Sumter's prompt evacuation, which he refused. On April 12, 1861, at dawn, the Confederate batteries in the harbour opened fire.

"Then, and thereby," Lincoln informed Congress when it met on July 4, "the assailants of the Government, began the conflict of arms." The Confederates, however, accused him of being the real aggressor. They said he had cleverly maneuvered them into firing the first shot so as to put upon them the onus of war guilt. Although some historians have repeated this charge, it appears to be a gross distortion of the facts. Lincoln was determined to preserve the Union, and to do so he thought he must take a stand against the Confederacy. He concluded he might as well take this stand at Sumter.

Lincoln's primary aim was neither to provoke war nor to maintain peace. In preserving the Union, he would have been glad to preserve the peace also, but he was ready to risk a war that he thought would be short.

After the firing on Fort Sumter, Lincoln called upon the state governors for troops. (Virginia and three other states of the upper South responded by joining the Confederacy). He then proclaimed a blockade of the Southern ports. These steps—the Sumter expedition, the call for volunteers, and the blockade—were the first important decisions of Lincoln as commander in chief of the army and navy. But he still needed a strategic plan and a command system for carrying it out.

General Scott advised him to avoid battle with the Confederate forces in Virginia, to get control of the Mississippi River, and, by tightening the blockade, hold the South in a gigantic squeeze. Lincoln had little confidence in Scott's comparatively passive and bloodless "Anaconda" plan. He believed the war must be actively fought if it ever was to be won. Overruling Scott, he ordered a direct advance on the Virginia front, which resulted in defeat and rout for the federal forces at Bull Run (July 21, 1861). After a succession of more or less sleepless nights, Lincoln produced a set of memorandums on military policy. His basic thought was that the armies should advance concurrently on several fronts and should move so as to hold and use the support of Unionists in Missouri, Kentucky, western Virginia, and eastern Tennessee. As he later explained:

> *I state my general idea of this war to be that we have the greater numbers, and the enemy has the greater facility of concentrating forces upon points of collision; that we must fail, unless we can find some way of making our advantage an over-match for his; and that this can only be done by menacing him with superior forces at different points, at the same time.*

This, with the naval blockade, comprised the essence of Lincoln's strategy.

Leadership in War

As a war leader, Lincoln employed the style that had served him as a politician—a description of himself, incidentally, that he was not ashamed to accept. He preferred to react to problems and to the circumstances that others had created rather than to originate policies and lay out long-range designs. In candour he would write, "I claim not to have controlled events, but confess plainly that events have controlled me." His guiding rule was, "My policy is to have no policy." It was not that he was unprincipled; rather, he was a practical man, mentally nimble and flexible, and, if one action or decision proved unsatisfactory in practice, he was willing to experiment with another.

From 1861 to 1864, while hesitating to impose his ideas upon his generals, Lincoln experimented with command personnel and organization. Accepting the resignation of Scott (November 1861), he put George B. McClellan in charge of the armies as a whole. After a few months, disgusted by the slowness of McClellan ("He has the slows," as Lincoln put it), he demoted him to the command of the Army of the Potomac alone. He questioned the soundness of McClellan's plans for the Peninsular Campaign, repeatedly compelled McClellan to alter them, and, after the Seven Days' Battles to capture Richmond, Virginia (June 25–July 1, 1862), failed, ordered him to give them up. Then he tried a succession of commanders for the army in Virginia —John Pope, McClellan again, Ambrose E. Burnside, Joseph Hooker, and George Gordon Meade—but was disappointed with each of them in turn. Meanwhile, he had in Henry W. Halleck a general in chief who gave advice and served as a liaison with field officers but who shrank from making important decisions.

For nearly two years the Federal armies lacked effective unity of command. President Lincoln, General Halleck, and War Secretary Edwin M. Stanton acted as an informal council of war. Lincoln, besides transmitting official orders through Halleck, also communicated directly with the generals, sending personal suggestions in his own name.

To generals opposing Robert E. Lee, he suggested that the object was to destroy Lee's army, not to capture Richmond or to drive the invader from Northern soil.

Finally Lincoln looked to the West for a top general. He admired the Vicksburg Campaign of Ulysses S. Grant in Mississippi. Nine days after the Vicksburg surrender (which occurred on July 4, 1863), he sent Grant a "grateful acknowledgment for the almost inestimable service" he had done the country. Lincoln sent also an admission of his own error. He said he had expected Grant to bypass Vicksburg and go on down the Mississippi, instead of crossing the river and turning back to approach Vicksburg from the rear. "I feared it was a mistake," he wrote in his letter of congratulations. "I now wish to make the personal acknowledgment that you were right, and I was wrong."

In March 1864 Lincoln promoted Grant to lieutenant general and gave him command of all the federal armies. At last Lincoln had found a man who, with such able subordinates as William T. Sherman, Philip Sheridan, and George H. Thomas, could put into effect those parts of Lincoln's concept of a large-scale, coordinated offensive that still remained to be carried out. Grant was only a member, though an important one, of a top-command arrangement that Lincoln eventually had devised. Overseeing everything was Lincoln himself, the commander in chief. Taking the responsibility for men and supplies was Secretary of War Stanton. Serving as a presidential adviser and as a liaison with military men was Halleck, the chief of staff. And directing all the armies, while accompanying Meade's Army of the Potomac, was Grant, the general in chief. Thus Lincoln pioneered in the creation of a high command, an organization for amassing all the energies and resources of a people in the grand strategy of total war. He combined statecraft and the overall direction of armies with an effectiveness that increased year by year. His achievement is all the more remarkable in view of his lack of training and experience in the art of warfare. This lack may have been an advantage as well as a handicap. Unhampered by outworn military dogma, Lincoln could all the better apply his practical insight and common sense—some would say his military genius—to the winning of the Civil War.

There can be no doubt of Lincoln's deep and sincere devotion to the cause of personal freedom. Before his election to the presidency he had spoken often and eloquently on the subject. In 1854, for example, he said he hated the Douglas attitude of indifference toward the possible spread of slavery to new areas. "I hate it because of the monstrous injustice of slavery itself," he declared. "I hate it because it deprives our republican example of its just influence in the world; enables the enemies of free institutions with plausibility to taunt us as hypocrites . . ." In 1855, writing to his friend Joshua Speed, he recalled a steamboat trip the two had taken on the Ohio River 14 years earlier. "You may remember, as I well do," he said, "that from Louisville [Kentucky] to the mouth of the Ohio there were, on board, ten or a dozen slaves, shackled together with irons. That sight was a continual torment to me; and I see something like it every time I touch the Ohio, or any other slave-border."

Yet, as president, Lincoln was at first reluctant to adopt an abolitionist policy. There were several reasons for his hesitancy. He had been elected on a platform pledging no interference with slavery within the states, and in any case he doubted the constitutionality of federal action under the circumstances. He was concerned about the possible difficulties of incorporating nearly four million African Americans, once they had been freed, into the nation's social and political life. Above all, he felt that he must hold the border slave states in the Union, and he feared that an abolitionist program might impel them, in particular his native Kentucky, toward the Confederacy. So he held back while others went ahead. When Gen. John C. Frémont and Gen. David Hunter, within their respective military departments, proclaimed freedom for the slaves of disloyal masters, Lincoln revoked the proclamations. When Congress passed confiscation acts in 1861 and 1862, he refrained from a full enforcement of the provisions authorizing him to seize slave property. And when Horace Greeley in the *New York Tribune* appealed to him to enforce these laws, Lincoln patiently replied (Aug. 22, 1862):

> *My paramount object in this struggle is to save the Union, and is not either to save or to destroy slavery. If I could save the Union without freeing any slave I would do it; and if I could save it by freeing all the slaves I would do it; and if I could save it by freeing some and leaving others alone, I would also do that.*

Meanwhile, in response to the rising antislavery sentiment, Lincoln came forth with an emancipation plan of his own. According to his proposal, the slaves were to be freed by state action, the slaveholders were to be compensated, the federal government was to share the financial burden, the emancipation process was to be gradual, and the freedmen were to be colonized abroad. Congress indicated its willingness to vote the necessary funds for the Lincoln plan, but none of the border slave states were willing to launch it, and in any case few African American leaders desired to see their people sent abroad.

While still hoping for the eventual success of his gradual plan, Lincoln took quite a different step by issuing his preliminary (Sept. 22, 1862) and his final (Jan. 1, 1863) Emancipation Proclamation. This famous decree, which he justified as an exercise of the president's war powers, applied only to those parts of the country actually under Confederate control, not to the loyal slave states nor to the federally occupied areas of the Confederacy. Directly or indirectly, the proclamation brought freedom during the war to fewer than 200,000 slaves. Yet it had great significance as a symbol. It indicated that the Lincoln government had added freedom to reunion as a war aim, and it attracted liberal opinion in England and Europe to increased support of the Union cause.

Lincoln himself doubted the constitutionality of his step, except as a temporary war measure. After the war, the slaves freed by the proclamation would have risked re-enslavement had nothing else been done to confirm their liberty. But something else was done: the Thirteenth Amendment was added to the Constitution, and Lincoln played a large part in bringing about this change in the fundamental law. Through the chairman of the Republican National Committee he urged the party to include a plank for such an amendment in its platform of 1864. The plank, as adopted, stated that slavery was the cause of the rebellion, that the president's proclamation had aimed "a death blow at this gigantic evil," and that a constitutional amendment was necessary to "terminate and forever prohibit" it.

When Lincoln was reelected on this platform and the Republican majority in Congress was increased, he was justified in feeling, as he apparently did, that he had a mandate from the people for the Thirteenth Amendment. The newly chosen Congress, with its overwhelming Republican majority, was not to meet until after the lame duck session of the old Congress during the winter of 1864–65. Lincoln did not wait. Using his resources of patronage and persuasion upon certain of the Democrats, he managed to get the necessary two-thirds vote before the session's end. He rejoiced as the amendment went out to the states for ratification. His own Illinois led off the ratification, and other states followed one by one in acting favourably upon it.

Lincoln deserves his reputation as the Great Emancipator. His claim to that honour, if it rests uncertainly upon his famous proclamation, has a sound basis in the support he gave to the antislavery amendment. It is well founded also in his greatness as the war leader who carried the nation safely through the four-year struggle that brought freedom in its train. And, finally, it is strengthened by the practical demonstrations he gave of respect for human worth and dignity, regardless of colour. During the last two years of his life he welcomed African Americans as visitors and friends in a way no president had done before. One of his friends was the distinguished former slave Frederick Douglass, who once wrote, "In all my interviews with Mr. Lincoln I was impressed with his entire freedom from prejudice against the colored race."

Wartime Politics

To win the war, Lincoln had to have popular support. The reunion of North and South required, first of all, a certain degree of unity in the North. But the North contained various groups with special interests of their own. Lincoln faced the task of attracting to his administration the support of as many divergent groups and individuals as possible. Accordingly, he gave much of his time and attention to politics, which in one of its aspects is the art of attracting such support. Fortunately for the Union cause, he was a president with rare political skill. He had the knack of appealing to fellow politicians and talking to them in their own language. He had a talent for smoothing over personal differences and holding the loyalty of men antagonistic to one another. Inheriting the spoils system, he made good use of it, disposing of government jobs in such a way as to strengthen his administration and further its official aims.

The opposition party remained alive and strong. Its membership included war Democrats and peace Democrats, often called "Copperheads," a few of whom collaborated with the enemy. Lincoln did what he could to cultivate the assistance of the war Democrats, as in securing from Congress the timely approval of the Thirteenth Amendment. So far as feasible, he conciliated the peace Democrats. He heeded the complaints of one of them, Governor Horatio Seymour of New York, in regard to the draft quota for that state. He commuted the prison sentence of another, Congressman Clement L. Vallandigham of Ohio, to banishment within the Confederate lines. In dealing with those suspected of treasonable intent, Lincoln at times authorized his generals to make arbitrary arrests. He justified this action on the ground that he had to allow some temporary sacrifice of parts of the Constitution in order to maintain the Union and thus preserve the Constitution as a whole. He let his generals suspend several newspapers, but only for short periods, and he promptly revoked a military order suppressing the hostile *Chicago Times*. In a letter to one of his generals he expressed his policy thus:

> *You will only arrest individuals and suppress assemblies or newspapers when they may be working palpable injury to the military in your charge, and in no other case will you interfere with the expression of opinion in any form or allow it to be interfered with violently by others. In this you have a discretion to exercise with great caution, calmness, and forbearance.*

Considering the dangers and provocations of the time, Lincoln was quite liberal in his treatment of political opponents and the opposition press. He was by no means the dictator critics often accused him of being. Nevertheless, his abrogating of civil liberties, especially his suspension of the privilege of the writ of habeas corpus, disturbed Democrats,

Republicans, and even members of his own cabinet. In the opinion of a soldier from Massachusetts, the president, "without the people having any legal means to prevent it, is only prevented from exercising a Russian despotism by the fear he may have of shocking too much the sense of decency of the whole world." Even Lincoln's friend Orville Hickman Browning believed the arrests ordered by the president were "illegal and arbitrary, and did more harm than good, weakening instead of strengthening the government." Yet Lincoln defended his actions, arguing that the Constitution provided for the suspension of such liberties "in cases of Rebellion or Invasion, [when] the public Safety may require it." Moreover, posed Lincoln with rhetorical flare, "Must I shoot a simpleminded soldier boy who deserts" and "not touch a hair of a wilely agitator who induces him to desert?"

Within his own party, Lincoln confronted factional divisions and personal rivalries that caused him as much trouble as did the activities of the Democrats. True, he and most of his fellow partisans agreed fairly well upon their principal economic aims. With his approval, the Republicans enacted into law the essentials of the program he had advocated from his early Whig days—a protective tariff, a national banking system, and federal aid for internal improvements, in particular for the construction of a railroad to the Pacific Coast. The Republicans disagreed among themselves, however, on many matters regarding the conduct and purposes of the war. Two main factions arose: the "Radicals" and the "Conservatives." Lincoln himself inclined in spirit toward the Conservatives, but he had friends among the Radicals as well, and he strove to maintain his leadership over both. In appointing his cabinet, he chose his several rivals for the 1860 nomination and, all together, gave representation to every important party group. Wisely he included the outstanding Conservative, Seward, and the outstanding Radical, Salmon P. Chase. Cleverly he overcame cabinet crises and kept these two opposites among his official advisers until Chase's resignation in 1864.

Lincoln had to deal with even more serious factional uprisings in Congress. The big issue was the "reconstruction" of the South. The seceded states of Louisiana, Arkansas, and Tennessee having been largely recovered by the federal armies, Lincoln, late in 1863, proposed his "10 percent plan," according to which new state governments might be formed when 10 percent of the qualified voters had taken an oath of future loyalty to the United States. The Radicals rejected Lincoln's proposal as too lenient, and they carried through Congress the Wade-Davis Bill, which would have permitted the remaking and readmission of states only after a majority had taken the loyalty oath. When Lincoln pocket-vetoed that bill, its authors published a "manifesto" denouncing him.

Lincoln was already the candidate of the "Union" (that is, the Republican) party for reelection to the presidency, and the Wade-Davis manifesto signaled a movement within the party to displace him as the party's nominee. He waited quietly and patiently for the movement to collapse, but even after it had done so, the party remained badly divided. A rival Republican candidate, John C. Frémont, nominated much earlier by a splinter group, was still in the field. Leading Radicals promised to procure Frémont's withdrawal if Lincoln would obtain the resignation of his conservative postmaster general, Montgomery Blair. Eventually Frémont withdrew and Blair resigned. The party was reunited in time for the election.

In 1864, as in 1860, Lincoln was the chief strategist of his own electoral campaign. He took a hand in the management of the Republican Speakers' Bureau, advised state committees on campaign tactics, hired and fired government employees to strengthen party support, and did his best to enable as many soldiers and sailors as possible to vote. Most of the citizens in uniform voted Republican. He was reelected with a large popular majority (55 percent) over his Democratic opponent, Gen. George B. McClellan.

In 1864 the Democratic platform called for an armistice and a peace conference, and prominent Republicans as well as Democrats demanded that Lincoln heed Confederate peace offers, irregular and illusory though they were. In a public letter, he stated his own conditions:

> *Any proposition which embraces the restoration of peace, the integrity of the whole Union, and the abandonment of slavery, and which comes by and with an authority that can control the armies now at war against the United states will be received and considered by the Executive government of the United States, and will be met by liberal terms on other substantial and collateral points.*

When Conservatives protested to him against the implication that the war must go on to free the slaves, even after reunion had been won, he explained, "To me it seems plain that saying reunion and abandonment of slavery would be considered, if offered, is not saying that nothing else or less would be considered, if offered." After his reelection, in his annual message to Congress, he said, "In stating a single condition of peace, I mean simply to say that the war will cease on the part of the government, whenever it shall have ceased on the part of those who began it." On Feb. 3, 1865, he met personally with Confederate commissioners on a steamship in Hampton Roads, Virginia. He promised to be liberal with pardons if the South would quit the war, but he insisted on reunion as a precondition for any peace arrangement.

In his Second Inaugural Address he embodied the spirit of his policy in the famous words "with malice toward none; with charity for all." His terms satisfied neither the Confederate leaders nor the Radical Republicans, and so no peace was possible until the final defeat of the Confederacy.

Postwar Policy

At the end of the war, Lincoln's policy for the defeated South was not clear in all its details, though he continued to believe that the main object should be to restore the "seceded States, so-called," to their "proper practical relation" with the Union as soon as possible. He possessed no fixed and uniform program for the region as a whole. As he said in the last public speech of his life (April 11, 1865), "so great peculiarities" pertained to each of the states, and "such important and sudden changes" occurred from time to time, and "so new and unprecedented" was the whole problem that "no exclusive and inflexible plan" could "safely be prescribed." With respect to states like Louisiana and Tennessee, he continued to urge acceptance of new governments set up under his 10 percent plan during the war. With respect to states like Virginia and North Carolina, he seemed willing to use the old rebel governments temporarily as a means of transition from war to peace. He was on record as opposing the appointment of "strangers" (carpetbaggers) to govern the South. He hoped that the Southerners themselves, in forming new state governments, would find some way by which whites and blacks "could gradually live themselves out of their old relation to each other, and both come out better prepared for the new." A program of education for the freedmen, he thought, was essential to preparing them for their new status. He also suggested that the vote be given immediately to some African Americans—"as, for instance, the very intelligent, and especially those who have fought gallantly in our ranks."

On the question of reconstruction, however, Lincoln and the extremists of his own party stood even farther apart in early 1865 than a year before. Some of the Radicals were beginning to demand a period of military occupation for the South, the confiscation of planter estates and their division among the freedmen, and the transfer of political power from the planters to their former slaves. In April 1865 Lincoln began to modify his own stand in some respects and thus to narrow the gap between himself and the Radicals. He recalled the permission he had given for the assembling of the rebel legislature of Virginia, and he approved in principle—or at least did not disapprove—Stanton's scheme for the military occupation of Southern states. After the cabinet meeting of April 14, Attorney General James Speed inferred that Lincoln was moving toward the radical position. "He never seemed so near our views," Speed believed. What Lincoln's

The assassination of U.S. Pres. Abraham Lincoln by John Wilkes Booth, *April 14, 1865; lithograph by Currier & Ives.* Library of Congress, Washington, D.C. (digital file no. 3b49830u)

reconstruction policy would have been, if he had lived to complete his second term, can only be guessed at.

On the evening of April 14, 1865, 26-year-old John Wilkes Booth—a rabid advocate of slavery with ties to the South and the flamboyant son of one of the most distinguished theatrical families of the 19th century—shot Lincoln as he sat in Ford's Theatre in Washington. Early the next morning Lincoln died.

Thomas Nast

(b. Sept. 27, 1840, Landau, Baden [Germany]—d. Dec. 7, 1902, Guayaquil, Ecua.)

Although cartoonist Thomas Nast is best known for his attack on the political machine of William M. Tweed in New York City in the 1870s, he had already made a name for himself before the outbreak of the Civil War, during which he vigorously supported the cause of the Union and opposed slavery from his drawing board at *Harper's Weekly*.

Nast's cartoons "After the Battle" (1862), attacking Northerners opposed to energetic prosecution of the war, and his "Emancipation" (1863), showing the evils of slavery and the benefits of its abolition, were so effective that Pres. Abraham Lincoln called him "our best recruiting sergeant." During Reconstruction, Nast's cartoons portrayed Pres. Andrew Johnson as a repressive autocrat and characterized Southerners as vicious exploiters of helpless blacks, revealing his bitter disappointment in postwar politics.

Eliza Emily Chappell Porter

(b. Nov. 5, 1807, Geneseo, N.Y.—d. Jan. 1, 1888, Santa Barbara, Calif.)

Educator and welfare worker Eliza Emily Chappell Porter served as director of the Chicago Sanitary Commission (1861–62, and briefly in 1863; later the Northwestern Sanitary Commission), which was organized to solicit, collect, and distribute food, medical supplies, and other provisions for use by the Union army and in military hospitals. Porter abandoned office work for field service in 1862. She escorted a group of women volunteers to Cairo, Ill., and there and in nearby Mound City she helped organize hospitals and direct the work of caring for the large number of casualties from the Battle of Shiloh (Pittsburg Landing).

After recruiting more volunteer nurses, she assisted in hospitals in Savannah, Georgia, and Memphis, Tennessee. In the latter city, she also established a school for African American children. She then visited and distributed supplies to several hospitals before joining "Mother" Mary Ann Bickerdyke in Chattanooga, Tennessee, to care for the Union soldiers wounded in Gen. W.T. Sherman's march to Atlanta, Ga. Throughout the Civil War and afterward, Porter was involved with hospital inspection.

William H. Seward

(b. May 16, 1801, Florida, N.Y.—d. Oct. 10, 1872, Auburn, N.Y.)

William H. Seward served as secretary of state during the Civil War and the first years of Reconstruction.

In 1828 Seward became active in the Antimasonic Party, serving in the New York Senate from 1830 to 1834. At about this time he allied himself with other opponents of the Jacksonian Democrats in forming the new Whig Party. Under this banner Seward served as governor of New York for four years (1839–43), soon becoming recognized as leader of the antislavery wing of the party.

In 1849 Seward was elected to the U.S. Senate, where the antagonism between free and slave labour became the theme of many of his speeches. During the turbulent 1850s he increasingly resisted the Whig attempt to compromise on the slavery issue. When the party collapsed (1854–55), Seward joined the newly organized Republican Party, which took a firm stand against expansion of slavery into the territories. Although Seward was the recognized Republican leader, he was twice thwarted (1856, 1860) in his wish to be nominated for the presidency.

When Abraham Lincoln took office as president on the eve of the Civil War (March 1861), he promptly named Seward secretary of state. On most issues he was Lincoln's closest and most influential adviser, despite early differences over the reinforcement of Ft. Sumter, S.C., and Seward's irresponsible suggestion that a foreign war be provoked to distract the country from its civil conflict at home. Seward gradually rose to the challenge of the office and was particularly successful in preventing foreign governments from giving official recognition to the Confederacy. While he did not succeed in preventing the French occupation of Mexico or the acquisition by the Confederacy of the warship *Alabama* from England, his diplomacy prepared the way for a satisfactory adjustment of the difficulties with these powers at a later date. Although a treaty in 1862 for the suppression of the slave trade conceded to England the right to search U.S. vessels for slaves in African and Cuban waters, he secured a similar concession for U.S. war vessels from the British government. By his course in the *Trent* Affair, concerning the capture and imprisonment of two Confederate agents from a British ship, he virtually committed Great Britain to the U.S. attitude concerning the right of search of vessels on the high seas.

On April 14, 1865, nine days after he was severely injured in a carriage accident, the bedridden Seward was stabbed in the throat by Lewis Powell (alias Lewis Payne), a fellow conspirator of John Wilkes Booth, who had that night assassinated Lincoln. Seward made a remarkable recovery and retained his Cabinet post under Pres. Andrew Johnson until 1869. He chose to support Johnson's unpopular Reconstruction policies and had to share some of the bitter congressional obloquy bestowed upon his chief. Seward's last act of public renown was the purchase of Alaska from Russia for $7.2 million in 1867, called "Seward's Folly" at the time.

Edwin M. Stanton

(b. Dec. 19, 1814, Steubenville, Ohio—d. Dec. 24, 1869, Washington, D.C.)

As secretary of war under President Lincoln, Edwin M. Stanton tirelessly presided over the giant Union military establishment during most of the Civil War.

A lawyer and staunch Democrat who grew steadily more outspoken in support of antislavery measures, Stanton was appointed attorney general by Pres. James Buchanan in December 1860. In that capacity, as tension accelerated between North and South, he opposed the abandonment of Fort Sumter in the Charleston, S.C., harbour by Union forces. Fearing the success of secessionist influences, he secretly advised Republican leaders of the Cabinet's proceedings. Although he was a caustic critic of President-elect Lincoln in this period, he was, nevertheless, made legal adviser to Lincoln's secretary of war, Simon Cameron. When Cameron resigned under fire less than a year later, Stanton accepted appointment as his successor (Jan. 13, 1862).

During the remainder of the Civil War, he proved an able, energetic administrator, despite his nervous, asthmatic constitution and cranky, contradictory temperament. Exceedingly patriotic and zealous in his honesty, he insisted on tighter management of his department, gave short shrift to patronage seekers, and continually pushed for a more aggressive prosecution of the war. He provoked violent quarrels with nearly every important federal military commander.

After the assassination of Lincoln (April 1865), Stanton played a leading role in the investigation and trial of the conspirators, and for a short time he virtually directed the conduct of government in the stricken capital. He agreed to continue in his post under Pres. Andrew Johnson and skillfully managed the demobilization of Union forces. Stanton was soon at loggerheads with Johnson, however, over the nature of Reconstruction policy toward the defeated South. The secretary of war used his position to foster stricter Reconstruction measures than the president desired; in addition Stanton acted as the secret representative, within the Cabinet, of the Radical Republicans in Congress, who were Johnson's bitter enemies. The situation finally became so untenable that Johnson tried to remove Stanton from office, but the stubborn secretary refused to be dismissed, claiming that the Tenure of Office Act—passed by the Radicals in Congress (1867) over the president's veto—protected his official position. Johnson's persistence resulted in his impeachment by an unsympathetic House of Representatives. When the Senate vote fell one short of conviction, Stanton had no alternative but to surrender his office (May 26, 1868) and return to private law practice. He died four days after his appointment to the U.S. Supreme Court by Pres. Ulysses S. Grant.

Clement L. Vallandigham

(b. July 29, 1820, Lisbon, Ohio—d. June 17, 1871, Lebanon, Ohio)

While a member of the U.S. House of Representatives representing Ohio (1857–63), Clement L. Vallandigham was adamant against the principles and policies of the newly formed Republican Party, particularly as they related to the slavery issue.

Of Southern ancestry, Vallandigham idealized the Southern way of life, and he assumed leadership of the faction of Midwest Democrats, called Copperheads, who opposed the prosecution of the war against the South—a war they viewed as beneficial only to Eastern interests. During the Civil

War, he bitterly attacked the administration of Pres. Abraham Lincoln, charging that it was destroying not only the Constitution but civil liberty as well. He also became commander of the secret, antiwar Knights of the Golden Circle (later Sons of Liberty). In 1863 he made vigorous speeches in Ohio against the war and the government, and consequently grew to be one of the most suspected and hated men in the North. He was arrested in May by military authorities for expressing treasonable sympathy with the enemy. Tried and found guilty by a military commission, he was sentenced to imprisonment. Soon afterward Lincoln commuted his sentence to banishment behind Confederate lines.

Bored with exile in the South, Vallandigham made his way to Canada, where he continued his campaign of harassment from across the border. In September 1863 the Ohio Peace Democrats nominated him in absentia for governor, but resounding Union military victories at Gettysburg and Vicksburg in July ensured his decisive defeat at the polls. He returned illegally to Ohio in 1864 and took an active part in that year's election campaign. He also wrote part of the national Democratic platform in which the war was denounced as a failure.

After the war Vallandigham criticized the Radical Reconstruction policy of the Republicans as both unconstitutional and tyrannical, but in 1870 he recognized the uselessness of further opposition and urged his party to emphasize financial issues instead.

Elizabeth L. Van Lew

(b. Oct. 17, 1818, Richmond, Va.—d. Sept. 25, 1900, Richmond)

The daughter of a prosperous family of Northern antecedents who held strong antislavery views, Elizabeth L. Van Lew stayed in Richmond, Va., during the Civil War and gathered important intelligence for the Union.

During the 1850s, under her influence, the family's domestic servants were freed. At the outbreak of the Civil War she remained firmly and publicly loyal to the United States. She made many visits to Union prisoners in Libby Prison in Richmond, Va, bringing in food, clothing, and other items and often carrying away military information that she was able to transmit to federal authorities. On occasion she hid escaped prisoners in her house.

In March 1864, following Gen. Hugh J. Kilpatrick's unsuccessful attempt to open Libby Prison during a cavalry raid on Richmond (a raid apparently planned in response to information gathered by Van Lew that the prisoners were soon to be moved farther south), she and her agents daringly spirited out of the city the body of Colonel Ulric Dahlgren, Kilpatrick's second-in-command and the son of Admiral John A.B. Dahlgren, who had been killed in the raid. His remains had suffered indignities at the hands of an outraged Richmond citizenry.

During the yearlong siege of Richmond and Petersburg in 1864–65, Van Lew performed invaluable services in intelligence gathering. Her assumed manner of mental aberration, which gained her the indulgent nickname of "Crazy Bet" around Richmond, enabled her to carry on unsuspected. Her contacts reached even into Jefferson Davis's home, where she had placed one of her former servants.

After the fall of Richmond in April 1865, Van Lew was personally thanked and given protection by Gen. Ulysses S. Grant.

Benjamin F. Wade

(b. Oct. 27, 1800, Springfield, Mass.—d. March 2, 1878, Jefferson, Ohio)

A U.S. senator from Ohio, Benjamin F. Wade was an outspoken opponent of slavery whose radical views brought him into conflict with Presidents Abraham Lincoln and Andrew Johnson.

Wade was first elected to the Senate in 1851 as a Whig. He was reelected to the Senate as a Republican in 1857 and 1863. In the Senate during the 1850s, Wade was an uncompromising foe of the extension of slavery and vigorously opposed the passage of the Kansas-Nebraska Act (1854). During the Civil War he took his stand with the Radical Republicans, a congressional group that favoured vigorous prosecution of the war, emancipation of the slaves, and severe punishment for the South. As chairman of the Joint Congressional Committee on the Conduct of the War, Wade played a prominent but controversial role in investigating all aspects of the Union military effort. In 1864, as cosponsor of the Wade-Davis Bill, which declared that reconstruction of the Southern state governments was a legislative rather than an executive concern, he came into direct conflict with President Lincoln.

When Andrew Johnson became president after Lincoln's assassination, Wade at first cooperated with him. But when Johnson made it clear that he favoured a lenient plan of reconstruction, Wade became his caustic critic. Elected president pro tempore of the Senate on March 2, 1867, Wade would have succeeded to the presidency had Johnson been removed by the Senate in the impeachment trial of May 1868. Certain of success, Wade actually began to select his cabinet. Johnson's acquittal bitterly disappointed him. When the Democratic majority in the Ohio legislature denied him a fourth senatorial term, Wade retired to his Ohio law practice in 1869.

Mary Edwards Walker

(b. Nov. 26, 1832, near Oswego, N.Y.—d. Feb. 21, 1919, Oswego)

American physician and reformer Mary Edwards Walker is thought to have been the only woman surgeon formally engaged for field duty during the Civil War.

At the outbreak of the war, Walker traveled to Washington, D.C., to offer her services. She worked as a volunteer nurse in the Patent Office Hospital there while attempting to gain a regular appointment to the army medical service. In 1862 Walker took time away from Washington to earn a degree from the New York Hygeio-Therapeutic College in New York City. In that year she began working in the field, and in September 1863 she was appointed assistant surgeon in the Army of the Cumberland by Gen. George H. Thomas.

Walker was apparently the only woman so engaged in the Civil War. She was assigned to the 52nd Ohio Regiment in Tennessee, and she quickly adopted standard officers' uniform, suitably modified. From April to August 1864, she was a prisoner in Richmond, Va. In October she was given a contract as "acting assistant surgeon," but she was assigned to a women's prison hospital and then to an orphanage.

She left government service in June 1865 and a short time later was awarded a Medal of Honor. She remains the only woman to have won the medal in wartime. Feminist organizations widely publicized Walker's Civil War service, but she became estranged from them over the years because of her growing eccentricity.

THURLOW WEED

(b. Nov. 15, 1797, Cairo, N.Y.—d. Nov. 22, 1882, New York, N.Y.)

After realizing that anti-Masonry was not a strong enough issue for a national party, journalist Thurlow Weed became active with the Whig Party organization, and his paper, the Albany Evening Journal, became a leading Whig organ.

Weed allied himself with William H. Seward, a leading New York Whig, and was influential in Seward's election as governor of the state (1838). When the Whig Party disintegrated, Weed joined the new Republican Party and helped manage Seward's unsuccessful campaign for the Republican presidential nomination in 1860. He eventually became a staunch supporter of Pres. Abraham Lincoln.

In 1861, Seward, then Lincoln's secretary of state, sent Weed as a special agent to England, where he was a propagandist for the United States. Following Lincoln's death (1865) and the rise of the Radical Republicans, Weed's influence in the Republican Party declined. In 1863 he sold his paper and retired from politics.

GIDEON WELLES

(b. July 1, 1802, Glastonbury, Conn.—d. Feb. 11, 1878, Hartford, Conn.)

Gideon Welles, who served as secretary of the navy under presidents Abraham Lincoln and Andrew Johnson, began his political career as a Jacksonian Democrat, but in 1854 he quit the Democrats and switched to the Republican Party. In 1856 he founded the *Hartford Evening Press*, one of the first Republican papers in New England, and wrote for it extensively.

In 1861 Lincoln made Welles secretary of the Navy, in part fulfilling a political obligation to put a New Englander in the Cabinet. Welles proved to be a highly competent administrator and a surprisingly keen military strategist. He quickly built a large and effective navy from a few ships and a force reduced by the departure of Confederate sympathizers. Undisturbed by criticism, he authorized the construction of ironclads, kept his department as free from graft as possible, and promoted officers of merit over those with great seniority. He was largely responsible for implementing the "Anaconda plan" of slowly squeezing the South into submission, and he effectively directed the naval blockade that isolated the South and severed it in half.

In 1869 Welles left the Cabinet, having completed the longest term as Navy secretary to that time. He then drifted from the Republican Party, backing the Liberal Republicans in 1872 and Democrat Samuel Tilden in 1876. He spent his final years writing magazine articles and a book, *Lincoln and Seward* (1874). Long after his death the *Diary of Gideon Welles*(1911) was published, a work highly regarded by historians for its insights into the people and events of the Civil War era.

Walt Whitman

(b. May 31, 1819, West Hills, Long Island, N.Y.—d. March 26, 1892, Camden, N.J.)

Poet, journalist, and essayist Walt Whitman, one of the towering figures of American literature, was deeply affected by the Civil War and wrote about it extensively.

Early in the war, Whitman's brother was wounded at Fredericksburg, and Whitman went there in 1862, staying some time in the camp, then taking a temporary post in the paymaster's office in Washington. He spent his spare time visiting wounded and dying soldiers in the Washington hospitals, spending his scanty salary on small gifts for Confederate and Union soldiers alike and offering his usual "cheer and magnetism" to try to alleviate some of the mental depression and bodily suffering he saw in the wards.

In May 1865 a collection of war poems entitled *Drum Taps* showed Whitman's readers a new kind of poetry, moving from the oratorical excitement with which he had greeted the falling-in and arming of the young men at the beginning of the Civil War to a disturbing awareness of what war really meant. "Beat! Beat! Drums!" echoed the bitterness of the Battle of Bull Run, and "Vigil Strange I Kept on the Field One Night" had a new awareness of suffering, no less effective for its quietly plangent quality.

The Sequel to Drum Taps, published in the autumn of 1865, contained Whitman's great elegy on Pres. Abraham Lincoln, "When Lilacs Last in the Dooryard Bloom'd." His horror at the death of democracy's first "great martyr chief " was matched by his revulsion from the barbarities of war. Whitman's prose descriptions of the Civil War, published later in *Specimen Days & Collect* (1882–83), are no less effective in their direct, moving simplicity.

Fernando Wood

(b. June 14, 1812, Philadelphia, Pa.—d. Feb. 14, 1881, Hot Springs, Ark.)

First elected mayor of New York City in 1854 (and reelected in 1856 and 1859), Fernando Wood was the leader of the Northern Peace Democrats during the Civil War.

In 1860 Wood led a pro-Southern delegation to the Democratic National Convention. As civil war loomed early in 1861, he called for New York City to secede and become a free city. Although he briefly supported Pres. Abraham Lincoln and the Northern war effort, by 1863 he was organizing the Peace Democrats (called "Copperheads" by Republicans) and demanding that the North negotiate an immediate end to the war.

Elected to Congress in 1862 and again from 1866 to 1880, Wood opposed Republican Reconstruction policies but generally supported Republican fiscal measures. His independence alienated fellow Democrats, and they refused to elect him speaker of the House in 1875. But in 1877 Wood was elected majority floor leader and made chairman of the Ways and Means Committee.

THE CONFEDERACY

Judah P. Benjamin

(b. Aug. 6, 1811, St. Croix, Virgin Islands—d. May 6, 1884, Paris, France)

Judah P. Benjamin held high offices in the government of the Confederate States of America. The first professing Jew elected to the U.S. Senate (1852; reelected 1858), he is said to have been the most prominent American Jew during the 19th century.

Born a British subject, Benjamin was taken from the British Virgin Islands to Charleston, S.C., in his early youth. A successful New Orleans lawyer, prosperous sugar planter, and organizer of the Illinois Central Railroad, he was elected to the Louisiana legislature in 1842 and the U.S. Senate in 1852. In the Senate Benjamin was noted for his pro-slavery speeches. After his state had seceded from the Union, he was appointed attorney general in the Confederate government (Feb. 21, 1861). Later that year he was named secretary of war by his friend Pres. Jefferson Davis.

It was charged that Benjamin's mismanagement of the war office led to several major military defeats, and he resigned. Davis promptly named him secretary of state (Feb. 7, 1862). Late in the war Benjamin enraged many white Southerners by urging that slaves be recruited into the Confederate Army and emancipated after their term of service. At the end of the Civil War Benjamin escaped to England.

John Wilkes Booth

(b. May 10, 1838, near Bel Air, Md.—d. April 26, 1865, near Port Royal, Va.)

Abraham Lincoln's assassin, John Wilkes Booth, was a member of one of the United States' most distinguished acting families of the 19th century. Booth early showed excellent theatrical potential but also exhibited an emotional instability and a driving egocentricity that made it difficult for him to accept his brother Edwin's rise to acclaim as the foremost actor of the day. After an unsuccessful Baltimore theatrical debut in 1856, John was widely acclaimed on a tour of the Deep South in 1860 and remained in demand as an actor throughout the Civil War.

A vigorous supporter of the Southern cause, Booth was outspoken in his advocacy of slavery and his hatred of Lincoln. He was a volunteer in the Richmond militia that hanged the abolitionist John Brown in 1859. By the autumn of 1864 Booth had begun to plan a sensational abduction of President Lincoln. He recruited several coconspirators, and throughout the winter of 1864–65, the group gathered frequently in Washington, D.C., where they mapped out a number of alternative abduction plans. After several attempts had miscarried, Booth resolved to destroy the president and his officers no matter what the cost.

On the morning of April 14, 1865, he learned that the president was to attend an evening performance of the comedy *Our American Cousin* at Ford's Theatre in the capital. Booth hurriedly assembled his band and assigned each member his task, including the murder of Secretary of State William Seward. He himself would kill Lincoln. About 6 PM, Booth entered the deserted theatre, where he tampered with the outer door of the presidential box so that it could be jammed shut from the inside.

He returned during the play's third act to find Lincoln and his guests unguarded. Entering the box, Booth drew a pistol and shot Lincoln through the back of the head. He grappled briefly with a patron, swung himself over the balustrade, and leaped off it, reportedly shouting, "Sic semper tyrannis!" (the motto of the state of Virginia, meaning "Thus always to tyrants!") and "The South is avenged!" He landed heavily on the stage, breaking a bone in his left leg, but was able to make his escape to the alleyway and his horse. The attempt on Seward's life failed, but Lincoln died shortly after seven o'clock the following morning.

Eleven days later, on April 26, Federal troops arrived at a farm in Virginia, just south of the Rappahannock River, where a man said to be Booth was hiding in a tobacco barn. David Herold, another conspirator, was in the barn with Booth. He gave himself up before the barn was set afire, but Booth refused to surrender. After being shot, either by a soldier or by himself, Booth was carried to the porch of the farmhouse, where he subsequently died. The body was identified by a doctor who had operated on Booth the year before, and was then secretly buried, though four years later it was reinterred. There is no acceptable evidence to support the rumours, current at the time, doubting that the man who had been killed was actually Booth.

Belle Boyd

(b. May 9, 1844, Martinsburg, Va. [now W.Va.]—d. June 11, 1900, Kilbourne [now Wisconsin Dells], Wis.)

When her hometown, Martinsburg, Va., was occupied by Union forces in July 1861, Belle Boyd associated freely with officers, gleaning bits of military information that she sent by messenger to Confederate authorities.

Boyd and her mother denied entry to Union soldiers who wanted to raise a flag over their house in Martinsburg. When one of the soldiers tried to force his way in, Boyd shot and killed him. She was tried and was acquitted on a defense of justifiable homicide. Union officers under the command of Gen. James Shields were quartered in the same residence as Boyd in Front Royal, and Boyd overheard their plans for a withdrawal from that town. She undertook a hazardous journey through the lines to inform Gen. Thomas J. "Stonewall" Jackson of the Union plans to destroy the town's bridges as part of their retreat. This was the only major success she is known to have had as a Confederate spy. After her return to Martinsburg, Boyd continued to spy openly for the Confederacy and served also as a courier and scout with J.S. Mosby's guerrillas.

In 1862 Boyd was arrested on a warrant signed by U.S. Secretary of War Edwin Stanton. She was eventually released as part of an exchange of prisoners. Arrested again after her return to Union-held Martinsburg, Boyd was again released, in 1863, after a bout with typhoid fever in prison. Her usefulness in the North at an end, she was thenceforth employed as a courier.

In 1864 she sailed on a blockade runner to England bearing letters from Confederate president Jefferson Davis. After her ship was intercepted by a Union vessel, she utterly distracted an officer named Hardinge who was placed

Belle Boyd. Library of Congress, Washington, D.C. (neg. no. LC BH 82 4864A)

aboard as prize master. He allowed the Confederate captain of the vessel to escape, and for that was court-martialed and discharged from the navy, after which he went to England, where he married Boyd in August 1864. After he died early in 1865, she published her two-volume memoir, *Belle Boyd in Camp and Prison*.

Mary Boykin Miller Chesnut

(b. March 31, 1823, Pleasant Hill, S.C.—d. Nov. 22, 1886, Camden, S.C.)

Mary Boykin Miller Chesnut was the author of *A Diary from Dixie*, an insightful view of Southern life and leadership during the Civil War.

The daughter of a prominent South Carolina politician and the wife a one-time U.S. senator who served as an aide to Gen. P. G. T. Beauregard and as the commanding general of the South Carolina reserves, Chesnut accompanied her husband on his military missions during the Civil War. She began recording her views and observations on Feb. 15, 1861, and closed her diary on Aug. 2, 1865. After the war she reworked her manuscript many times in anticipation of publication. But *A Diary from Dixie* was not published until 1905, long after her death. Although not a day-by-day account, *A Diary* is regarded highly by historians for its perceptive views of Confederate military and political leaders and for its insight into Southern society during the Civil War.

Howell Cobb

(b. Sept. 7, 1815, Jefferson County, Ga.—d. Oct. 9, 1868, New York City)

Georgia politician Howell Cobb championed Southern unionism during the 1850s but then advocated immediate secession following the election of Abraham Lincoln.

Cobb served in Congress from 1842 to 1851 and again from 1855 to 1857; he supported the annexation of Texas, the war with Mexico, and the extension of slavery into the territories. But he broke with the most extreme pro-slavery Southerners when he advocated extending the Missouri Compromise line to the Pacific, opposed the creation of a sectional political party, and supported the Compromise of 1850.

In 1851 Cobb ran for governor of Georgia on the ticket of the newly formed Constitutional Union Party and won a solid victory over a pro-secession candidate. In so doing, he severed all ties with pro-secessionist Democrats, became politically isolated, and was overwhelmingly defeated when he ran for a seat in the U.S. Senate in 1854. His pro-Union district returned Cobb to Congress in 1855, and the following year he played a major role in the nomination and election of James Buchanan as president. Buchanan made Cobb secretary of the treasury, a position Cobb held until Lincoln was elected president in 1860.

Immediately following Lincoln's election, Cobb resigned his Cabinet post, returned to Georgia, and became an ardent spokesman for secession. He served as chairman of the Montgomery, Ala., convention called to organize the Confederacy, then organized his own regiment and led it to the front. He eventually rose to the rank of major general and commanded the District of Georgia until forced to surrender at the end of the war.

A bitter opponent of Reconstruction, Cobb in his last years practiced law in Macon, Ga.

Howell Cobb. Library of Congress, Washington, D.C.

JEFFERSON DAVIS

(b. June 3, 1808, Christian county, Ky.—d. Dec. 6, 1889, New Orleans, La.)

Jefferson Davis served as the president of the Confederacy throughout its existence during the Civil War.

Davis was the 10th and last child of a Georgia-born planter of Welsh ancestry. He graduated from the U.S. Military Academy at West Point, N.Y. (1828), and served as a lieutenant in the Wisconsin Territory and later in the Black Hawk War. In 1835 he became a planter in Mississippi. Elected to the U.S. House of Representatives (1845–46), he resigned to serve in the war with Mexico as colonel in command of the First Mississippi volunteers. He became a national hero for winning the Battle of Buena Vista (1847) with tactics that won plaudits even in the European press. After returning, severely wounded, he entered the Senate and soon became chairman of the Military Affairs Committee. Pres. Franklin Pierce made him secretary of war in 1853. Davis enlarged the army, strengthened coastal defenses, and directed three surveys for railroads to the Pacific.

During the period of mounting intersectional strife, Davis spoke widely in both North and South, urging harmony between the sections. When South Carolina withdrew from the Union in December 1860, Davis still opposed secession, though he believed that the Constitution gave a state the right to withdraw from the original compact of states. He was among those who believed that the newly elected president, Abraham Lincoln, would coerce the South and that the result would be disastrous.

President of the Confederacy

On Jan. 21, 1861, twelve days after Mississippi seceded, Davis made a moving farewell speech in the Senate and pleaded eloquently for peace. Before he reached his Brierfield plantation, he was commissioned major general to head Mississippi's armed forces and prepare its defense. But within two weeks the Confederate Convention in Montgomery, Ala., chose him as provisional president of the Confederacy. He was inaugurated on Feb. 18, 1861, and his first act was to send a peace commission to Washington, D.C., to prevent an armed conflict. Lincoln refused to see his emissaries and the next month the president sent armed ships to Charleston, S. C., to resupply the beleaguered Union garrison at Fort Sumter. Davis reluctantly ordered the bombardment of the fort (April 12–13), which marked the beginning of the Civil War. Two days later Lincoln called for 75,000 volunteers, a move that brought about the secession of Virginia and three other states from the Union.

Davis faced a dire crisis. A president without precedent, he had to mold a brand-new nation in the midst of a war. With only one-fourth the white population of the Northern states, a small fraction of the North's manufacturing capacity, and inferior railroads, no navy, no powder mills, no shipyard, and an appalling lack of arms and equipment, the South was in poor condition to withstand invasion. Its only resources seemed to be cotton and courage. But at Bull Run (Manassas, Va.), on July 21, 1861, the Confederates routed Union forces. In the meantime, with makeshift materials, Davis created factories for producing powder, cannon, side arms, and quartermaster stores. In restored naval yards gunboats were constructed, and the South's inadequate railroads and rolling stock were patched up repeatedly. Davis sent agents to Europe to buy arms and ammunition, and he dispatched representatives to try to secure recognition from England and France.

Davis made the inspired choice of Robert E. Lee as commander of the Army of Northern Virginia in June 1862. While Davis's military judgment was occasionally at fault, he wisely gave Lee wide scope in conducting the war over the next three years. Perhaps Davis's most serious mistake as commander in chief was the excessive importance he attached to defending the Confederate capital at Richmond, Va., at the expense of operations farther west, including the defense of the key Confederate fortress at Vicksburg, Miss.

Davis had innumerable troubles during his presidency, including a squabbling Congress, a dissident vice president, and the constant opposition of extreme states-rights advocates, who objected vigorously to the conscription law he had enacted over much opposition in 1862. But despite a gradually worsening military situation, unrelieved internal political tensions, continuing lack of manpower and armament, and skyrocketing inflation, he remained resolute in his determination to carry on the war.

Capture and Imprisonment

When Lee surrendered to the North without Davis's approval, Davis and his cabinet moved south, hoping to reach the trans-Mississippi area and continue the struggle until better terms could be secured from the North. At dawn on May 10, 1865, Davis was captured near Irwinville, Ga. He was imprisoned in a damp casemate at Fort Monroe, Va., and was put in leg irons. Though outraged Northern public opinion brought about his removal to healthier quarters, Davis remained a prisoner under guard for two more years. Finally, in May 1867, he was released on bail and went to Canada to regain his shattered health. Several notable Northern lawyers offered their free services to defend him in a treason trial, for which Davis longed. The government, however, never forced the issue, many believe because it feared that such a trial might establish that the original Constitution gave the states a right to secede. The case was finally dropped on Dec. 25, 1868.

In 1877 Davis retired to Beauvoir, a small Gulf-side estate near Biloxi, Miss. There he wrote his *Rise and Fall of the Confederate Government*. Though pressed to enter the U.S. Senate, he declined to "ask for amnesty," for he felt he had done nothing wrong in fighting for states' rights under the Constitution, and he never regained his citizenship. He remained the chief spokesman and apologist for the defeated South. Davis' citizenship was restored posthumously in 1978.

Though dedicated to the principles of democracy, Davis was by nature a benevolent aristocrat. He was diplomatic to a degree, but he did not possess the pliancy of the professional politician. His sensitivity to criticism stood in stark contrast to the single-minded imperturbability with which his greater counterpart, Abraham Lincoln, pursued his own war aims. Davis died in 1889 in New Orleans of a complicated bronchial ailment. At his temporary interment he was accorded the greatest funeral the South had ever known. On May 31, 1893, he was buried permanently in Hollywood Cemetery in Richmond.

Rose O'Neal Greenhow

(b. *c.* 1815, probably Montgomery county, Md.—d. Oct. 1, 1864, near Wilmington, N.C.)

Rose O'Neal Greenhow used her social position as a leading hostess in Washington, D.C., and her shrewd judgment to cloak her espionage for the Confederacy during the Civil War.

Greenhow was a confidante of several powerful political figures, notably John C. Calhoun and James Buchanan. After her husband's death in 1854, she returned to Washington, D.C., from Mexico City. Although she was a Southerner who had long been staunchly pro-slavery, she remained in Washington, D.C. after the outbreak of the Civil War. She was soon recruited as a Confederate spy.

Rose O'Neal Greenhow. Library of Congress, Washington, D.C. (neg. no. LC BH82 4513)

In July 1861 Greenhow secured and forwarded information about the movements of Gen. Irvin McDowell's army toward Manassas Junction, Virginia. In August she was arrested by Allan Pinkerton, head of the Union secret service, and confined to her home. She somehow managed to continue sending information from there and, after her incarceration in January 1862, even from Old Capitol Prison. In March she was examined by a War Department commission, and in June she was exiled south. Greeted as a heroine in the Confederacy, she was handsomely rewarded by Pres. Jefferson Davis.

In August 1863 Greenhow sailed for Europe as an unofficial agent of the Confederacy, and later that year she published her prison diary, *My Imprisonment and the First Year of Abolition Rule* at Washington. On Oct. 1, 1864, weighed down by gold sovereigns, she drowned upon the sinking of a small boat in which she was attempting to run the federal blockade of Wilmington, N.C.

Paul Hamilton Hayne

(b. Jan. 1, 1830, Charleston, S.C.—d. July 6, 1886, Grovetown, Ga.)

Paul Hamilton Hayne was one of the best-known Confederate poets. During the Civil War, Hayne contributed verse supporting the Southern cause—notably "The Battle of Charleston Harbor"—to the *Southern Illustrated News of*

Richmond. Hayne's published works include *Sonnets and Other Poems* (1857), *Legends and Lyrics* (1872), *The Mountain of the Lovers* (1875), and *The Broken Battalions* (1885).

James Murray Mason

(b. Nov. 3, 1798, Fairfax County, Va.—d. April 28, 1871, Alexandria, Va.)

During his tenure in the U.S. Senate representing Virginia, James Murray Mason allied himself closely with other states-rights Southern Democrats in the Senate.

With Abraham Lincoln's election in 1860, Mason advocated Southern secession and resigned his Senate seat to join the Confederacy. He accepted appointment by Pres. Jefferson Davis to serve as Confederate commissioner to England. Accompanied by John Slidell, he sailed for England aboard the British ship *Trent*. The *Trent* was captured at sea by a U.S. naval vessel, and the two Confederate diplomats were imprisoned for two months in Boston.

The *Trent* Affair nearly caused a severance of diplomatic relations between the U.S. and Great Britain. But on Jan. 1, 1862, Pres. Lincoln ordered the release of Mason and Slidell, and the two emissaries made their way to Europe. In England, however, Mason was able to make little progress in winning official support for the Confederate cause. Mason did not return to North America until 1866, and he stayed in Canada—afraid of being arrested as an important official of the defeated Confederacy—until 1868.

John Slidell

(b. 1793, New York, N.Y.—d. July 29, 1871, London, Eng.)

John Slidell was a Confederate diplomat whose seizure with James M. Mason precipitated the *Trent* Affair during the Civil War.

Slidell represented Louisiana in the U.S. Senate from 1853 to 1861. There he was a staunch supporter of Pres. James Buchanan and a vigorous opponent of Stephen A. Douglas. When Louisiana seceded, Slidell cast his lot with the Confederacy. Entering the Confederate foreign service, he was sent to France in late 1861, but on his way there he and fellow envoy James M. Mason were removed by a Federal man-of-war from the British steamer *Trent* and imprisoned at Fort Warren in Boston harbour. The British government strongly protested this action, and the two men were released in January 1862 at Pres. Abraham Lincoln's insistence and over Secretary of State William H. Seward's objections.

In France, Slidell's relations with Napoleon III, though cordial, remained unofficial. Thus this second mission, had little result, save that financial negotiations with the Erlangers of Paris and Frankfurt led to the Confederate cotton loan of 1863.

Alexander H. Stephens

(b. Feb. 11, 1812, Wilkes County, Ga.—d. March 4, 1883, Atlanta, Ga.)

Alexander H. Stephens served as vice president of the Confederate States of America during the Civil War.

He was called "Little Ellick" by his colleagues because he weighed only about 100 pounds. A Whig who served in the Georgia House of Representatives (1837–41), the state Senate (1842–43), and the U.S. House of Representatives (1843–59), Stephens urged the annexation of Texas and supported the Compromise of 1850 and the Kansas-Nebraska Act (1854), both of which attempted to establish criteria for the extension of slavery to U.S. territories. He defended slavery but opposed the dissolution of the Union. When Georgia seceded, however (1861), he followed his state and was shortly elected vice president of the Confederacy.

Throughout the war Stephens opposed the exercise of extraconstitutional war powers by Confederate president Jefferson Davis lest the freedom for which the South was ostensibly fighting should be destroyed. The policy he advocated was to preserve constitutional government in the South and to strengthen the antiwar party in the North by convincing it that the Lincoln administration had abandoned such government. To the same end he urged, in 1864, the unconditional discharge of Federal prisoners. Stephens headed the Confederate commission to the abortive peace conference at Hampton Roads, Va., in February 1865.

After the fall of the Confederacy, Stephens was confined for five months at Fort Warren, Boston. In 1866 he was elected to the U.S. Senate but was denied his seat because his state had not been properly reconstructed according to the congressional guidelines. He did serve again in the U.S. House of Representatives (1873–82), however. His book *A Constitutional View of the Late War Between the States*, 2 vol. (1868–70), is perhaps the best statement of the Southern position on state sovereignty and secession.

Robert A. Toombs

(b. July 2, 1810, Wilkes County, Ga.—d. Dec. 15, 1885, Washington, Ga.)

A Southern antebellum politician who became an ardent secessionist, Robert A. Toombs served briefly as Confederate secretary of state and later sought to restore white supremacy in Georgia during and after Reconstruction.

Toombs served in the Georgia legislature before joining the U.S. House of Representatives in 1844. In 1850 Toombs, a Whig, began to emerge as a states' rights, and ultimately secession, advocate. In his "Hamilcar" speech, he demanded that the South not be denied its rights in the newly acquired territories. Yet he worked for passage of the Compromise of 1850 and its acceptance in Georgia, and he helped organize the Constitutional Union Party in Georgia as a political vehicle for conservatives unhappy with the Whigs but not ready to support the secession-minded Democrats.

Running on the Constitutional Union ticket in 1852, Toombs won election to the U.S. Senate. Shortly thereafter he joined the Democrats, but he remained a moderate on the states' rights issue until 1860.

Not until Abraham Lincoln's election as president and the failure of the Crittenden Compromise of 1860 did Toombs publicly call for secession. He led the movement for a Georgia convention to vote to secede from the Union. In 1861 he resigned from the Senate and was a delegate to the Montgomery convention that established the Confederacy. Severely disappointed at not being selected president of the Confederate States of America, he nonetheless accepted appointment by Jefferson Davis to become secretary of state. Within a few months, however, he broke with Davis and left the government.

In July 1861 Toombs took command of a Georgia brigade as a brigadier general. His military experience was undistinguished, though he did take a bullet in his left hand at Antietam. When no promotion followed, Toombs angrily resigned his commission. He stayed out of the war until near the end, and he continually criticized Davis's leadership and Confederate policies—especially conscription, suspension of habeas corpus, and reliance upon credit to finance the war effort.

In May 1865 Toombs fled—by way of New Orleans and Havana—to London. He returned to Georgia in 1867, but refused to seek a pardon or take the oath of allegiance. Instead, he devoted himself to rebuilding his law practice and to overthrowing Radical Reconstruction in Georgia. In 1877 he broke with other Democrats in welcoming Pres. Rutherford Hayes's plans to end Reconstruction. The same year, he played a prominent role at the convention that revised the state constitution in favour of white supremacy.

William Lowndes Yancey

(b. Aug. 10, 1814, Warren County, Ga.—d. July 27, 1863, Montgomery, Ala.)

There is no evidence that southern political leader and "fire-eater" (pro-slavery extremist) William Lowndes Yancey was a proponent of secession prior to the Mexican War, but in his later years he consistently urged the South to secede in response to Northern antislavery agitation.

A lawyer, editor, and state legislator, Yancey was first elected to represent Alabama in the U.S. House of Representatives in 1844. In 1848 he drafted the Alabama Platformin response to the Wilmot Proviso, which was a proposed ban on slavery in the territories newly acquired from Mexico. The

Alabama Platform insisted that slave-owners had the right to take their chattel property with them into the territories, that Congress had the duty to protect the rights of slaveholders everywhere, that a territorial legislature could not ban slavery, and that the Democratic Party should endorse only pro-slavery candidates for national office.

Although it was endorsed by the Alabama legislature, Yancey's Alabama Platform was overwhelmingly rejected when he presented it at the 1848 Democratic National Convention.

Yancey, however, was resolute, and, after the Compromise of 1850, he added secession to his creed. For the next decade he sought to arouse Southerners to the peril of remaining in the Union. He organized Southern-rights associations and in 1858 assisted in the creation of the League of United Southerners. He delivered hundreds of speeches, trying to draw Southerners of all parties and persuasions into a movement backing his uncompromising pro-slavery states' rights position.

By 1860 the Alabama Platform had won substantial support throughout the South. At the Democratic National Convention in Charleston, a slightly revised version won only qualified acceptance, prompting the Southern delegates to withdraw and nominate a rival ticket. In essence, therefore, Yancey was responsible for the dissolution of the last national institution of the antebellum era.

Yancey then campaigned for John C. Breckinridge, nominee of the Southern wing of the party, the Constitutional Democrats. Following Lincoln's election, it was Yancey who drafted Alabama's secession ordinance. Early in 1861, he went to England and France in quest of official recognition of the new Confederate government, but his mission proved unsuccessful. He returned in 1862 and was elected to the Confederate Senate, where he served until his death.

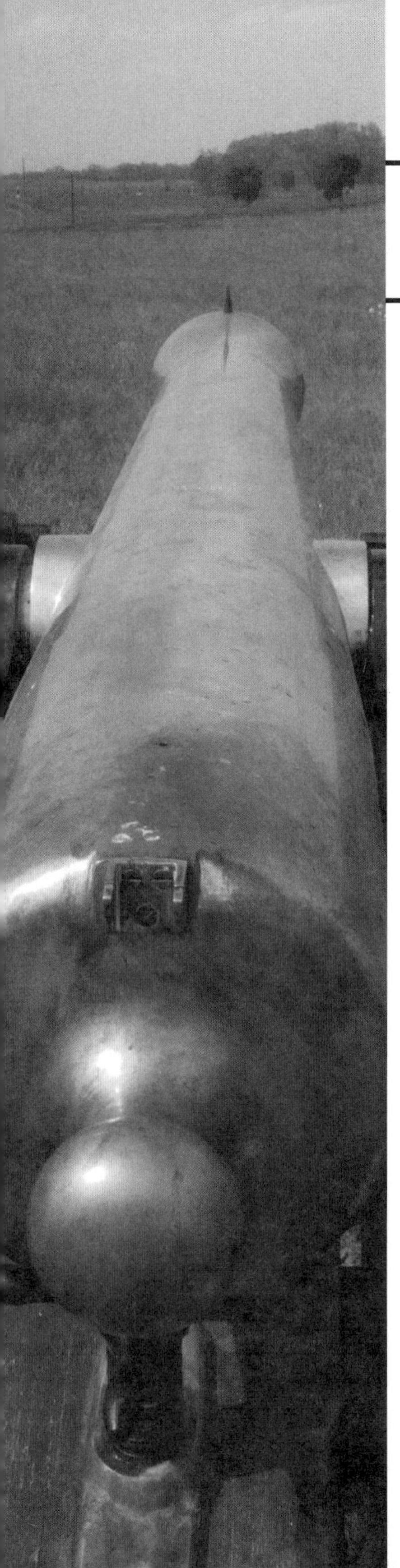

CHAPTER 9

The Aftermath

The Era of Reconstruction

Reconstruction under Abraham Lincoln

The original Northern objective in the Civil War was the preservation of the Union, a war aim with which virtually everybody in the free states agreed. As the fighting progressed, the Lincoln government concluded that emancipation of the slaves was necessary in order to secure military victory; thereafter, freedom became a second war aim for the members of the Republican Party. The more radical members of that party—men like Charles Sumner and Thaddeus Stevens—believed that emancipation would prove a sham unless the government guaranteed the civil and political rights of the freedmen; thus, equality of all citizens before the law became a third war aim for this powerful faction. The fierce controversies of the Reconstruction era raged over which of these objectives should be insisted upon and how these goals should be secured.

Conflicting Plans

Lincoln himself had a flexible and pragmatic approach to Reconstruction, insisting only that the Southerners, when defeated, pledge future loyalty to the Union and emancipate their slaves. As the Southern states were subdued, he appointed military governors to supervise their restoration. The most vigorous and effective of these appointees was Andrew Johnson, a war Democrat whose success in reconstituting a loyal government in Tennessee led to his nomination as vice president on the Republican ticket with Lincoln in 1864.

In December 1863 Lincoln announced a general plan for the orderly Reconstruction of the Southern states, promising to recognize the government of any state that pledged to support the Constitution and the Union and to emancipate the slaves if it was backed by at least 10 percent of the number of voters in the 1860 presidential election. In Louisiana, Arkansas, and Tennessee loyal governments were formed under Lincoln's plan. They sought readmission to the Union with the seating of their senators and representatives in Congress.

The Republican Party, at its formation during the 1850s, was a coalition that included Northern altruists, industrialists, former Whigs, and practical politicians. While not publicly committed to abolition of slavery prior to the Civil War, the party nonetheless attracted the most zealous antislavery advocates. When Abraham Lincoln declared restoration of the Union to be his aim during the Civil War, the antislavery advocates in Congress pressed for emancipation as a stated war aim as well. Then, in December 1861, frustrated at the poor showing of the Union Army and the lack of progress toward abolition, the Radical Republicans (that is, those most committed to emancipation of the slaves and later to the equal treatment and enfranchisement of the freed blacks) formed the Joint Committee on the Conduct of the War. They agitated for the dismissal of Gen. George B. McClellan and favoured the enlistment of black troops.

Radical Republicans were outraged at Lincoln's plan for the South, which favoured executive usurpation of congressional powers, required only minimal changes in the Southern social system, and left political power essentially in the hands of the same Southerners who had led their states out of the Union. They broke with the president completely over Reconstruction policy and put forth their own plan of Reconstruction in the Wade-Davis Bill, which Congress passed on July 2, 1864. The plan required not 10 percent, but a majority of the white male citizens in each Southern state to participate in the reconstruction process, and insisted upon an oath of past, not just of future, loyalty.

Finding the bill too rigorous and inflexible, Lincoln pocket vetoed it; the Radicals bitterly denounced him. During the 1864–65 session of Congress, they in turn defeated the president's proposal to recognize the Louisiana government organized under his 10 percent plan. At the time of Lincoln's assassination, therefore, the president and the Congress were at loggerheads over Reconstruction.

Reconstruction under Andrew Johnson

At first it seemed that the new president, Andrew Johnson, might be able to work more cooperatively with Congress in the process of Reconstruction. A former representative and a former senator, Johnson understood congressmen. A loyal Unionist who had stood by his country even at the risk of his life when Tennessee seceded, he was certain not to compromise with secession. His experience as military governor of that state showed him to be politically shrewd and tough toward the slaveholders. "Johnson, we have faith in you," Radical Benjamin F. Wade assured the new president on the day he took the oath of office. "By the gods, there will be no trouble running the government."

Johnson's Policy

Such Radical trust in Johnson proved misplaced. The new president was, first of all, himself a Southerner. He was a Democrat who looked for the restoration of his old party partly as a step toward his own reelection to the presidency in 1868. Most important of all, Johnson shared the white Southerners' attitude toward African Americans, considering black people innately inferior and unready for equal civil or political rights. On May 29, 1865, Johnson made his policy clear when he issued a general proclamation of pardon and amnesty for most Confederates and authorized the provisional governor of North Carolina to proceed with the reorganization of that state. Shortly afterward he issued similar proclamations for the other former Confederate states. In each case a state constitutional convention was to be chosen by the voters who pledged future loyalty to the U.S. Constitution. The conventions were expected to repeal the ordinances of secession, to repudiate the Confederate debt, and to accept the Thirteenth Amendment, abolishing slavery. The president did not, however, require them to enfranchise African Americans.

"Black Codes"

Given little guidance from Washington, Southern whites turned to the traditional political leaders of their section for guidance in reorganizing their governments; and the new regimes in the South were suspiciously like those of the antebellum period. To be sure, slavery was abolished, but each reconstructed Southern state government proceeded to adopt a "Black Code," regulating the rights and privileges of freedmen. Varying from state to state, these codes in general treated African Americans as inferiors, relegated to a secondary and subordinate position in society. Their right to own land was restricted, they could not bear arms, and they might be bound out in servitude for vagrancy and other offenses. The conduct of white Southerners indicated that they were

In focus: Thirteenth Amendment

Although the words slavery and slave are never mentioned in the Constitution, the Thirteenth Amendment abrogated those sections of the Constitution that had tacitly codified the "peculiar institution": Article I, Section 2, regarding apportionment of representation in the House of Representatives, which had been "determined by adding to the whole Number of free Persons, including those bound to Service for a Term of Years, and excluding Indians not taxed, three fifths of all other Persons provided for the appointment," with "all other persons" meaning slaves; Article I, Section 9, which had established 1807 as the end date for the importation of slaves, referred to in this case as "such Persons as any of the States now existing shall think proper to admit"; and Article IV, Section 2, which mandated the return to their owners of fugitive slaves, here defined as persons "held to Service or Labour in one State, under the Laws thereof, escaping into another."

The Emancipation Proclamation, declared and promulgated by Pres. Abraham Lincoln in 1863, freed only those slaves held in the Confederate States of America. In depriving the South of its greatest economic resource—abundant free human labour—Lincoln's proclamation was intended primarily as an instrument of military strategy; only when emancipation was universally proposed through the Thirteenth Amendment did it become national policy. Moreover, the legality of abolition by presidential edict was questionable.

The full text of the amendment reads:

> Neither slavery nor involuntary servitude, except as a punishment for crime whereof the party shall have been duly convicted, shall exist within the United States, or any place subject to their jurisdiction. Congress shall have power to enforce this article by appropriate legislation.

The amendment was passed by the Senate on April 8, 1864, but did not pass in the House until Jan. 31, 1865. The joint resolution of both bodies that submitted the amendment to the states for approval was signed by Lincoln on Feb. 1, 1865; however, he did not live to see its ratification. Assassinated by John Wilkes Booth, he died on April 15, 1865, and the amendment was not ratified by the required number of states until Dec. 6, 1865.

not prepared to guarantee even minimal protection of African American rights. In riots in Memphis (May 1866) and New Orleans (July 1866), African Americans were brutally assaulted and promiscuously killed.

The Freedmen's Bureau and Civil Rights Legislation

Watching these developments with forebodings, Northern Republicans, during the congressional session of 1865–66,

A group of freedmen, Richmond, Va. Library of Congress, Washington, D.C.

inevitably drifted into conflict with the president. Congress attempted to protect the rights of African Americans by extending the life of the Freedmen's Bureau, the popular name for the U.S. Bureau of Refugees, Freedmen, and Abandoned Lands, established to provide practical aid to 4 million newly freed black Americans in their transition from slavery to freedom. Johnson vetoed the bill. Though Congress initially failed to override his veto, the second time around they succeeded.

Headed by Major General Oliver O. Howard, the Freedmen's Bureau might be termed the first federal welfare agency. Despite handicaps of inadequate funds and poorly trained personnel, the bureau built hospitals for, and gave direct medical assistance to, more than 1 million freedmen. More than 21 million rations were distributed to impoverished blacks as well as whites.

Its greatest accomplishments were in education: more than 1,000 black schools were built and over $400,000 spent to establish teacher-training institutions. All major black colleges were either founded by, or received aid from, the bureau. Less success was achieved in civil rights, for the bureau's own courts were poorly organized and short-lived, and only the barest forms of due process of law for freedmen could be sustained in the civil courts. The most notable failure concerned the land itself. Thwarted by Pres. Andrew Johnson's restoration of abandoned lands to pardoned Southerners and by the adamant refusal of Congress to consider any form of land redistribution, the bureau was ultimately forced to oversee sharecropping arrangements that inevitably became oppressive.

An act to define and guarantee African Americans' basic civil rights was also vetoed by Johnson, but, again, Republicans succeeded in passing it over the president's veto. While the president, from the porch of the White House, denounced the leaders of the Republican Party as "traitors," Republicans in Congress tried to formulate their own plan to reconstruct the South. Their first effort was the passage of the Fourteenth Amendment, which guaranteed the basic civil rights of all citizens, regardless of colour, and which tried to persuade the Southern states to enfranchise African Americans by threatening to reduce their representation in Congress.

The president, the Northern Democrats, and the Southern whites spurned this Republican plan of Reconstruction. Johnson tried to organize his own political party in the National Union Convention, which met in Philadelphia in August 1866. In August and September of that year, he visited many Northern and Western cities in order to defend his policies and to attack the Republican leaders. At the president's urging, every Southern state except Tennessee overwhelmingly rejected the Fourteenth Amendment.

Victorious in the fall elections, congressional Republicans moved during the 1866–67 session to devise a second, more stringent program for reconstructing the South. After long and acrimonious quarrels between Radical and moderate Republicans, the party leaders finally produced a compromise plan in the First Reconstruction Act of 1867. Expanded and clarified in three supplementary Reconstruction acts, this legislation swept away the regimes the president had set up in the South, put the former Confederacy back under military control, called for the election of new constitutional conventions, and required the constitutions adopted by these bodies to include both African American suffrage and the disqualification of former Confederate leaders from holding office. Under this legislation, new governments were established in all the former Confederate states

In Focus: Fourteenth Amendment

The Fourteenth Amendment to the Constitution of the United States granted citizenship and equal civil and legal rights to African Americans and slaves who had been emancipated after the Civil War, including them under the umbrella phrase "all persons born or naturalized in the United States." In all, the amendment comprises five sections, four of which began in 1866 as separate proposals that stalled in legislative process and were amalgamated into a single amendment.

This so-called Reconstruction Amendment prohibited the states from depriving any person of "life, liberty, or property, without due process of law" and from denying anyone within a state's jurisdiction equal protection under the law. Nullified by the Thirteenth Amendment, the section of the Constitution apportioning representation in the House of Representatives based on a formula that counted each slave as three-fifths of a person was replaced by a clause in the Fourteenth Amendment specifying that representatives be "apportioned among the several states according to their respective numbers, counting the whole number of persons in each state, excluding Indians not taxed." The amendment also prohibited former civil and military office holders who had supported the Confederacy from again holding any state or federal office—with the proviso that this prohibition could be removed from individuals by a two-thirds vote in both Houses of Congress. Moreover, the amendment upheld the national debt while exempting the federal government and state governments from any responsibility for the debts incurred by the rebellious Confederate States of America. Finally, the last section, mirroring the approach of the Thirteenth Amendment, provided for enforcement.

The full text of the amendment reads:

> All persons born or naturalized in the United States, and subject to the jurisdiction thereof, are citizens of the United States and of the state wherein they reside. No state shall make or enforce any law which shall abridge the privileges or immunities of citizens of the United States; nor shall any state deprive any person of life, liberty, or property, without due process of law; nor deny to any person within its jurisdiction the equal protection of the laws. Representatives shall be apportioned among the several states according to their respective numbers, counting the whole number of persons in each state, excluding Indians not taxed. But when the right to vote at any election for the choice of electors for President and Vice President of the United States, Representatives in Congress, the executive and judicial officers of a state, or the members of the legislature thereof, is denied to any of the male inhabitants of such state, being twenty-one years of age, and citizens of the United States, or in any way abridged, except for participation in rebellion, or other crime, the basis of representation therein shall be reduced in the proportion which the number of such male citizens shall bear to the whole number of male citizens twenty-one years of age in such state.
>
> No person shall be a Senator or Representative in Congress, or elector of President and Vice President, or hold any office, civil or military, under the United States, or under any state, who, having previously taken an oath, as a member of Congress, or as an officer of the United States, or as a member of any state legislature, or as an executive or judicial

officer of any state, to support the Constitution of the United States, shall have engaged in insurrection or rebellion against the same, or given aid or comfort to the enemies thereof. But Congress may by a vote of two-thirds of each House, remove such disability. The validity of the public debt of the United States, authorized by law, including debts incurred for payment of pensions and bounties for services in suppressing insurrection or rebellion, shall not be questioned. But neither the United States nor any state shall assume or pay any debt or obligation incurred in aid of insurrection or rebellion against the United States, or any claim for the loss or emancipation of any slave; but all such debts, obligations and claims shall be held illegal and void. The Congress shall have power to enforce, by appropriate legislation, the provisions of this article.

Among those legislators responsible for introducing the amendment's provisions were Rep. John A. Bingham of Ohio, Sen. Jacob Howard of Michigan, Rep. Henry Demig of Connecticut, Sen. Benjamin G. Brown of Missouri, and Rep. Thaddeus Stevens of Pennsylvania. The Congressional Joint Resolution proposing the amendment was submitted to the states for ratification on June 16, 1866. On July 28, 1868, having been ratified by the requisite number of states, it entered into force. However, its attempt to guarantee civil rights was circumvented for many decades by the post-Reconstruction-era black codes, Jim Crow laws, and the "separate but equal" ruling of Plessy v. Ferguson *(1896).*

(except Tennessee, which had already been readmitted); and by July 1868 Congress agreed to seat senators and representatives from Alabama, Arkansas, Florida, Louisiana, North Carolina, and South Carolina. By July 1870 the remaining Southern states had been similarly reorganized and readmitted.

Suspicious of Andrew Johnson, Republicans in Congress did not trust the president to enforce the Reconstruction legislation they passed over his repeated vetoes, and they tried to deprive him of as much power as possible. Congress limited the president's control over the army by requiring that all his military orders be issued through the general of the army, Ulysses S. Grant, who was believed loyal to the Radical cause, and in the Tenure of Office Act (1867) they limited the president's right to remove appointive officers. When Johnson continued to do all he could to block the enforcement of Radical legislation in the South, the more extreme members of the Republican Party demanded his impeachment. The president's decision in February 1868 to remove the Radical secretary of war Edwin M. Stanton from the Cabinet, in apparent defiance of the Tenure of Office Act, provided a pretext for impeachment proceedings. The House of Representatives voted to impeach the president, and after a protracted trial the Senate acquitted him by the margin of only one vote.

KEY PLAYERS IN THE RECONSTRUCTION

Efforts to stitch the nation back together politically were begun even as the war raged. The following key figures were instrumental in trying to solve the political, social, and economic problems arising from the readmission to the Union of the 11 Confederate states.

George Sewall Boutwell

(b. Jan. 28, 1818, Brookline, Mass.—d. Feb. 27, 1905, Groton, Mass.)

Although elected the governor of Massachusetts by a coalition of antislavery Democrats and Free Soilers, George Sewall Boutwell found it impossible to remain a Democrat as the antislavery controversy intensified, and in 1855 he helped organize the Republican Party in Massachusetts.

From 1863 to 1869, Boutwell occupied a leadership position among the Radical Republicans in the House of Representatives. He served on the Joint Committee on Reconstruction, and he helped frame and pass the Fourteenth and Fifteenth Amendments to the U.S. Constitution, relating to former slaves and rebels.

Among the most vehement critics of Pres. Andrew Johnson's Reconstruction policies, Boutwell led in the movement for Johnson's impeachment in 1867. Two years later, Pres. Ulysses S. Grant named him secretary of the treasury, a position he held until 1873, when he entered the Senate.

George Sewall Boutwell. Library of Congress, Washington, D.C.

William G. Brownlow

(b. Aug. 29, 1805, Wythe county, Va.—d. April 29, 1877, Knoxville, Tenn.)

The editor of the last pro-Union newspaper in the antebellum South, William G. Brownlow served as governor of Tennessee during the early years of Reconstruction.

After spending a decade as an itinerant preacher, in 1838 Brownlow began his long career as a newspaper editor, starting with the *Tennessee Whig* (1838) and continuing with the *Jonesboro Whig and Independent* (1839–49) and the *Knoxville Whig* (1849–69 and 1875–77). An outspoken and unconditional advocate of the Union, Brownlow continued to ridicule secession until Confederate authorities suppressed the *Knoxville Whig* and caused its editor to flee in the fall of 1861. His press and type were destroyed, putting an end to the last pro-Union paper in the South.

The Confederate secretary of war, Judah Benjamin, banished Brownlow to the North, where the former editor regained his health (after having suffered from typhoid), made a successful lecture tour, and wrote a book, *Sketches of the Rise, Progress, and Decline of Secession; With a narrative of Personal Adventure Among the Rebels* (1862).

When eastern Tennessee was brought under the control of Federal forces in 1863, Brownlow returned to his home state and was instrumental in restoring civil government there. Then, in 1865, he was elected governor of that state. Determined to punish pro-secessionists, he advocated disenfranchising all who had fought against the Union, and he mobilized 1,600 state guards in order to crush the newly organized Ku Klux Klan. Despite failing health, he was elected to a second term by a large majority.

Toward the end of his second term as governor, Brownlow was elected to the U.S. Senate. In 1875 he returned to Knoxville, bought back the Whig (which he had sold in 1869), and edited the paper until shortly before his death.

Blanche K. Bruce

(b. March 1, 1841, Prince Edward county, Va.—d. March 17, 1898, Washington, D.C.)

Blanche K. Bruce was the son of a slave mother and white planter father who rose to become a U.S. senator during Reconstruction in Mississippi. He was well educated as a youth. After the Civil War, he moved to Mississippi, where in 1869 he became a supervisor of elections.

Blanche K. Bruce. Library of Congress, Washington, D.C.

By 1870 he was an emerging figure in state politics. After serving as sergeant at arms in the state senate, he held the posts of county assessor, sheriff, and member of the Board of Levee Commissioners of the Mississippi River. Through these positions he amassed enough wealth to purchase a plantation in Floreyville, Miss.

In 1874 Mississippi's Republican-dominated state legislature elected Bruce, a Republican, to a seat in the U.S. Senate. He served from 1875 to 1881, advocating just treatment for both blacks and Indians, and opposing the policy excluding Chinese immigrants. He sought improvement of navigation on the Mississippi and advocated better relations between the races. Much of his time and energy he devoted to fighting fraud and corruption in federal elections.

Bruce lost his political base in Mississippi with the end of Reconstruction governments in the South. He remained in Washington when, at the conclusion of his Senate term, he was appointed register of the Treasury.

Zachariah Chandler. Library of Congress, Washington, D.C.

Zachariah Chandler

(b. Dec. 10, 1813, Bedford, N.H.—d. Nov. 1, 1879, Chicago, Ill.)

Zachariah Chandler was a leader of the Radical Republicans during the Civil War and Reconstruction.

Chandler served as mayor of Detroit from 1851 to 1852. He was defeated when he ran as the Whig candidate for governor of Michigan in 1852. With the collapse of the Whig Party, Chandler became one of the founders of the Republican Party, signing the call for the historic meeting at Jackson, Mich. (July 6, 1854).

A delegate to the Republican national convention in 1856, he became a member of the party's national committee. He was elected to the U.S. Senate and served there from 1857 to 1875.

During his Senate tenure, Chandler emerged as a leader of the Radical

Republicans. He urged President Lincoln to prosecute the Civil War more forcefully, he vigorously advocated emancipation of the slaves, and he later backed the Reconstruction Acts. He was a member of the Joint Committee on the Conduct of the War and a leading supporter of a new national bank.

In spite of the efforts of a patronage army that gave him complete control over the Republican Party in Michigan throughout his senatorial career, Chandler was defeated by his Democratic opponent in 1874. Appointed secretary of the interior by Pres. Ulysses S. Grant in October 1875, Chandler reorganized the department before his brief tenure ended in March 1877.

Roscoe Conkling. Library of Congress, Washington, D.C.

Roscoe Conkling

(b. Oct. 30, 1829, Albany, N.Y.—d. April 18, 1888, New York City)

Known for his support of severe Reconstruction measures toward the South and his insistence on the control of political patronage in his home state of New York, Roscoe Conkling was a prominent Republican leader in the post–Civil War period. Having established a reputation as a lawyer, orator, and Whig Party leader, Conkling ran as a Republican in 1858 and was elected to the U.S. House of Representatives, serving for six years. In 1867 he won a seat in the Senate, where he held office for 14 years.

While in Congress, Conkling consistently upheld the administration of Pres. Abraham Lincoln in his conduct of the Civil War. He became a leader of the Radical Republicans, who advocated firm military supervision of the defeated Confederate states and broader rights for freedmen. In addition, he was an avid supporter of the Fourteenth (due process) Amendment to the Constitution (1868). Conkling influenced the administration of Pres. Ulysses S. Grant (1869–77) in its overall policy toward the South.

Ebenezer R. Hoar

(b. Feb. 21, 1816, Concord, Mass.—d. Jan. 31, 1895, Concord)

A leading antislavery Whig in Massachusetts, Ebenezer R. Hoar was briefly attorney general in Pres. Ulysses S. Grant's administration.

Born into a distinguished New England family, Hoar rose rapidly to prominence as a lawyer, and his outspoken opposition to slavery made him a leading public figure in his home state. By the mid-1840s, he was an antislavery Whig member of the state senate. It was there that he described himself as a "Conscience Whig," in contrast to the pro-slavery "Cotton Whigs." Hoar opposed the Whigs' nomination of Zachary Taylor for president in 1848, and he was instrumental in the formation of the Free Soil and Republican parties in Massachusetts when the Whig Party declined.

Ebenezer R. Hoar. Encyclopædia Britannica, Inc.

In 1859 Hoar became an associate justice of the Massachusetts Supreme Court, a position that he held until 1869, when President Grant appointed him U.S. attorney general. His tenure was brief, however. He alienated the Senate when he insisted that nine newly created federal judgeships be filled according to merit rather than through patronage. As a consequence, the Senate refused to confirm Hoar when Grant nominated him for a seat on the U.S. Supreme Court. In 1870 Hoar resigned from Grant's cabinet.

George W. Julian

(b. May 5, 1817, Wayne County, Ind.—d. July 7, 1899, Irvington, Ind.)

Reform politician George W. Julian was an abolitionist, served in Congress as a Radical Republican during the Civil War and Reconstruction eras, and later championed women's suffrage and other liberal measures.

By the mid-1840s Julian was a Whig member of the Indiana state legislature and a frequent author of antislavery newspaper articles. His abolitionist views prompted him to switch to the Free Soil Party, and in 1848 he won a seat in the U.S. House of Representatives, running on the Free Soil ticket.

In Congress, Julian opposed the Compromise of 1850. Defeated for reelection that year, he returned to his law practice and antislavery agitation in Indiana. In 1852 Julian was the vice presidential nominee of the Free Soil Party, and four years later he was a prominent figure in the formation of the Republican Party.

Elected to Congress as a Republican in 1860, Julian played an important role in passage of the Homestead Act and in making emancipation a Northern war aim during the Civil War. He served on the Joint Committee on the Conduct of the War, and he became well known for his advocacy of such Radical Reconstruction measures as punishment of Confederate leaders (including confiscation of their lands) and suffrage for the former slaves.

During the Reconstruction era, Julian joined with other Republican Radicals in blocking Pres. Andrew Johnson's Reconstruction policies. In 1867 he was one of seven representatives selected to prepare articles of impeachment against Johnson.

Julian was defeated for renomination in 1870 and two years later broke with the Republican Party to support the Liberal Republicans and their presidential nominee, Horace Greeley.

George W. Julian. Library of Congress, Washington, D.C. (Digital File Number: cwpbh-04616)

John Willis Menard

(b. April 3, 1838, Kaskaskia, Ill.—d. Oct. 8, 1893, Washington, D.C.)

John Willis Menard was the first African American elected to the U.S. Congress. However, he was denied his seat by that body.

During the Civil War he served as a clerk in the U.S. Department of the Interior.

In 1865 he moved to New Orleans, where he became active in the Republican Party, serving as inspector of customs and later as a commissioner of streets. He also published a newspaper, *The Free South,* later named *The Radical Standard.* Elected to Congress from Louisiana in 1868 to fill an unexpired term, Menard failed to overcome an election challenge by the loser, and Congress refused to seat either man.

Pinckney Benton Stewart Pinchback

(b. May 10, 1837, Macon, Ga.—d. Dec. 21, 1921, Washington, D.C.)

Born into freedom, African American Pinckney Benton Stewart Pinchback was a Union officer in the Civil War and a leader in Louisiana politics during Reconstruction.

Pinchback was one of 10 children born to a white Mississippi planter and a former slave. When the father died in 1848, the family fled to Ohio, fearing that white relatives might attempt to re-enslave them.

Pinchback found work as a cabin boy on a canal boat and worked his way up to steward on the steamboats plying the Mississippi, Missouri, and Red rivers. After war broke out between the states in 1861, he ran the Confederate blockade on the Mississippi to reach Federal-held New Orleans. There he raised a company of black volunteers for the North, called the Corps d'Afrique. When he encountered racial discrimination in the service, however, he resigned his captain's commission.

Returning to New Orleans after the war, Pinchback organized the Fourth Ward Republican Club and served as a delegate to the convention that established a new constitution for Louisiana. He was elected to the state senate in 1868 and then was named its president pro tempore; as such he became lieutenant governor upon the death of the incumbent in 1871. From Dec. 9, 1872, to Jan. 13, 1873, he served as acting governor while impeachment proceedings were in progress against Henry Clay Warmoth. In the meantime he went into business and acquired control of a Republican paper, the *New Orleans Louisianian.*

In 1872 Pinchback was elected to Congress, but his Democratic opponent contested the election and won the seat. A year later he was elected to the U.S. Senate, but he was again refused the seat amid charges and countercharges of fraud and election irregularities—although some observers said it was the colour of his skin that counted against him. He was appointed to his last office in 1882 as surveyor of customs in New Orleans.

Joseph Hayne Rainey

(b. June 21, 1832, Georgetown, S.C.—d. Aug. 2, 1887, Georgetown)

A former American slave, Joseph Hayne Rainey was the first African American to serve in the U.S. House of Representatives (1870–79).

The son of a barber who bought the family's freedom, Rainey received some private schooling and took up his father's trade in Charleston, S.C. During the Civil War he was forced to work on the fortifications in Charleston harbour but managed to escape to the West Indies, where he remained until the end of the war (1865). Upon his return to South Carolina, he was a delegate to the state constitutional convention (1868) and served briefly in the state Senate before his election to the U.S. House of Representatives in 1870. He was reelected four times, the longest tenure in the House of any black during the Reconstruction era.

While in office Rainey dedicated himself to the passage of civil-rights legislation, pressing the interests not only of blacks but of other minorities such as the Indians and the Chinese in California. Upon leaving the House in 1879, he was appointed U.S. internal revenue agent of South Carolina. He resigned that post in 1881 to engage in banking and brokerage enterprises in Washington, D.C.

James T. Rapier

(b. Nov. 13, 1837, Florence, Ala.—d. May 31, 1883, Montgomery, Ala.)

African American planter and labour organizer James T. Rapier was a member of the U.S. House of Representatives from Alabama during Reconstruction.

Born in affluence—his father was a wealthy planter—Rapier was educated by private tutors and later studied at Montreal College (Canada), the University of Glasgow (Scotland), and Franklin College (Nashville, Tenn.).

Rapier returned to Alabama after the Civil War and became a successful cotton planter. He began his career in public life by serving as a delegate to Alabama's first Republican state convention; he was a member of the platform committee. In 1867 he participated in the convention called to rewrite the state constitution, and, after losing a campaign in 1870 to become Alabama's secretary of state, he won a congressional seat in 1872. In Washington he worked for the passage of the Civil Rights Act of 1875, although he was defeated for reelection in 1874.

Except for service as collector of internal revenue in Alabama's second district, Rapier did not again hold public office. But he continued as an active labour organizer, seeking to unite poor urban workers and rural sharecroppers, and he wrote prolabour editorials for the *Montgomery Sentinel*, of which he was the publisher.

THE SOUTH DURING RECONSTRUCTION

In the South, the Reconstruction period was a time of readjustment accompanied by disorder. Southern whites wished to keep African Americans in a condition of quasi-servitude, extending few civil rights and firmly rejecting social equality. African Americans, on the other hand, wanted full freedom and, above all, land of their own. Inevitably, there were frequent clashes. Some erupted into race riots, but acts of terrorism against individual African American leaders were more common.

During this turmoil, Southern whites and blacks began to work out ways of getting their farms back into operation and of making a living. Indeed, the most important developments of the Reconstruction era were not the highly publicized political contests but the slow, almost imperceptible changes that occurred in Southern society. African Americans could now legally marry, and they set up conventional and usually stable family units; they quietly seceded from the white churches and formed their own religious organizations, which became centres for the African American community. Without land or money, most freedmen had to continue working for white masters, but they were now unwilling to labour in gangs or to live in the old slave quarters under the eye of the plantation owner.

Sharecropping gradually became the accepted labour system in most of the South Planters, short of capital, favoured the system because it did not require them to pay cash wages; African Americans preferred it because they could live in individual cabins on the tracts they rented and because they had a degree of independence in choosing what to plant and how to cultivate. The South as a whole, however, was desperately poor throughout the Reconstruction era. A series of disastrously bad crops in the late 1860s, followed by the general agricultural depression of the 1870s, hurt both whites and blacks.

The governments set up in the Southern states under the congressional program of Reconstruction were, contrary to traditional clichés, fairly honest and effective. Though the period has sometimes been labeled "Black Reconstruction," the Radical governments in the South were never dominated by African Americans. There were no black governors, only two black senators and a handful of congressmen, and only one legislature controlled by blacks. Those African Americans who did hold office appear to have been similar in competence and honesty to the whites. It is true that these Radical governments were expensive, but large state expenditures were necessary to rebuild after the war and to establish—for the first time in most Southern states—a system of common schools. There certainly was corruption, though nowhere on the scale of the Tweed Ring, which at that time was busily looting New York City. But it is not possible to show that Republicans were more guilty than Democrats, or blacks than whites, in the scandals that did occur.

Though some Southern whites in the mountainous regions and some planters in the rich bottomlands were willing to cooperate with the African Americans and their Northern-born "carpetbagger" allies in these new governments, there

In Focus: Carpetbaggers and Scalawags

During the Reconstruction period, any Northern politician or financial adventurer accused of going South to use the newly enfranchised freedmen as a means of obtaining office or profit was likely to be labeled a "carpetbagger." The epithet originally referred to an unwelcome stranger coming, with no more property than he could carry in a satchel (carpetbag), to exploit or dominate a region against the wishes of some or all of its inhabitants. Although carpetbaggers often supported the corrupt financial schemes that helped to bring the Reconstruction governments into ill repute, many of them were genuinely concerned with the freedom and education of black citizens.

Southerners who supported the federal plan of Reconstruction or who joined with black freedmen and carpetbaggers in support of Republican Party policies were pejoratively branded scalawags. These individuals came from various segments of Southern society. In the Deep South, many were apt to be former Whigs of the planter-merchant aristocracy. In the upper South, they were often hill-country farmers whose sympathies during the war had been Unionist. Altogether, during the Reconstruction era, scalawags constituted perhaps 20 percent of the white electorate, a sizable force in any election or constitutional convention. The origin of the term is unclear, but it was known in the United States from at least the 1840s, at first denoting a worthless farm animal and then denoting a worthless person.

were relatively few such "scalawags." The mass of Southern whites remained fiercely opposed to African American political, civil, and social equality. Most often their hostility was manifested through support of the Democratic Party, which gradually regained its strength in the South and waited for the time when the North would tire of supporting the Radical regimes and would withdraw federal troops from the South.

Ku Klux Klan

Sometimes racial hostility was expressed through such terrorist organizations as the Ku Klux Klan. The Klan was originally organized as a social club by Confederate veterans in Pulaski, Tenn., in 1866. They apparently derived the name from the Greek word *kyklos*, from which comes the English "circle"; "Klan" was added for the sake of alliteration and Ku Klux Klan emerged. The organization quickly became a vehicle for Southern white underground resistance to Radical Reconstruction. Klan members sought the restoration of white supremacy through intimidation and violence aimed at the newly enfranchised black freedmen. A similar organization, the Knights of the White Camelia, began in Louisiana in 1867.

In the summer of 1867, the Klan was structured into the "Invisible Empire of the South" at a convention in Nashville,

Tenn., attended by delegates from former Confederate states. The group was presided over by a grand wizard (Confederate cavalry general Nathan Bedford Forrest is believed to have been the first grand wizard) and a descending hierarchy of grand dragons, grand titans, and grand cyclopes. Dressed in robes and sheets designed to frighten superstitious blacks and to prevent identification by the occupying federal troops, Klansmen whipped and killed freedmen and their white supporters in nighttime raids.

The 19th-century Klan reached its peak between 1868 and 1870. A potent force, it was largely responsible for the restoration of white rule in North Carolina, Tennessee, and Georgia. But Forrest ordered it disbanded in 1869, largely as a result of the group's excessive violence. Local branches remained active for a time, however.

The Ulysses S. Grant Administrations (1869–77)

During the two administrations of President Grant there was a gradual attrition of Republican strength. As a politician the president was passive, exhibiting none of the brilliance he had shown on the battlefield. His administration was tarnished by the dishonesty of his subordinates, whom he loyally defended. As the older Radical leaders—men like Sumner, Wade, and Stevens—died, leadership in the Republican Party fell into the hands of technicians like Roscoe Conkling and James G. Blaine, men devoid of the idealistic fervour that had marked the early Republicans. At the same time, many Northerners were growing tired of the whole Reconstruction issue and were weary of the annual outbreaks of violence in the South that required repeated use of federal force.

Efforts to shore up the Radical regimes in the South grew increasingly unsuccessful. The adoption of the Fifteenth Amendment (1870), prohibiting discrimination in voting on account of race, had little effect in the South, where terrorist organizations and economic pressure from planters kept African Americans from the polls. Nor were three Force Acts passed by the Republicans (1870–71), giving the president the power to suspend the writ of habeas corpus and imposing heavy penalties upon terroristic organizations, in the long run more successful. If they succeeded in dispersing the Ku Klux Klan as an organization, they also drove its members, and their tactics, more than ever into the Democratic camp.

In 1882, the Supreme Court declared the Ku Klux Act unconstitutional, but by that time the Klan had practically disappeared, though it would revive in the 20th century.

Growing Northern disillusionment with Radical Reconstruction and with the Grant administration became evident in the Liberal Republican movement of 1872, which resulted in the nomination of the erratic Horace Greeley for president. Though Grant was overwhelmingly reelected, the true temper

In Focus: Fifteenth Amendment

The Fifteenth Amendment (1870) to the Constitution of the United States guaranteed that the right to vote could not be denied based on "race, color, or previous condition of servitude." The amendment complemented and followed in the wake of passage of the Thirteenth and Fourteenth amendments, which abolished slavery and guaranteed citizenship, respectively, to African Americans. The passage of the amendment and its subsequent ratification (Feb. 3, 1870) effectively enfranchised African American men, while denying that right to women of all colours. Women would not receive that right until the ratification of the Nineteenth Amendment in 1920.

The full text of the Fifteenth Amendment reads:

> The right of citizens of the United States to vote shall not be denied or abridged by the United States or by any State on account of race, color, or previous condition of servitude—
> The Congress shall have power to enforce this article by appropriate legislation.

During Reconstruction, the amendment was successful in encouraging African Americans to vote. Many African Americans were even elected to public office during the 1880s in the states that formerly had comprised the Confederate States of America. By the 1890s, however, efforts by several states to enact such measures as poll taxes, literacy tests, and grandfather clauses—in addition to widespread threats and violence—had completely reversed these trends. By the beginning of the 20th century, nearly all African Americans in the states of the former Confederacy were again disenfranchised. Although the Supreme Court and Congress attempted to strike down such actions as unconstitutional, it was not until Pres. Lyndon B. Johnson introduced the Voting Rights Act of 1965 that Congress was able to put an end to this violence and discrimination. The act abolished voter prerequisites and also allowed for federal supervision of voter registration. With the passage of the Voting Rights Act, the Fifteenth Amendment was finally enforceable, and voter turnout among African Americans improved markedly.

of the country was demonstrated in the congressional elections of 1874, which gave the Democrats control of the House of Representatives for the first time since the outbreak of the Civil War. Despite Grant's hope for a third term in office, most Republicans recognized by 1876 that it was time to change both the candidate and his Reconstruction program. The nomination of Rutherford B. Hayes of Ohio, a moderate Republican of high principles and of deep sympathy for the South, marked the end of the Radical domination of the Republican Party.

The circumstances surrounding the disputed election of 1876 strengthened Hayes's intention to work with the Southern whites, even if it meant abandoning the few Radical regimes that remained in the South. In an election marked by widespread fraud and many irregularities, the Democratic candidate, Samuel J. Tilden, received the majority of the popular vote; but the vote in the electoral college was long in doubt. In order to resolve the impasse, Hayes's lieutenants had to enter into agreement with Southern Democratic congressmen, promising to withdraw the remaining federal troops from the South, to share the Southern patronage with Democrats, and to favour that section's demands for federal subsidies in the building of levees and railroads. Hayes's inauguration marked, for practical purposes, the restoration of "home rule" for the South—i.e., that the North would no longer interfere in Southern elections to protect African Americans and that the Southern whites would again take control of their state governments.

RECONSTRUCTION IN RETROSPECT

At the beginning of the 20th century, many historians viewed the Reconstruction governments as an abyss of corruption resulting from Northern vindictiveness and the desire for political and economic domination. Later, revisionist historians noted that not only was public and private dishonesty widespread in all regions of the country during Reconstruction, but also that a number of constructive reforms actually were introduced into the South during that period. In addition to the extension of civil rights and the participation of African Americans in government, courts were reorganized, judicial procedures improved, public-school systems established, and more feasible methods of taxation devised. Many provisions of the state constitutions adopted during the postwar years have continued in existence.

The Reconstruction experience led to an increase in sectional bitterness and the development of one-party politics in the South. Scholarship has suggested that the most fundamental failure of Reconstruction was in not effecting a distribution of land in the South that would have offered an economic base to support the newly won political rights of black citizens.

> *"It seemed like it took a long time for freedom to come. Everything just kept on like it was. We heard that lots of slaves was getting land and some mules to set up for theirselves. I never knowed any what got land or mules nor nothing."*
>
> —Millie Freeman, former slave

Glossary

aberration The act of deviating from the normal.

antebellum Before or existing before a war, especially in reference to the American Civil War.

armistice A temporary suspension of wartime hostilities by agreement of both parties; truce.

attrition The act of weakening or exhausting by constant harassment or attack.

barbarism An uncivilized state or condition.

brevet An honorary promotion wherein a military officer's rank, but not pay, is raised.

bulwark A wall or other protection against external danger or attack; rampart.

commissary A store selling food and supplies at a military post, mining camp, or other place of work.

conscription Compulsory enrollment in military service; draft.

excoriate To denounce severely or berate.

flotilla A group of small naval vessels.

howitzer A short-barreled cannon.

impenitent Not repentant.

indemnification The act of compensating for damage or loss sustained.

insurrection An act of rising in revolt against civil authority or organized government.

interpolation Something introduced (usually something extraneous) between other parts; something interjected or interposed.

ironclad An iron- or steel-plated wooden warship.

littoral Having to do with a shore or coastal region.

lyceum An institution for public education through discussions and lectures.

magnanimity Generosity in forgiving an insult or injury.

martinet Someone, especially in the military, who strictly adheres to rules and procedures.

materiel The equipment, arms, and general supplies of a military force.

myrmidon A person who unquestionably follows commands, without concern for ethics or scruples.

ordnance Military supplies, including weapons and ammunition.

peculiar institution With peculiar meaning, unique or distinctive. This phrase was used as a euphemism for slavery.

pejorative Having a belittling effect or force.

pontoon Floating structure used as a temporary bridge over a river.

popular sovereignty In regard to American history, the doctrine that held that the people of the federal territories should decide for themselves whether to enter the Union as free or slave states..

promiscuously Indifferently or indiscriminately.

promulgation A declaration or proclamation that may have the force of law.

provincialism Narrow-mindedness, ignorance, specifically as is considered to be a result of lack of exposure to cultural or intellectual activity.

quiescent Inactive; motionless; still.

sobriquet A nickname.

suasion A persuasive effort or attempt or the act of doing so.

tatterdemalion A person in ragged, tattered clothing.

untenable Unsound; groundless, unable to be defended, as an argument.

verbosity The state or quality of using an excess of words; wordiness.

Bibliography

The Peculiar Institution

On slavery in the United States, see John W. Blassingame, *The Slave Community: Plantation Life in the Antebellum South*, rev. ed. (1979); Helen Tunnicliff Catterall (ed.), *Judicial Cases Concerning American Slavery and the Negro*, 5 vol. (1926–37, reprinted 1968); Paul Finkelman, *An Imperfect Union: Slavery, Federalism, and Comity* (1981), and his *Slavery in the Courtroom: An Annotated Bibliography of American Cases* (1985); Robert William Fogel and Stanley L. Engerman, *Time on the Cross: The Economics of American Negro Slavery* (1974); David W. Galenson, *White Servitude in Colonial America: An Economic Analysis* (1981); Eugene D. Genovese, *The Political Economy of Slavery: Studies in the Economy & Society of the Slave South* (1965), *Roll, Jordan, Roll: The World the Slaves Made* (1974), and *The World the Slaveholders Made*, rev. ed. with a new introduction (1988); Claudia Dale Goldin, *Urban Slavery in the American South, 1820–1860* (1976); Herbert G. Gutman, *The Black Family in Slavery and Freedom, 1750–1925* (1976); Winthrop D. Jordan, *White over Black: American Attitudes Toward the Negro, 1550–1812* (1968, reissued 1977); Peter Kolchin, *Unfree Labor: American Slavery and Russian Serfdom* (1987); Allan Kulikoff, *Tobacco and Slaves: The Development of Southern Cultures in the Chesapeake, 1680-1800* (1986); Lawrence W. Levine, *Black Culture and Black Consciousness: Afro-American Folk Thought from Slavery to Freedom* (1977); Leon F. Litwack, *Been in the Storm So Long: The Aftermath of Slavery* (1979); Edmund S. Morgan, *American Slavery, American Freedom: The Ordeal of Colonial Virginia* (1975); Gerald W. Mullin, *Flight and Rebellion: Slave Resistance in Eighteenth-Century Virginia* (1972); James Oakes, *The Ruling Race: A History of American Slaveholders* (1982); Ulrich Bonne Phillips, *American Negro Slavery: A Survey of the Supply, Employment, and Control of Negro Labor as Determined by the Plantation Régime* (1918, reissued 1966); Kenneth M. Stampp, *The Peculiar Institution: Slavery in the Ante-bellum South* (1956, reprinted 1975); Eric Williams, *Capitalism & Slavery* (1944, reissued 1980); and Peter H. Wood, *Black Majority: Negroes in Colonial South Carolina from 1670 Through the Stono Rebellion* (1974).

Civil War

Essential multivolume works include Shelby Foote, *The Civil War: A Narrative*, 3 vol. (1958–74; reissued in 14 vol., 1998–2000); Allan Nevins, *The War for the Union*, 4 vol. (1959–71, reissued 2000); and Bruce Catton, *The Centennial*

History of the Civil War, 3 vol. (1961–65). Two books by James M. McPherson, *Ordeal by Fire: The Civil War and Reconstruction*, 3rd ed. (2000) and *Battle Cry of Freedom: The Civil War Era* (1988), are excellent; the former places the war into broad context, while the latter focuses on the war years. Russell F. Weigley, *A Great Civil War: A Military and Political History, 1861–1865* (2000), is equally good. Frank E. Vandiver, *Their Tattered Flags: The Epic of the Confederacy* (1970, reprinted 1987); and Emory M. Thomas, *The Confederate Nation, 1861–1865* (1979, reissued 1993), concentrate on the South. Charles P. Roland, *An American Iliad: The Story of the Civil War*, 2nd ed. (2002), is a fine survey of the conflict. William M. Fowler, Jr., *Under Two Flags: The American Navy in the Civil War* (1990, reprinted 2001), covers sea combat.

INDEX

A

B

C

D

I

J

K

L

O

P

Q

R

S

T

U

V

W

Y